# AT THE HELM

# AT THE HELM

*A Memoir*

V. Krishnamurthy

COLLINS
BUSINESS

First published in India in 2014 by Collins Business
An imprint of HarperCollins *Publishers* India



ISBN: 978-93-5029-859-6

2 4 6 8 10 9 7 5 3 1



**HarperCollins *Publishers***
A-75, Sector 57, Noida 201301, India
77-85 Fulham Palace Road, London W6 8JB, United Kingdom
Hazelton Lanes, 55 Avenue Road, Suite 2900, Toronto, Ontario M5R 3L2
*and* 1995 Markham Road, Scarborough, Ontario M1B 5M8, Canada
25 Ryde Road, Pymble, Sydney, NSW 2073, Australia
31 View Road, Glenfield, Auckland 10, New Zealand
10 East 53rd Street, New York NY 10022, USA

Typeset in 12/14.7 Joanna MT at
SŪRYA

Printed and bound at
Thomson Press (India) Ltd.

Dedicated to the memory of my wife Rajam,
who continues to be my strength and inspiration.

# CONTENTS

# FOREWORD

It gives me immense pleasure to write this Foreword to the memoir of Dr V. Krishnamurthy. The joy arises from many aspects of his personality—the roles he played and the invaluable contributions he made to Indian industry, the public sector, government, national policy and the social sector.

The single most important aspect of his career is that he has been an outstanding chief executive officer (CEO) of Indian industry. He compares most favourably with other leading Indian CEOs of his generation, including giants like Sumant Moolgaonkar of Telco, Prakash Tandon of Hindustan Lever, Ajit Haksar of ITC and others. It was his mission to work in and for the Indian economy. If he had chosen to work globally, in my view, he would have matched, if not exceeded, the performance of the world's big CEOs such as Jack Welch of GE, Percy Barnevik of ABB, Akio Morita of Sony and others at that level.

He has shown greater versatility than most comparable Indian and foreign CEOs. He first built power equipment manufacturer BHEL in the capital goods sector. Then, he brought to life Maruti in the automobile and consumer durables sector. He went on to turn around steel giant SAIL. Even any one of these successes would have been enough to qualify him as a great CEO. Two of them would have made him the best Indian CEO. All three make him virtually beyond reach and comparison.

Krishnamurthy has been a path-breaking CEO in both the

public and private sectors. In BHEL, he did many things considered impossible not only by his predecessor but also by Mrs Indira Gandhi, the then prime minister. He demonstrated, for the first time in India, the ability of a CEO to lead a large, multi-unit, high technology, capital intensive, long gestation company to high performance. He did this through professional management interventions such as India's first formal corporate plan, a multi-functional corporate structure, delegation with accountability, budgetary control, performance appraisal and other management systems.

His success in BHEL was rewarded by his elevation as secretary to the Government of India in the department of heavy industries in the ministry of industry. While having to manage new political and bureaucratic relationships in his ministry and with other ministries, he brought much needed management concepts and practices to the ministry. Due to differences with the minister, he had to leave office without completing his term. But his contributions to Indian industry and the public sector were to continue.

Prime Minister Mrs Indira Gandhi requested him to revive the moribund Maruti. He ran Maruti, a joint venture with Suzuki Motors of Japan, virtually as a private enterprise. Without any prior exposure to the automotive sector, he blazed new trails. He not only saved Maruti but also transformed the entire automobile industry in India. Nothing less. He gave the Indian car buyer an undreamt-of world class product and service experience. Even if the core technology came from Suzuki, he led the absorption, skill training, vendor and dealer development, etc. to produce quality cars which not only delighted Indian customers but were also taken by Suzuki to its export markets. He revolutionized car sales and service in India. He also fostered the growth of many private sector auto component manufacturers, many of whom have since grown, been listed on the stock market and delivered high value to all their respective stakeholders.

Even as he was blazing new trails in Maruti, the new, young prime minister, Rajiv Gandhi, wanted him to turn around SAIL. Krishnamurthy brought about several deep changes in the attitudes, culture, technology, and systems of SAIL. He made the huge organization sensitive, for the first time, to issues of customer satisfaction, quality, timely delivery and competitive pricing. This was a revolution for a near monopoly producer of steel.

When he became chairman of BHEL, he was in his forties. This was a welcome departure from the then general Indian organizational culture and public sector ethos that one had to be older and more senior to become chairman. Another characteristic of the public sector at that time was blind compliance with the directions, orders, instructions, hints and even unstated desires and expectations of civil servants and the minister concerned. The typical PSU CEO was involved mostly in project implementation and, after commissioning, he was preoccupied with production. Without being insubordinate in any way, Krishnamurthy changed the culture by simply taking charge, giving comfort to employees and delivering results through his leadership and managerial competence. In a top-down milieu, where planning for PSUs was done primarily by the Planning Commission with some involvement of the ministry, Krishnamurthy took the bull by its horns and produced corporate plans for all the three PSUs he helmed. It was not just a statistical extrapolation but a strategic plan.

There was also a feeling in the public sector in the 1970s that each enterprise had to be small to be manageable by Indian executives, who were perceived to have limited managerial experience and talent. Krishnamurthy changed that by demonstrating that BHEL can be run more successfully as a multi-unit enterprise under the same corporate management. The PSU head office was then very lean. It consisted mainly of the CMD and the financial adviser and chief accounts officer (FACAO). In the PSU ethos, the FACAO was a very powerful position, sometimes even more so than the CMD. If the FACAO disagreed on any issue of investment or expenditure, the matter had to go to the board. The power was primarily negative—to delay and even stop things. The FACAO could not be a prime mover of strategy and operations in the PSU.

Krishnamurthy resolved this problem in many innovative ways. He inspired the board's confidence, and even admiration, by presenting corporate plans—a meaningful big picture within which all investments and major expenditures could be seen in their proper perspective and approved in principle. Later, in SAIL, he started the system of signing memorandums of understanding with the ministry. This concept killed two birds with one stone—high autonomy for the PSU management as well as accountability with specified deliverables.

Krishnamurthy also created a new organizational structure essential for the implementation of key principles such as setting goals for units, policy guidance, delegation, accountability, MIS, management by exception, performance-based rewards and recognition, etc. He created, for the first time in the public sector, all relevant functional departments—marketing, operations, purchase and HR besides the already existent finance department. He also set up major, central R&D facilities in BHEL, Maruti and SAIL.

CEOs and managers, both in the public and private sectors, can continue to learn much from Krishnamurthy and his work in the two PSUs, BHEL and SAIL, the virtual private sector joint venture Maruti, as well as his supportive role as secretary, heavy industries. An important lesson is to keep learning at every opportunity, growing and widening one's managerial repertoire.

Krishnamurthy was an avid and fast learner. Even during short spells of postings and projects, he soaked in a great deal. This began with his stint in the Tamil Nadu Electricity Board and continued through the Planning Commission, BHEL, Maruti, the heavy industries department, SAIL and later. He learnt from all the relevant stakeholders. Examples are his learning from Appadurai in TNEB, national leaders like Nehru and Indira Gandhi, planners like Mahalanobis, collaborators like the Russians, Czechs, Americans, Germans, Japanese, and others.

Managers can imbibe Krishnamurthy's sense of mission. He was not working for the modest salaries of the government and the public sector. He was motivated by the goal of building the Indian public and manufacturing sectors.

Then there is his self-confidence, bordering on audacity. He believed that Indian managers could be as good as anyone. He went on to prove it by personal example in several sectors.

Not only CEOs but also industrialists and entrepreneurs need to adopt Krishnamurthy's commitment to modern professional management. He ran all three companies almost by the book—with a focus on strategy, organizational development, HRD and controls.

A key message of Krishnamurthy's lifetime of work is the vital importance and power of vision. He was not daunted by the most serious problems, difficulties, constraints, setbacks and criticisms on the ground. He set his sights high and lifted those of the organizations he helmed. In BHEL, it was through a strategic year plan, aspiring for higher ratings of power equipment, new technologies, total power plant erection and commissioning, exports, etc. In Maruti, it was a car of world class quality but affordable to the Indian consumer. In terms of sustained quality, volume and resale value, the Maruti 800 he launched has in effect been the Indian 'People's Car'. In SAIL, he went further out into the future. He got the organization to prepare, through a highly participative process, a fifteen-year plan. It has continued to be a guiding light for his successors in SAIL.

Krishnamurthy's sustained, relentless, uncompromising high performance orientation is extremely relevant in today's world of fierce domestic and global competition. A business survival mantra to learn from Krishnamurthy is customer orientation. He was not satisfied with success through total or semi monopoly, government pricing and purchase preferences. I think he was not suited to being a monopolist. He relished competition. It gave him more pleasure to satisfy, win and retain the customer. He got BHEL to compete for international tenders. He prepared SAIL for impending domestic and import competition. He achieved Maruti's success with a product seen as superior to the two incumbent offers of the entrenched competition.

The secret to Krishnamurthy's ability to resurrect the near-dead Maruti or turn around the then white elephant SAIL or build a struggling BHEL is his early insight that big things can be achieved only through people. For him, 'people' meant neither just his immediate direct reports, nor the senior management group, nor even the executive cadre, but the company's entire employee population. He invested a lot of his time and energy in direct communication—from one-on-one to group and very large group interactions, what are now called town hall meetings. He would invite people's views on their difficulties, their diagnosis of the organization's problems, and their suggestions. He would share his vision for the organization, what he and the management would do for it, and what they needed to do for it. It was through this deep communication process that he could achieve quantum changes.

The management of change is another lesson to learn from Krishnamurthy. He often told change resisters, 'It is better to go through painful, planned change than to have traumatic change imposed on us from above or by outside forces.' The longer change was postponed, the tougher it became to handle. That was the legacy Krishnamurthy inherited in all three organizations. But he got the plants and the national unions to agree to unprecedented changes in Indian industry such as stoppage of overtime, large scale voluntary retirement, manpower reduction, retraining, multi-skilling, redeployment and so on. He was not just a change agent but a change master. Almost a change magician!

The final acid test of the legacy of any CEO is institution building. After his exit, does the company decline or just about survive? Or does it continue to flourish, go from strength to strength, keep going back and drawing from the leader's foundations, philosophy, vision, inspiration and strategic direction? All three companies—BHEL, Maruti and SAIL—have continued to grow and flourish. Their core values and strengths, founded by Krishnamurthy, have endured, enabling all three enterprises to weather storms and keep coming back up. The entrepreneurial and managerial capital and personal energy that Krishnamurthy invested in them qualifies him to be called their founder, similar to a G.D. Birla, Jamshedji Tata, J.K. Singhania or Rama Prasad Goenka. Moreover, the human capital that he started developing in these companies is now adding value to many Indian private sector companies in the power, automobile, steel and other sectors.

One final attribute of the man I would like to highlight is stamina. Today's bright managers look forward to long careers of forty years and more. They can learn from a CEO who has been working for over six decades and is still wrestling with the national challenge of uplifting India's manufacturing, which is way behind that of its northern neighbour, China. Metaphorically speaking, Krishnamurthy is not just a long distance runner, not even just a marathoner, but an ultra-marathoner, the kind who can run 150 miles and more.

I end with the hope that generations of Indian and global managers will study Krishnamurthy's memoir, learn from it and act on its lessons, and maximize their potential to benefit their internal and external stakeholders.

Dr Mrityunjaya B. Athreya,
Management Advisor.
March 2014.

# INTRODUCTION

One day in the middle of 2002, I got a call from Dr A.P.J. Abdul Kalam. At that time, there was no talk about his becoming President of India. A week or so earlier, he had addressed managers at the Human Resource Development Institute of Bharat Heavy Electricals Ltd (BHEL). In his interactions after his presentation, he found that people at BHEL were still talking about various initiatives I had taken during my stint as chairman and managing director—twenty-five years after I had left the organization. He said he had then tried to find out more and had searched for books written about my work in BHEL but could not find any. 'Isn't it time you wrote about your work?' he asked.

Since then, friends and family members have been requesting me to document my working life, which to most of them appeared unique and full of experiments. But I never got down to the task. I used to advise active professionals to spend at least 20 per cent of their time documenting their work for future generations. This lack of documentation is one of the shortcomings of the professional world in India.

I realized that I was also guilty of the same lapse. I am glad that I have attempted to write this book before my memory fades. I have tried my best to recollect most of the incidents in my working life and sincerely hope this book captures the philosophy behind my actions and decisions.

I have received numerous national and international awards for my work. I am both honoured and humbled by such recognition, but what I really cherish is the immense satisfaction I get when I look back at the three organizations whose course I helped shape and the contributions I have made to policy making relating to the economy, public sector and the country's technological landscape.

As I reflect on my life and work, the one thing that strikes me is how what I did in the normal course turned out to be path-breaking in many ways. But at the time when I did all that, there was no sense of creating history; it just seemed the natural and most sensible thing to do.

In each of my three public sector assignments, I was put in a challenging situation. In the case of BHEL, I had to save the company from imminent disintegration and dispel the impression that Indian managers do not have the ability to manage large organizations. In Maruti Udyog, I was given the responsibility of not just manufacturing a car but of modernizing the automobile industry itself. Steel Authority of India Ltd (SAIL) was almost a sunset company when I took over, and the challenge was to shake up the organization from its very foundations and put it back in a leadership position. In each case, I battled a negative image. In each case, doubts were raised about my ability to make a difference. In each case, I was able to prove everyone wrong.

It is a sad comment on the way the public sector is managed that I am feted for something that should have been par for the course. The public sector has some of the best brains in the country. Why, then, were they not able to deliver results—to the shareholders (the public at large) or to the customers? To a large extent, the system is to blame. Over time, the public sector has come to be synonymous with the absence of identified ownership, leading to lack of accountability and insecurity in the tenure of the chief executive. This was not always the case.

I am a great believer in the public sector and the Nehruvian model of development of which it was an intrinsic part. Though I am a strong advocate of economic freedom, I feel the post-1991 economic policies resulted in an excessive dependence on the market economy and in the government giving up its role in many areas. At that point of time, I felt that was the right approach. But over a period of time, I have come to believe that the free market can take the country only up to a point, and the government and the public sector do have a role to play.

Contrary to popular perception, the concept of the public sector that Nehru envisaged was not akin to the Soviet model, where private industry was practically non-existent. In the Nehruvian model of a mixed economy, only the manufacture of arms and ammunition was reserved entirely for the public sector. In a number of manufacturing industries that required large investment—like iron and steel, heavy machines and telecommunications equipment—new projects were assigned to the public sector with a view to securing accelerated economic growth. There was no attempt to bar private industry from these areas. The public sector was meant to help develop a self-reliant economy, and there is no denying that it did play this role in areas as diverse as manufacturing steel, power equipment, and professional education as well as building a scientific temper in the country through the thirty-odd national research centres. Like Nehru, I also believe that human resource development is best done through the efforts of the public sector.

Jawaharlal Nehru's vision for the public sector was also one in which the companies would be free from day-to-day interference by the government, and state-owned companies had a large measure of operational freedom in the early days. The character of state-owned public enterprises got distorted only after Nehru's death, when populism led to the state getting into areas that hardly qualified for its presence. In addition, the autonomy of the public sector got eroded over time, leading to diffused accountability.

I had always been perturbed by the control regime that took hold of the Indian economy and public sector after the late sixties. The management of large state-owned enterprises was the subject of my Ph.D. thesis for the Soviet Academy of Sciences. One of the first calls for more freedom for public sector companies was made in the 'Outline of a Corporate Plan' that was drawn up in BHEL in 1974.

I got a chance to articulate my ideas in a much more cogent manner when I was appointed chairman of the working group on the management of public sector enterprises for the Eighth Five-Year Plan and when Rajiv Gandhi asked me to draw up a white paper on the public sector, a commitment he had made in his budget speech in 1987. The draft white paper categorically stated that operational autonomy is a must for all public enterprises and had sought non-interference on decisions taken by public sector managers relating to location, technology, equipment, day-to-day administration and delegated financial and administrative powers. Unfortunately, the white paper was never tabled in Parliament. The draft was sent to a cabinet committee headed by P.V. Narasimha Rao in early 1989. He said that if the recommendations were accepted, the government's responsibility to oversee public sector undertakings would be diluted and it would also reduce accountability to Parliament.

It is not enough for state-owned companies to seek greater operational freedom. This freedom must be used in a way that companies perform better than they used to. It was my firm belief in this that led to SAIL being among the first four companies to sign memoranda of understanding (MoU) with the government in 1986. The MoU idea was floated by the Arjun Sengupta Committee to Review Policy for Public

Enterprises in 1984. The MoUs clearly set out obligations for both the government and the public sector enterprises. The government would give the companies greater autonomy in fixing prices, investment planning and financial management, in return for which the companies had to adhere to a performance contract which set out certain mutually agreed upon performance targets. This was in line with my thinking.

The public sector did not get the kind of freedom I argued for during my time, but I demonstrably proved that it is possible to do a lot within the constraints that existed while I helmed BHEL, Maruti and SAIL. Perhaps that is why the panel that chose me as the Business India Businessman of the Year in 1987 noted, in the context of my stint in SAIL, 'If for any reason at all he fails, virtually the entire public sector will have to be written off for the next twenty years.'

How did I do it? That is what this book sets out to relate through the stories of my various stints. The details may vary, but there is a common thread running through them. This thread has five strands, which form the core of my management philosophy: giving importance to people and treating them with dignity, constant communication with all stakeholders, creating awareness of productivity and quality, developing a marketing and customer culture, and constantly upgrading the technological status of the company.

These five principles put the organizations I headed on a firm footing. If this book can show young managers how to be fearless in the face of all challenges and hurdles and remain focussed on achieving their goals, if it can teach them to respect human dignity and treat people equally without any bias, if it can inculcate in them a deep faith in their capabilities and teach them how to be transformational leaders rather than transactional leaders, then I will feel that working on this book was worth the effort.

[illegible]

[illegible]

[illegible]

[illegible]

# 1

# FROM KARUVELI TO KARUVELI

As the car crossed the bridge over the dark waters of the Arasalar river—a tributary of the mighty Kaveri—I sat up and looked out of the window curiously.

On the face of it, there was nothing that distinguished the village we had just entered from all the other villages I had driven through on the six-hour journey from Chennai. There were the usual mud-walled houses with sloping thatched roofs that almost obscured the entrance as well as a few brick and mortar houses with red-tiled roofs. Elderly men lounged on the thinnai (the platform that is a staple outside most traditional Tamilian homes), women went about their chores and paddy was being dried on the road.

But this was Karuveli, in the Thanjavur district of Tamil Nadu, where, legend has it, Lord Shiva did his Kodukotti dance. Standing here is a 1,500-year-old temple patronized by the Chola kings. The village is referred to as Kottittai in the Tamil hymns composed by the Saivite saint Tirunaavukkarasar in praise of the presiding deity of the village, Sri Sarguneswara.

For me, this was a homecoming of sorts. This was the village that had been home to several generations of my family till the early 1930s, when we left after a reversal in our family fortunes, little knowing that we would not return for nearly sixty years. I was just five or six years old when we left and I had no memories of the village barring one—of reaching the river bank by bullock cart and then, since there was no bridge, crossing the river by boat.

It was a strange and fortuitous combination of events that brought me back to my village in 1996. That was the time I was at an extremely low point in my life. I had been detained by the Central Bureau of Investigation (CBI) in August 1992 and confined in a two-bedroom flat in the CBI complex for three weeks. The next few years were spent in legal battles to clear my name from the slew of charges slapped against me.

One day, a man called Vishnu Namboodiri, who had come to see T.N. Seshan—the then Chief Election Commissioner—dropped in to meet me. He looked at my face, took out some small shells from his bag, read them and then said, 'Your life is full of good acts; you have done nothing that is wrong. But some family commitments are yet to be completed. Find out what they are.' I tried to recollect but could remember nothing that anyone had spoken about. So I put it out of my mind.

A few months after this incident, a young engineering graduate in search of a job approached my elder son, Chandra. He had come home and, while chatting with my wife Rajam, got details of my date of birth from her. It turned out he was a numerologist. One Sunday, he came with a sheaf of papers and told me nearly everything that had happened in my life. At the end of it, he said, 'There is a temple in your village in a bad shape. What was expected of your family has not been fulfilled. You should do that.'

I didn't say anything. I knew that till my father's time, our family was the hereditary trustee of the Sarguneswara temple. After he left the village, we lost touch, and in 1959, following the enactment of the Tamil Nadu Hindu Religious and Charitable

Endowments Act, all temples (including this one) came under the control of the state Hindu Religious and Charitable Endowment Department. The role of our family became negligible.

The young man periodically reminded me about going to my village. He was unhappy that I had not paid heed to what he had said. 'You are ignoring what I have suggested,' he said. 'I know your wife is not well, but once you go, every step after that will bring health and mental peace.'

A few days later, I was talking to my elder brother Vaidyanathan in Chennai and mentioned what the young man had said. I wanted him to plan a visit to the temple as soon as possible. He said that around the same time that the young man had met me in Delhi, five village elders from Karuveli had met him and suggested that our family return to the village and assume leadership like in the old days. They had also mentioned that the Sarguneswara temple was in very bad shape and required attention.

We then decided to go to Karuveli. Would I have gone if the villagers had not met my brother around the same time the young man was badgering me to go to the village? I don't know. But it was too much of a coincidence, even for someone like me who was not a great believer in astrology or numerology.

My wife, brother and I received a ceremonial welcome at Karuveli, with nadaswaram players heralding our arrival. Karuveli is a small village of just about one thousand people. We were taken to our ancestral house (which now belonged to someone else) and then to the temple.

The temple was in ruins. The outer walls had crumbled and thick wild vegetation obscured the approach to the sanctum sanctorum, which was all that remained. Trees were beginning to grow out of cracks in the gopuram (temple tower). Priests stayed away from the temple because they were afraid of snakes. The daily rituals had stopped. It suddenly struck me that this could have been the unfulfilled commitment which Vishnu Namboodiri had spoken about. My brother and I immediately decided that we would take up the responsibility of restoring this temple to its original glory. It was a daunting task, both in physical and financial terms. The temple had to be entirely rebuilt.

We wondered if we would be able to raise enough resources for the task, but there was no going back on our commitment. In fact, it was my wife Rajam's conviction that paved the way for this project. She played a major role in raising funds for the construction and in bringing the entire family together for this purpose.

The Karuveli project finally started in 1996, and we were able to restore the temple. I was appointed as the hereditary trustee of the temple. Once the government realized we were not asking for money but generating it ourselves, it left us pretty much alone. We also started the Culture and Heritage Trust of Karuveli, set up a residential school to teach Vedic chanting and a computer training institute which, however, did not take off the way we expected. I also bought back a large part of the lands we had lost and constructed a large guest house with facilities for people to stay while on pilgrimage and for meditation. I could not, unfortunately, buy our house—diagonally opposite to the temple and next to the temple tank—back. It had changed hands twice, and the owner was not willing to sell it.

But the satisfaction I have got from the Karuveli project far exceeds the satisfaction I got from all my other challenging professional assignments. The young man's words proved prophetic. My wife's health improved and the unfair accusations against me fell flat one by one. The court dismissed all accusations levelled against me as baseless.

The Karuveli experience reinforced the belief that there is a divine dispensation in all that we do. 'Karuveli' means liberation from the fruits of one's karma—that endless cycle of births, deaths and rebirths. Maybe it was karma that caused a reversal in my family's fortunes and its departure from the village. It was perhaps karma again that had brought us back. I couldn't help thinking, 'Would I have been the person I was if the fortunes of my family hadn't changed so drastically when I was a little boy?'

~

I was born on 14 January 1925 and was the youngest of three sons. Ours was a wealthy family, my grandfather being the largest landowner of Karuveli at that time. The lands alone would have sustained us for a few generations. Perhaps that is why neither my father Venkataraman nor his brothers ever trained themselves for any vocation. Nor did they invest in education—all of them had studied only up to secondary school.

The tales of my grandfather's generosity were many. He would put up a pandal (marquee) outside the house, which was the first house of the Iyer agraharam (Brahmin locality), set up a swing and sit there for most of the day. No passerby who greeted him would be allowed to go without eating something. In fact, there were strict instructions to the women of the household to ensure something was offered to the guest without my grandfather having to ask for it.

But all this was not to last.

Around the time of the Great Depression of the 1930s, the agriculturists of the Thanjavur region also went through a difficult period. Floods in the Kaveri had ravaged their lands. My grandfather had incurred huge debts, and the family lost its lands since it was unable to repay the debts. There was litigation all around. We had to sell the house and leave.

My father decided to go to Chennai to start a business. I hardly saw him because the rest of us moved to Kuttalan village, also in Thanjavur district, to stay with my mother's elder brother, who was not so badly off. My early education was at the district board school in Kuttalan. When I was eleven years old, my mother died. That was a rude shock for me as I was the closest to her. I stayed on with my uncle and completed my school education, after which I moved to Chennai with Vaidyanathan, my elder brother. If anyone has had a role in shaping me it was him. My father had always been a distant and aloof figure in my life, and it was from Vaidyanathan, two years older than me, that I learnt the values of hard work and personal integrity.

My eldest brother Subramaniam, who was ten years older than me, was already in Chennai working with the Southern Railways. He had married. Both my brothers had to take up jobs after high school because of our financial circumstances. They could not study further. Vaidyanathan joined the newly launched Tamil weekly *Kalki* as its circulation manager. He was deeply involved in the freedom movement and, through him, I had the opportunity to see and interact with great personalities like C. Rajagopalachari and Kalki Sadasivam. Influenced by them, I started volunteering for small tasks in the freedom movement. I was keen to continue my studies after school, but no one in the family could guide me since education was not something anyone had ever been serious about. The only objective I had was to get some training that was adequate to land a job that was a little more than just run-of-the-mill.

In any case, getting into a good college was not easy. The anti-Brahmin movement had started, and I had the double handicap of being a Brahmin boy with a rural background. Though I had done well, my marks were not high enough to overcome these two obstacles. A relative who had retired as the principal of Patchiapas College then suggested an alternative—that I join an intermediate three-year course in engineering which would help me get employment.

The Second World War had broken out by then. The British government had started a programme called Bevin Boys, in which young boys were put through a shortened engineering course in order to train them to take up war-related activities. Modelled on that, a sandwich course in engineering had been designed in India. I got admission to the CNT Technical Institute for a three-year course in electrical engineering and got a diploma in 1943. During my free time, I continued to volunteer in the freedom struggle.

By then, the fortunes of my family had also started to change. From a time when people were unwilling to lend us Rs 100, we were now in a position to help others. We became a focal point for our extended family and friends living in the villages and wanting to move to the city. At 6 a.m. every day, a train would arrive at Chennai from Thanjavur. Four days of the week, some relative or the other would get off the train and come to our house—some for medical treatment, others for help in getting their children admitted to college, and so on. My brothers and I could never say no to anybody who approached us for help, no matter how difficult their request was.

There was an informal division of work among us. Subramaniam would look after the living arrangements, Vaidyanathan would handle whatever networking was required, and I would do the running around. Maybe that is where I learnt my first lessons in delegated responsibilities. I also picked up the values of trust and selflessness from my family. Initially, only my eldest brother was earning. The money would be kept in one place and everybody helped himself. By the twenty-fifth of the month, there would be no money left! But there were no recriminations from anyone. There were three watches between us, and all of us wore size 24 shirts. Neither the watches nor the shirts were identified with any one of us. We would just pick up whatever there was and wear it. There was never any question of yours or mine. I have never thought about it consciously, but maybe that was when I developed my penchant for making people think of their welfare and an organization's welfare as linked. The way we ran our household taught me many lessons in joint responsibility that would hold me in good stead in my later years and which I went on to incorporate into management practices.

When I finished college in 1943, there were hardly any employment opportunities in the civilian space, and even the jobs that we had thought were assured were not forthcoming. The British were constructing some airfields to meet the Japanese aggression and, with the help of some family friends, I got temporary employment as a technician in charge of electrical installations at two airfields at Kolar and Chettinad. This was good practical training for me. However, by the end of 1944, the war effort started winding down. I realized that this job would not last and that I had to look for other opportunities. With some difficulty, I got into the design and drawing office of the electricity department of what was then Madras Presidency. I was initially posted with the Mettur hydroelectrical project as a trainee. After a year's training there, I was posted to Chennai in a junior supervisory position.

For the next two years, I was involved in the design of several hydroelectric projects, including the Periyar and Kundah projects. Around this time, the British were preparing to leave, and I was put in the division meant to take over the assets of the British-owned Madras Electricity Supply Corporation as supervisor, with a brief to value the assets. After that, there was no looking back. I grabbed every opportunity to learn and grow professionally.

I was posted as junior engineer to the prestigious technical directorate headed by V.P. Appadurai, chief engineer of the electricity department. He took a liking to me and made a huge difference to my life at that time. Anti-Brahmin sentiments were running high but that did not stop Appadurai—himself from the non-Brahmin Mudaliar community—from encouraging me. I never let him down. Appadurai was always the first to enter office. Soon he found I was there before him. He also found that I had an aptitude for solving the most difficult problems with speed, and he started entrusting me with more and more responsibilities. That only earned me the envy of my peers. At one point, those among the old guard at the technical directorate complained to Appadurai that he was favouring me unduly and not giving them opportunities to prove themselves. Appadurai, on his part, ignored such protests and said that he would encourage anyone coming up to the same standards. It did not bother me either, because at a very young age I got important responsibilities like working on the designs of the Periyar and Kundah hydroelectrical projects and making a presentation to then Prime Minister Jawaharlal Nehru on the achievements of the erstwhile Madras Electricity Department. My stint there gave me the opportunity to be associated with the beginning of the development activity of independent India. In addition, I had forged a very strong relationship with a few of my colleagues—N. Gopalan, C. Sanjeevi and K.R. Radhakrishnan—and we were a formidable force within the organization.

But, in my bones, I felt I would not get a good deal in the future because of my caste. When Appadurai sent my name to the Madras Service Commission for an accelerated promotion, the papers were returned to him, raising all kinds of questions just because I was not from the preferred community. Appadurai did not give up and argued my case before the commission members and got my promotion through. However, that revealed to me the kind of problems I would face as my career progressed, and that disturbed me.

At that time, the Planning Commission wanted to start work on the Second Five-Year Plan. The Government of India put out a circular that invited applications for research officers with experience of planning and designing power projects on a deputation basis in the Planning Commission's natural resources division. I happened to fit the bill but was in two minds about applying. Some friends egged me on, and I applied for the job. Appadurai was not happy that I was planning to leave, but I convinced him to let me try my luck. He forwarded my application and, fortunately, I got selected without much problem. A letter was sent to the state government, asking it to place my services at the disposal of the Planning Commission.

This was a great opportunity to join the Central Engineering Services (CES), though initially on deputation. I had missed that opportunity earlier because I had not taken the competitive examination for the CES. But the state government proved very uncooperative. Questions were raised about how I was selected, how my application was forwarded, and whether others had also been given the opportunity. Appadurai once again came to my help and pleaded my case, getting me to give an assurance that I would return to the state government after my deputation was over. The Planning Commission also put pressure on the state government, saying it could not stand in my way after having forwarded my application. In 1954, I joined the Planning Commission as a research officer in the natural resources division.

I had no difficulty in establishing myself there and getting noticed. The division was formulating a national plan for power generation, and the experience I had gained in the Madras Electricity Department came in handy. Soon Appadurai and others in the state realized that my being in the Planning

Commission was useful for them, since they never had the kind of support and guidance that I could give them from Delhi. They tapped me a lot on issues they had to deal with, and that gave me more opportunities to prove myself.

I was on a one-year deputation and, at the end of the period, I had to make a choice about whether to return to Chennai and the state electricity department or stay back in Delhi. I opted for the latter. I appeared for a competitive examination held by the Union Public Service Commission (UPSC) and, in 1955, I joined the CES as a regular employee of the central government. I was promoted as senior research officer and allotted to the Planning Commission to work specifically on power development.

Joining the Planning Commission was *the* turning point in my life. It was during my five-year stint there that I got a ringside view of policy making and learnt to think big and to look at problems in a wider perspective. I doubt if I would have been able to achieve the successes I did later in my professional life if it were not for my years there.

The Planning Commission in those days was an intellectually vibrant place, where a fledgling country's development story was being written by the finest Indian minds—Prime Minister Jawaharlal Nehru, who was the chairman; Sir V.T. Krishnamachari, the first deputy chairman; P.C. Mahalanobis; J.J. Anjaria, who was the first chief economic adviser in the finance ministry and chief of the economic division of the commission; and administrators like Tarlok Singh (from whom I learnt the art of drafting notes), Penderel Moon and Pitambar Pant. The full Planning Commission (which included ministers) would meet frequently, and those meetings were attended by heavyweight ministers like Chintamani Deshmukh, T.T. Krishnamachari (known as T.T.K.), V.K. Krishna Menon, Rafi Ahmed Kidwai as well as chief ministers like Govind Ballabh

Pant of Uttar Pradesh, Dr Bidhan Chandra Roy of West Bengal, Ravi Shankar Shukla of Madhya Pradesh, Partap Singh Kairon of Punjab, K. Kamaraj of Tamil Nadu and S. Nijalingappa of Karnataka. I attended these meetings as a representative of the natural resource division and I was often deputed to take notes at various meetings. The quality of those discussions was outstanding and completely non-partisan. National interest always prevailed over everything else.

I particularly remember a discussion on a proposal by the West Bengal chief minister, Dr Bidhan Chandra Roy, for a steel mill in Durgapur. The member, industry, in the Commission, K.C. Neogy, though hailing from the state, was not in favour of the idea. He was not sure there would be sufficient demand in the country for steel. He was also not sure whether a young country had the wherewithal to take up one more steel plant apart from the ones at Bhilai and Rourkela. But Roy said he had refugees from erstwhile East Pakistan pouring into the state and needed to develop Durgapur as an industrial belt to provide employment. The proposal was strongly backed by T.T.K., who hailed from Tamil Nadu. T.T.K. even said he would quit the government if the proposal was not sanctioned. There were three hours of impassioned discussion, with no personal, regional or political factors making their presence felt. Finally, in the national interest, it was decided to approve the steel plant.

Of my years in the Planning Commission what I treasured most was the close interaction with people like Mahalanobis and being spotted by people like Moon and L.K. Jha, who would later play a role in several of my important assignments. These people had a knack of identifying juniors with potential and giving them opportunities to grow. Perhaps that stayed with me and was behind my initiatives in my later assignments to identify and encourage talent in every organization.

The natural resources division was also associated with the drawing up of the First Ten Year Plan for the development of atomic power, a subject that Pandit Nehru himself handled. I often—again as a sort of clerk of the court—sat in on the meetings he had on the subject with Homi J. Bhabha, the father of India's nuclear programme. It was a treat to watch such a distinguished person unfold his plans. Visiting state capitals during discussions on the annual plans also gave me a deep insight into the national perspective on development issues confronting the states and, more particularly, issues relating to power. Since I had done a stint in the state electricity department, I could also relate to what state-level officials said much better than the macro economists.

The natural resources division also had the responsibility of formulating the long-term priorities for power development. We wrestled with issues of the optimum mix of thermal and hydro power and came to the conclusion that since there were limitations on hydro power, that could account for only 40 per cent of generation; 60 per cent would have to come from thermal power, where coal would be the mainstay of generation. Given this, in order to cut down the cost of carrying coal to power plants, we came up with the concept of pit-head power plants (locating power generation stations at or close to coal mines), which was to become the order of the day later. This was the seminal paper on long-term planning for power that I worked on along with S. Swayambhu, who was the head of the power wing in the natural resources division, and my colleague K.R. Paramesvar, who became a lifelong friend. A lot of new ideas were being thrown up, and the Planning Commission gave us the opportunity to air them.

While the Planning Commission was debating about the need for accelerated and enhanced development of the power sector in the Second Plan, Pandit Nehru expressed concern that such large scale power development would not be possible in the country with heavy dependence on imported equipment. In those days, the annual addition contemplated was 4,000 MW for the whole country. The government had been thinking about the need for domestic production of power equipment for some years, and it finally decided to examine the feasibility of this. A committee headed by S.A. Gadkary, who had retired as member, power, in the Central Water and Power Commission, was set up.

I was assigned to assist the committee in an informal manner in addition to my official responsibilities. I collected information on future demand, the capacity of transformers, and the type and quantity of switchgear required for every megawatt of power to be generated. All this gave me tremendous insight into the problems relating to the manufacturing industry and the issues relating to skills and training. Though I was in the natural resources division, I also closely worked with the industry division, and so I was aware of the issues facing Indian industry as well. All this sparked off an interest in getting my hands dirty by being involved in a manufacturing operation and the development of an industry.

The Gadkary Committee recommended that the manufacture of power equipment be taken up in the public sector. Accordingly, Heavy Electricals (India) Ltd (HE(I)L) was set up in 1956 in collaboration with a British firm, Associated Electrical Industries (AEI), with a manufacturing plant in Bhopal. I was quick to apply for a job in the new venture, hopeful that my experience in working with the Gadkary Committee would stand me in good stead. It did, and I was selected to work in the commercial department of HE(I)L. But work on drafting the Third Five-Year Plan had just started, and the Planning Commission refused to release me. I was shattered, but there was nothing I could do. I continued to work in the Planning

Commission. Little did I know that better things were in store for me.

As the Third Five-Year Plan unfolded, the government found HE(I)L's planned capacity was not adequate for the country's growing need for power equipment. It appointed another committee headed by H.R. Bhatia of the Punjab Electricity Board to review the Gadkary report and estimate the country's future power equipment needs. Based on the recommendations of this committee, the industry ministry decided to set up two more power equipment manufacturing plants under HE(I)L. By this time, K.B. Mathur, who had retired as chairman of the Railway Board, had been appointed chairman of HE(I)L.

I was finding my job in the Planning Commission routine and wanted to move on. I had spent five years there and been associated with two five-year plans. Meanwhile, Swayambhu had left to join HE(I)L, and my division was headed by another person with whom I was not getting along. I had mentioned earlier to Jha, who was dealing with these matters in the prime minister's office, that I would like to move to manufacturing operations whenever there was an opportunity. Since Mathur was not familiar with the power equipment sector, Jha and Moon suggested my name as an officer on special duty to assist him on a deputation basis for a year.

It was a risk leaving the secure CES and joining a fledgling public sector organization. But I decided to take the plunge. Having done macro planning in the Planning Commission, I wanted to do planning for a specific industry. I felt it would be more exciting.

After my appointment became public, I had gone to the Railway Board on some work. There I met a friend of mine who said, 'I thought you were a sensible man, but clearly you are not.' He said nobody liked to work with Mathur, since he did not tolerate any dissent. I was a bit disturbed since I had a habit of being very frank in airing my opinions. But there was no going back. In 1960, I quit the Planning Commission and joined HE(I)L.

As it turned out, my misgivings were unfounded. After Appadurai, Mathur was my next mentor, and I not only got along very well with him but he also helped shape me as a manager.

A new chapter in my life was about to begin.

# 2

# MY TRYST WITH MANAGEMENT

I joined HE(I)L in 1960, as officer on special duty, with a wee bit of trepidation. After all, I was giving up a secure job as a regular employee of the CES to join a relatively new public sector organization. Besides, the words of my friend who had warned me about my new boss, K.B. Mathur, were still ringing in my ears. Was I making the right choice?

I quickly realized that the picture of Mathur that my friend had painted was not correct. Mathur was a wonderful boss, and it was he who helped hone my managerial capabilities. He delegated responsibilities and made people working under him feel empowered, a lesson which I put to practical use when I reached positions of authority later. Between four and six every evening, over tea, he would review with me all that had happened during the day and discuss what else needed to be done over the following week or so. The next morning, it was left to me to convey all that needed to be done to the general managers of the three plants. He never kept any files or papers on his desk, and work never got stalled.

The choice of the three general managers for the three plants showed Mathur's foresight in picking a multi-disciplinary team. Kohli, a retired additional director of the Railway Board, was a civil engineer; Appa, a serving chief engineer of HE(I)L, was an electrical engineer; and Krishnan, who was from the Indian Railways and was serving as chief engineer at the Durgapur steel plant, was a mechanical engineer. How he handled the general managers was in itself a wonderful lesson in man management. D.R. Kohli, the general manager of the Haridwar plant, was a trifle indecisive and a bit slow to act, referring matters to the head office for decisions at the slightest pretext. N.D.M. Appa, general manager of the Hyderabad plant, would take decisions, but Mathur always had a nagging doubt about the financial propriety of some of them. R.S. Krishnan, general manager of the Trichy plant, was extremely quick in taking decisions, and Mathur feared he would trip up somewhere along the line. A run-of-the-mill manager would treat all of them in the same manner, but not Mathur. Mathur would prod Kohli into action, carefully check the financial aspects of any contract Appa signed so as to avoid any embarrassment to the organization later, and would caution Krishnan not to rush into decisions. It was something that stayed with me, and all through my professional life as a manager, I identified the strengths and weaknesses of individuals and dealt with them in a manner that honed the former and neutralized the latter.

I plunged into the excitement of being involved in the building of indigenous power equipment manufacturing plants. A year after I joined, I was designated project officer and given the responsibility of preparing the initial project reports for the two new plants and was to assist Mathur in implementing them. Another year later, my responsibilities were further increased, and I became chief of planning and development. I was given complete freedom to shape the project, and I made full use of it. Such freedom and autonomy is unimaginable today.

The first task related to the new projects was to identify

locations for the plants. One plant was to manufacture large steam turbines, turbo generators and hydro generators, and the other plant was to manufacture small and medium turbines and boilers. Mathur, O.S. Murthy (director of the Railway Planning Board*), Kohli and I were put on a committee to identify sites.

The only brief we had from the government was that one plant should be located in the north and one in the south, and that they should help in opening up an underdeveloped area to industrialization. On our checklist were two additional requirements—the availability of 6,000 acres of land and access to water; and availability of adequate labour force as well as skilled employees.

When we invited proposals, state governments vied with each other to offer suitable sites. But the competition was not an unhealthy one; there were no parochial arguments or pressuring that one sees today. Perhaps that had something to do with the fact that several other large projects—steel mills, fertiliser plants, power plants—were being planned, and the states knew that even if they lost out on one, they were likely to get something else.

After visiting and evaluating many sites in different states, we decided on Haridwar in the north for the Heavy Electrical Equipment Plant to manufacture larger turbines and generators. There were many reasons for this decision, the main being the opening up of an underdeveloped area for industrialization, specifically in Uttar Pradesh. The decision invited a lot of jibes and ridicule, and people wondered what a place whose only claim to fame was as a pilgrimage centre could offer for a plant meant to manufacture sophisticated equipment. But we remained

---

*The involvement of the railways was natural because its civil engineering wing had immense experience in scouting for locations for manufacturing facilities for the railways.

firm on Haridwar, and our decision proved right. The Haridwar plant now produces the most sophisticated of power equipment that stands up to stiff international competition.

The selection of a site 30 km from Hyderabad city, with nothing but rocky outcrop in between, for the Heavy Power Equipment Plant was also jeered. But once again, the future proved us right. There was more criticism in store when we decided to split the Heavy Power Equipment Plant into two—one manufacturing turbines to be located in Hyderabad and another manufacturing high pressure boilers to be located in Tiruchirappalli (Trichy) in Tamil Nadu. The decision was based on sound logic. There was nothing in common in the technology for manufacturing turbines and boilers, and splitting the manufacturing operations would ensure that both the lines of production would grow without any constraint on resources. Besides, two different areas would reap the benefits of industrialization, along with enabling both the plants to grow faster. Critics questioned why a boiler plant should be located so far down south when boilers were needed in the coal belts up north. My response to that was that the manufacture of boilers required high-order engineering skills which were easily available near Trichy, as south India was known for its rich engineering talent at that time. The cost of transporting boilers from Tamil Nadu to the northern parts of India would admittedly be high, but even a one per cent higher efficiency in the operation of the plant would offset any extra cost of transportation. Time has proved that these decisions were correct.

The decision also set off a political storm. It invited a lot of criticism from the Andhra Pradesh government, which wanted both the turbine and boiler plants to be set up in the state. The state of Andhra Pradesh had been formed a few years earlier, in 1956 (following the division of the Madras Presidency), and the state government and people felt that by taking the boiler plant away from Hyderabad, the state was being denied its due by Tamilians—C. Subramaniam, the steel and heavy industries minister, was from Tamil Nadu, and Tamil Nadu Chief Minister K. Kamaraj was an influential Congress leader. All Andhra Pradesh political leaders made their displeasure public. The matter then reached Prime Minister Nehru. He suggested that the investment in the Trichy plant be less than that of the Hyderabad plant, thus mollifying Andhra Pradesh with higher investment. In spite of all the opposition, the Government of India accepted our recommendations as it felt that they were based on sound technological and managerial considerations. Once this ticklish question of location had been settled, we sat down to define the projects.

The government had, when deciding to set up these plants, selected the technical collaborators as well—Prommashexport of the Soviet Union for the heavy electrical equipment plant at Haridwar and First Brno Engineering Works represented by Skoda Export of Czechoslovakia for the small and medium turbines plant at Hyderabad and the high pressure boiler plant at Trichy. We had no role to play in this. We also had to go along with what the government had broadly agreed on with the collaborating countries with regard to the product mix and scope of technology in the economic cooperation agreement signed with them. Keeping the scope of the economic cooperation agreement that the governments had signed in mind, the collaborators prepared detailed project reports on the basis of detailed information we provided on sites, market requirements and skills availability, among other things. I was the main person involved in coordination during the preparation of these reports, and the year-long interaction with the collaborators gave me very good insight into the various stages of project formulation and implementation.

At the project report preparation stage, negotiations with the collaborating firms revolved around the products that the plants were to manufacture and the technology they were to use within the scope defined by the government. Mathur nominated me as the main negotiator and I, in turn, took the help of many experts. A young country did not have the resources to go shopping for equipment, and despite the government-level understanding on collaboration, I had to bargain hard to get the best technology and equipment at the lowest cost from these firms and also try and maximize the indigenous content. These negotiations were to prove extremely challenging, and I was fortunate that Mathur gave me a lot of freedom to conduct them, even though I was relatively inexperienced.

The negotiations with the Czechs were comparatively easier because they were not overbearing by nature. But those with the Soviets proved to be extremely tough, mainly because of political factors. The Cold War was at its peak, and India had aligned itself with the Soviet Union-led eastern bloc. The Soviets were always trying to get India to buy more of the components supplied by them instead of letting India manufacture them; their argument was that the components in question were very complicated products and could not be manufactured here and should, therefore, be imported. I would then have to counter this and see that Indian interests were safeguarded. The moment I asked for the price of some equipment or component to be reduced, negotiations would drag, with no fruitful result emerging. Both sides would keep repeating the arguments. Sometimes I gave in, sometimes they did. When a complete deadlock was reached, the Soviet government machinery would take over.

The economic minister at the Soviet embassy would seek an appointment with Mathur. He, knowing quite well what it was about since I used to keep him informed, would fix the meeting for 12 p.m. When the meeting started, he would indulge in extended pleasantries and then discuss everything under the sun except the scheduled topic. A favourite subject would be the details of the renovation of the marshalling yard at the Mughalsarai railway station when he was in the railways. As the clock ticked closer to 1 p.m. and the exasperated diplomat brought up the negotiations, Mathur would say, 'Oh I am sure Krishnamurthy is handling everything well. Continue talking to him. These are matters on which he will take decisions; I don't interfere.' With that, he would get up and end the meeting and leave at 1 p.m. sharp for his lunch!

Sometimes the Soviet representatives would then approach the industry or power minister, asking them to intervene. To the credit of the politicians of that time, they rarely ever did. Only once, on a matter related to the pricing of machinery, did a minister ask me to go a bit easy. That was the time some crucial negotiations relating to the Bokaro steel plant were underway, again with the Soviet Union, and the fate of that plant was at stake. Subramaniam asked me not to be rigid beyond a point with the Russians in this case as their help in setting up the Bokaro Steel Plant was indispensable and that some compromise on HE(I)L's part would help the Bokaro project. It would be pertinent to recall that this was during Nehru's time, and there was a political commitment to making the public sector a success. Ministers saw the public sector as a responsibility they needed to nurture, not a fiefdom they had to exploit for their personal or political ends.

Negotiations with the Russians and Czechs were confined to equipment and services available in their respective countries. In addition to these, HE(I)L had to obtain a host of other equipment and services both domestically as well as from other countries. It was again my responsibility to procure these to complete the project.

While the civil and infrastructure work at the plant was in

progress, our next big challenge was to get and train people in designing and manufacturing power equipment. Trained engineers were in short supply those days. It was a new nation and the Indian Institutes of Technology (IITs) had been set up only in the early 1950s and were just about ten years old. The power equipment industry was even younger. Getting experienced people was out of the question. The only trained engineers were in the railways, defence services and in some state electricity boards. So we had little choice but to hire a large number of fresh engineering graduates and send them for training abroad. We got an enthusiastic response to our recruitment advertisements. All the applicants wanted to do hard core engineering, opportunities for which were still limited in India. At the same time, there was some uncertainty in their minds because no one knew what shape the industry would take or how robust its future would be. Many also joined because we were sending them abroad for training.

We had a rigorous recruitment drill, with a retired member of the Union Public Service Commission and two others in charge of the process. There was complete transparency in the way the selections were made and no one could complain of nepotism or favouritism. We recruited around 1,400 engineers and sent them to the Soviet Union or Czechoslovakia for training in the fundamentals of the design and manufacture of power equipment. The training, which lasted between two and three years, was of superior quality, and soon we had a bunch of highly qualified engineers who could design and manufacture a sophisticated product from scratch, meeting global standards.

In all this, Mathur gave me complete freedom and trusted me implicitly. It reached a point where, in a replay of what happened when I was in the Madras Electricity Department and colleagues complained about Appadurai giving me too much importance, several contemporaries at BHEL approached Lal

Bahadur Shastri, who was then the minister for commerce and industry, and told him that I called the shots in the company and that Mathur was ignoring others. I learnt all this later. One day, Mathur told me to meet Shastri and explain the progress on the projects and how the negotiations with the collaborators were proceeding. I was a bit puzzled by this but went and briefed the minister and answered whatever questions he put to me. When I came back and told Mathur about what transpired, it was then that he told me that the minister had asked him why he was giving me so much importance and that Mathur had told him to assess me himself. After this, throughout the project, I periodically reported the progress to the then industries minister.

But even as the early stages of construction were well underway in all the three new units, the main unit at Bhopal was still floundering, several years after the project had been started. Subramaniam felt that the reason for the Bhopal unit not doing well was that Mathur was unable to manage all four units and that the three new units under construction should be separated from the operating unit at Bhopal. He felt that the four units would be better managed if they were split into two entirely different corporate entities under two different managements. He mentioned this to me during one of my regular briefings on the progress of the projects. I took the extraordinary step of arguing with him that his reasoning was wrong and that the plants would benefit from being under a common chairman, as that would facilitate a free exchange of ideas and people and better customer service. But the government was firm, and in November 1964, Bharat Heavy Electricals Ltd (BHEL) was incorporated as a new company, with the three units at Haridwar, Hyderabad and Trichy. Mathur gave up his post as chairman of HE(I)L and became chairman and managing director of BHEL, while K.C. Lall replaced him at HE(I)L.

Naturally, I became a part of BHEL under Mathur and remained chief of planning and development.

Through meticulous planning, I was able to coordinate the completion of the civil and construction work at the sites with the commissioning of plants and equipment by engineers trained in the Soviet Union and Czechoslovakia. This I would consider my unique achievement at a time when the Indian public sector was characterized by inefficiency, inordinate delays and cost overruns in project planning and implementation.

Around that time, international manufacturers had developed a new type of circuit breakers called the 'air blast circuit breakers'. This product was different from the oil circuit breakers produced by HE(I)L at Bhopal. Logically, the Bhopal unit should have picked up this new technology. But for a variety of reasons, including that of its engagement with its British consultant, it could not enter this line. We at BHEL saw this as an opportunity. I successfully negotiated with Swedish electric company ASEA and got it to collaborate with BHEL. As switching equipment was not part of the planned products of the Haridwar, Hyderabad and Trichy units, we decided to set up a switchgear unit at the Hyderabad campus. This switchgear manufacturing unit became the fourth unit of BHEL and was highly successful. We got C.V. Cariappa, working then at Bharat Electronics, to head this new unit as general manager.

Some months later, Mathur retired, and another former chairman of the Railway Board, D.C. Baijal, replaced him. By that time, sections of the three plants were in different stages of commissioning, and the one in Trichy had started production. Decisions on a lot of operational details that needed to be taken locally at the site were being passed up to the chairman's office. In many cases, I felt the decisions in the chairman's office were being taken in an ad hoc manner, without keeping the long-term interests of the company in mind. Since Baijal was on a short-term contract, his risk-taking ability was seen to be low. Although he was a very competent and fair-minded person, Baijal's comprehension of the manufacturing industry was comparatively low, and this often led to a difference of opinion between us on the methods of management of large enterprises. The role of a chairman of an organization in an operational phase is different from that of one in a construction phase. In the organizational phase, the aspirations of the young engineers and technologists at the plant had to be addressed by projecting future policies in terms of technology, marketing, customer penetration, etc. I found myself differing with Baijal on these issues. The feedback I received from the plants was that the chairman was not taking a long-term view of the organization.

It was at this juncture that I told Baijal that I wanted to quit the head office and move to one of the plants. In any case, I had spent seven years planning and managing at the macro level, and I now wanted the challenge of implementing a project at the micro level. Initially, he did not agree but came around when I kept insisting. He wanted me to go to Haridwar, which was considered the largest of the three units. But I was reluctant, since a new general manager, Jagdish Prasad, had only recently been appointed. I would have gone there as his deputy and would have to wait till he retired to take charge. The other problem was that I did not know Hindi. How could I run a plant without being able to communicate with my workers? In spite of my apprehensions, however, I was considering his offer.

In the last year of Baijal's three-year tenure, he said he wanted Krishnan, who had done an outstanding job in completing the Trichy plant and operationalizing it within the stipulated time frame, to succeed him. Krishnan agreed but on one condition—that I should head the Trichy plant when he shifted to Delhi. Baijal was reluctant, since Trichy was the smallest of the three plants. I was also a bit hesitant. Normally, Trichy would have been an ideal place to go to since it had already gone into operation and I would get experience in building it up. Besides, it was also the place where one could experiment the most. But it would involve returning to Tamil Nadu. Caste politics was at its peak at that time, and I remembered what I had faced during my stint at the Madras Electricity Department. Moreover, Trichy was not very far from Thanjavur, the district from which my family hailed, and I was worried that every action of mine would be scrutinized for personal considerations or nepotism, even if I was scrupulously professional in my decisions. My wife was also unhappy since our eldest son, Chandra, was in the final year of school at that time. But Krishnan was adamant on his condition and, finally in 1967, I moved to Trichy.

That was to prove to be another tipping point for my career. It was there that I was able to blossom as a manager.

~

When I went to Trichy, the only brief was to take over the baton from Krishnan. I was concerned about how the new organization would receive me. After all, there were two deputy general managers senior to me already in place. How would they react?

I was designated senior deputy general manager, so that my position in the hierarchy became clear. However, Krishnan did not issue any order detailing my responsibilities. People thought I had been imposed upon them by the head office. One week later, Zdnek Kuchler, the representative of Skoda Exports (the Czech firm that was coordinating between First Brno and BHEL), asked Krishnan what papers he should refer to me. Krishnan told him that whatever matters were referred to him should be sent to me. If I could handle them, I would, or else I would send them on to him. That sent out a message about my role. Later, I was given the responsibility of all departments except civil construction, which was under P.V.K. Achan. I got busy in organizing the different departments and setting out their responsibilities, discussions with state electricity boards (which were our main customers) and in coordinating with the headquarters in Delhi. In addition, since I had been chief of development and planning of all the three plants, I would often get queries and requests for help from the Haridwar and Hyderabad plants. Other public sector undertakings would also approach me for help because of my experience in dealing with Soviets and Czechs. In a way, I felt satisfied that my work in HE(I)L and BHEL had been recognized.

Soon I realized that Krishnan did not have a homogenous team. One day, the financial adviser and chief accounts officer, P.T. Venugopal, came to see me with around thirty files. He said they related to issues on which he did not agree with Krishnan. In those days, if the general manager and the financial adviser differed on a matter, it had to be referred to the chairman or to the board. Venugopal told me to go through them and take a decision. Invariably, he went by my suggestions. K.G. Belliappa, a mechanical engineer who was the works manager and whom Krishnan had brought along with him from the railways, did not adhere to organizational discipline. Krishnan would commit to a customer to give a certain quantity of boiler components, but three months down the line, Belliappa would reduce it by half. He did not like Krishnan asking him why production was low or looking into how the workshop was functioning or insisting that the commitment made to the customer be met. Krishnan could not do much about it as Belliappa was a senior officer of the railways, and he did not want to take action against him. But I tried to make Belliappa see reason—that as a commercial organization, we needed to fulfil our commitment to the customers. Belliappa proved to be intractable, and later I had to ask him to leave. These two incidents with Venugopal and Belliappa gave me the confidence that I had the authority to implement my ideas. At the same time, the trust reposed in me put a lot of responsibility on me. My initial apprehension about how I would be received seemed to melt away.

I was also familiarizing myself with operational issues. Although the plant had started production in May 1965 (the first BHEL unit to do so), business was extremely slow to pick up. The rated capacity of the plant was 30,000 tonnes a year. It had logged production of less than 3,000 tonnes in the first year. Perhaps it could have done 10,000 tonnes, but there were not enough orders. Instead of increasing staff gradually as production increased, Krishnan had recruited as if the plant would operate at full capacity at the outset itself. So there were 7,000 people on the rolls. As a result, people were working at sub-optimal levels. I realized there was a need to build up the tempo of work. But that required going out and getting orders. There was no dedicated sales team in any of the three plants, and Krishnan, V.R. Deenadayalu (who was in charge of planning), and I would go to different state electricity boards and pitch for contracts. Our first large contract was for the Ennore power plant in Tamil Nadu. Interestingly, my old mentor, Appadurai, was heading the Tamil Nadu Electricity Board, and our old chemistry helped the deal go through with a speed unknown in government circles at that time.

I was just settling in and learning the ropes when tragedy struck. One morning at 5 a.m., I got a call saying Krishnan had been taken ill. I rushed to his house. He was asthmatic and had suffered a heart attack. I was next to him when he passed away. I was very upset. We had become very friendly, and I had a lot of respect for him as a professional. I seriously considered whether I should continue or return to Delhi. It is always difficult to succeed a successful person. Krishnan was worshipped in Trichy. Because of my designation, people knew that I would succeed Krishnan as managing director when he moved to the headquarters, but doing so practically overnight in such tragic circumstances was a different matter. Baijal, however, said I should continue and did not lose time in appointing me as general manager of the unit. After all, this was the only plant that was in production, and it had to be made a success. I was already being trained for the job and was familiar with the issues the unit was facing. So I had to stay on, but I was a bit nervous about whether I would be able to fill his shoes. There was a general doubt among the team in Trichy, too, about whether I would succeed in my new role.

~

So there I was, the managing director of a plant at forty-one years, and perhaps the youngest person to hold that post. Till then, I had held only non-executive positions and had no experience of any micro-level work. I had been involved in planning in the Madras Electricity Department; in the Planning Commission, I had been engaged in analyzing and formulating policy; and since I moved to BHEL, I was involved in planning, project formulation and overseeing the plants at a macro level. Now I was the business head for an entire plant. At the headquarters, I had only a few people reporting to me. Now I had to deal with 7,000 employees, ensuring that they were kept busy and motivated.

Having observed over the past few months the way the plant functioned, I knew that some of the policies that Krishnan had followed had to change. But I also knew that any radical and noticeable departure would create resentment towards me. I had to change things but give the impression it was only a continuation of Krishnan's legacy.

I personally felt that Krishnan had to be honoured for what he had achieved in Trichy. I genuinely believed that he had done a great job of getting the plant to the production stage in the face of great challenges while the other two plants were floundering, and I wanted to perpetuate his memory. Many public sector managers remain anonymous and uncelebrated despite having done yeoman service to the country, and I did not want that to happen in Krishnan's case. Hence, one of the first things I did on taking over was to collect a subscription from each of the 7,000 employees, contribute a substantial amount myself and install a bust of Krishnan at the centre of the factory. I also announced that his birthday would be observed as founder's day. It was unheard of—how could a public sector factory have a founder? But I went ahead. I also renamed the missionary school on the BHEL campus, which Krishnan had been instrumental in starting, R.S. Krishnan Memorial School. Some time later, I started the R.S. Krishnan Bridge Tournament. This was my way of recognizing a man who did pioneering work in the public sector. All these actions endeared me to the employees, and they began seeing me as someone who was prepared to respect what had been done earlier and unlikely to undo anything that would hurt their pride.

On the work front, my immediate challenge was to enlarge the order book, ramp up production and improve upon the production schedule. This could only be done by eliminating the inefficiency and sloth that was considered normal for any government organization and that required me to first turn my attention to the employees at all levels and inculcate an entrepreneurial spirit. Trichy was to become the laboratory for many new initiatives, which I later scaled up at the national level in BHEL and replicated in my other assignments.

I set about attempting to usher in a new work culture in the organization, emphasizing higher degrees of discipline, team work and productivity. I faced some resistance here. Though I had inherited very senior and experienced managers, quite a few of them came with a hierarchical and bureaucratic mindset that was not in sync with the kind of work culture I wanted to inculcate. Many of them had been hired from the railways, a service to which Krishnan originally belonged.

Nevertheless, I worked on motivating people, explaining to them that they were not just cogs in a wheel producing boilers but were working for a larger cause of the nation. Merely giving pep talks was not enough, however. I had to demonstrate that I meant what I was saying. I had learnt very early in life, thanks to the ups and downs my family had seen, the need to treat people with dignity. I also realized I could not be an ivory tower manager and interacted with both senior executives and workers regularly.

I would ask workers about their work and invite suggestions on how to improve their efficiency. I am a firm believer in the fact that even unskilled workers can make extremely useful suggestions. In the evenings on my way home, I used to walk into a different shop floor every day, address workers by their first names, ask after their families and other personal problems and try to help in whatever way I could. I take pride in saying that I knew all employees of mine by name and was aware of their personal problems. The fact that the general manager knew them personally made a huge difference to them. I also said that anyone was free to approach me and air their grievances. If someone said he had not got his promotion or increment, I considered it an insult to me. Why should they have to ask? Why did the management not know that the promotion or increment was due and do something about it?

Earlier, workers had to approach the trade union with any grievance, individual or collective. The union would then represent the matter to the personnel department, which would then take its time to address the problem. The general manager would get information that was filtered through the personnel department. My approach cut through this hierarchy. Some of my managers did not like this. One of them was P.A. Menon, the chief personnel manager. He objected to my being accessible to the workers or attending union meetings and sorting out issues on the spot. He felt it undermined his authority. It was not my intention to do that or even give that impression. I would have happily let him handle his responsibilities on his own. But he had an extremely bureaucratic approach, asking one of his junior officers to talk to the workers, not explaining why a particular decision was taken or not taken and being abrupt with them and the union. That attitude may have worked in the railways. It was out of place in a commercial organization which still had to prove itself.

One major challenge on the employee front was dealing with the trade unionism. The Indian National Trade Union Congress (INTUC), the apex trade union backed by the Congress, was the recognized union at Trichy, but it was being challenged by the Centre for Indian Trade Unions (CITU), which was affiliated to the Communist Party of India (Marxist) or CPM. The CITU was very active in the railways workshop in Trichy and was making inroads into BHEL. Now, the Dravida Munnetra Kazhagam (DMK), which had come into power in Tamil Nadu, also wanted to establish its own trade union wing, and the large BHEL workforce was a huge attraction. The CITU and the DMK's trade union wings were constantly engaged in a game of one-upmanship with the recognized union and with each other in their attempt to woo workers. In doing so, they were constantly upping the ante on several issues, from punctuality to overtime to bonus, and fomenting trouble.

The presence of multiple trade unions made negotiations with workers difficult. Since even the recognized union did not enjoy the allegiance of every worker, I was looking for a way to engage with a truly representative body. I found this in something called the works committee, which every factory was required to have. This committee was a far more representative body, to which workers in each building and shop floor sent their elected representatives. The committee, which met once a month, was supposed to discuss only issues relating to working conditions, canteen facilities and the like. I, however, did away with this restriction and said it was free to discuss any issue relating to the company. I would attend meetings of the committee and explain the status of the business, the kinds of issues we faced and how we were tackling them, even discussing subjects that managements considered their prerogative.

For example, the unions objected to the occasional ad hoc appointments the management would make to oblige people. Normally, this was done to help friends or relatives. I came to an informal agreement with the employees that a certain number of such appointments would be made in a year, but it would only be done to further the interests of the company. For example, I explained, if the chairman of a state electricity board recommended someone, I needed to oblige him because we depended on orders from the electricity boards. At the same time, I assured, no one would be appointed to a job for which he or she was not qualified. Once the logic was explained and I was seen following it, and people realized that I was not obliging my family or friends, the union never resisted such appointments.

But I still had to deal with the competitive politics of the different apex unions. In 1967-68, its third year of operation, the Trichy plant made a profit of Rs 42 lakh, a sizeable profit at that time. This was a truly commendable achievement, since the project report prepared by the Czech collaborators had projected losses for the first four years after production. That led naturally to a demand for bonus. It was a valid demand—this achievement could not have been possible without the efforts of the workers—but there was a rule about new units enjoying a six-year bonus holiday. However, I believed that the management should show some gesture to the workers. I had informally promised the workers that I would discuss the issue with the board and get a favourable decision. I had also taken up the matter with O.S. Murthy, who had succeeded Baijal as chairman. He, however, felt that granting the demand would lead to more demands for relaxing other rules and did not agree to my proposal.

Even as I was continuing my efforts to persuade him and the board, different unions—mainly CITU—instigated a tool-down agitation. I dealt with the situation strongly. Though I supported the workers in their demand for bonus, I refused to tolerate indiscipline even if it was for a legitimate cause. The man suspected of instigating the agitation was identified and suspended.

But I realized the demand for bonus could not be ignored any more. I then announced that bonus would be paid to all the employees. Murthy was upset that I had made the announcement without the approval of the board of directors, which had to clear the proposal. I admit I should not have done this, but I needed to establish my authority and neutralize the negative influence of the unions. I was called to Delhi, and Murthy and the board opposed my proposal strongly, saying I was setting a bad precedent. I, however, refused to give in and argued my case strongly. Finally, the board yielded but sanctioned a smaller amount as a lump sum to be distributed as bonus. Unfortunately, that amount was not sufficient to give the statutory 8 per cent bonus to all the employees. But I realized this was the best I could get. This was a challenge to my ability to get out of a tricky situation. I decided to take a gamble.

On my return to Trichy after the meeting with the board, I called a meeting of all the 330 executives and managers. I told them very frankly what had happened in the meetings in Delhi and then made a request—that they should forego their share of the money sanctioned by the board and allow me to use it to give a bonus to the staff and workers since the needs of that particular section of employees was greater. I promised these executives and managers that I would take care of their interests separately at the right time. All but five agreed. I went ahead with my proposal.

The fact that my tough stance on the strike was accompanied by a positive gesture on the part of the management, and that there was continuous interaction between the management and the workers through the works committee, created a lot of mutual trust among the two sections which were normally antagonistic towards each other. Importantly, all disputes were settled bilaterally and never went to the labour commissioner. As a result, barring this one problem, Trichy never faced any serious industrial unrest. Occasionally, some processions were taken out, accompanied by slogans of 'Krishnamurthy murdabad'. But beyond disturbing the tranquillity at home, there was never any serious fallout of this.

There were some other tough measures that I took in the interest of discipline and decorum. I did not allow the trade unions to have gate meetings, as they were invariably noisy, with sloganeering and union leaders delivering rabble-rousing speeches. I carved out a piece of ground close to the factory, got a dais constructed, put up a mike, and said unions were free to use that at any time of day but they should not disrupt the working of the factory.

This was a leaf I had taken from Krishnan's book. He had not allowed any politician or political party to hold public meetings or processions inside the township or paste bills and posters anywhere. I enforced it strictly. The CPM and CITU politicians protested that we were infringing on their fundamental rights. I stood firm, pointing out that the township was a private place, with a strong presence of foreigners; raucous public meetings would give a bad impression about the country. I also made the point that the people inside the township were educated people and politicians could communicate with them through pamphlets without disturbing anyone.

Apart from looking after the interests of all workers, I had to pay special attention to particular groups that required very careful handling and extra concessions. One such group was of high pressure welders, who played a critical role in the manufacture of boilers. It was a high-skill job, and the welders, who had to be certified by competent authorities, were paid more than supervisors. They had some problems unique to them, and we had to ensure that no grievance grew beyond a point. The unions were constantly trying to instigate them, and any unrest on the part of welders would bring the plant to a standstill. Besides, the attrition rate of these welders was also high. They were in great demand in West Asia for welding of oil pipes and other installations. So we had to go the extra mile to retain them and spent a lot on training them and later setting up a Welding Research Institute in Trichy. The seeds for this institute were sown when I was general manager, though it finally got established in 1975 when I was chairman.

I noticed that the eyesight of the high-pressure welders started weakening after some years, reducing their working life. I then pulled out two of the doctors led by Dr Sadhananda Moorthy at the Factory Medical Centre from their routine work and got them to sit with the welders, assess how many hours a day they should work, how much rest they should have between welding sessions, and what kind of diet they should have, among other things. I then got them to do a similar exercise for all other activities in the plant. After I became chairman and managing director, I got an occupational health physician to join the Factory Medical Centre, and in 1976, BHEL started an enterprise-wide occupational health services (OHS) programme with Trichy as the base. It was the first of its kind, at least in the public sector in India, and a year later the International Labour Organization acknowledged that the OHS programme at Trichy could be the base for similar programmes at factories across the country.

Thanks to these welfare-oriented steps, I found it easier to enforce measures to bring about higher levels of discipline and productivity. The work culture in Trichy was different from that in the rest of the industry.

~

If sensitive human relations management—treating people with dignity, motivating them, making even the junior-most employees feel they matter to the organization—became one pillar of my personal management style, customer orientation was the other. Once again, it was Trichy that helped me develop this.

In those days, customer orientation was missing even in the private sector. India was a seller's market in almost everything from consumer goods to heavy machinery, and the customer counted for little. The public sector, which was not profit-driven, was even less bothered about the customer, secure in the knowledge that he had no choice but to come to it. I did not want customers to come to us out of compulsion but out of choice. That involved both chasing customers aggressively as well as changing the way we worked.

I had realized that the lack of a dedicated sales team was coming in the way of an aggressive pitching for orders. Soon after becoming general manager, I floated a proposal for setting up a commercial manager's post in all the three plants to look after sales. The other general managers felt there was no need, when all that was required was to approach the state electricity boards and sign a purchase agreement. This was the result of the Soviet mindset—that a government organization did not need to go out and market itself or pursue customers. I argued that they were only looking at the present needs of the state electricity boards when they should be looking at future requirements and also the need to cater to the private sector. Fortunately, the board and Baijal saw my point of view on this matter, a commercial division was sanctioned, and I got Deenadayalu appointed as commercial manager in Trichy. The planning department was then taken over by S. Balasubramanian.

We now had a dedicated team for sales. But the odds were stacked against us. Our Czech collaborator was not known as a major boiler manufacturer, so we could not fall back on its brand value to pull in customers. Our customers were state electricity boards and large industries who saw us as an inexperienced organization. They were not entirely off the mark, as none of our products was in operation. Valves were the first products to roll out of the factory (plants were producing individual items till the entire project was complete), and we produced a complete boiler only in 1968. It took twenty-four months after a boiler had been supplied for it to be commissioned. For example, the boiler produced in 1968 for the Ennore power plant was commissioned, along with a turbo generator produced in Hyderabad, only in 1970. So we were not able to prove as yet that our products were of high quality.

Given the scepticism about our technical ability, we had to find other ways to prove to customers that we would be reliable suppliers. I got Lloyds and similar global quality inspection firms to inspect our facilities and certify them, as well as other agencies to conduct inspections of finished parts and processes to increase customer confidence. In addition, what we lacked in terms of actual design or proven efficiency of the product, we made up through service. During the installation and commissioning of boilers, I personally kept in close touch with the sites, and the engineers were always at hand to solve whatever problem occurred till the time of commissioning and sometimes even later. We need not have done this, since we were a manufacturing organization and, in line with the prevailing mindset, could have stopped at supplying our products. This ready availability of the entire organization to solve problems proved to our customers that we were serious and reliable players. Slowly, our order books started getting filled up.

Our major success came soon after the commercial manager's post was filled. Madras Fertilizers Ltd, a joint venture between the Government of India and American oil firm AMOCO, had decided to import a new package boiler. When I came to know this, we approached Madras Fertilizers and offered to supply the boiler. However, the consultants, Engineers India Ltd, raised doubts about our ability to do so. It had to complete the project in eighteen months and doubted our ability to deliver on time since we had not supplied a whole boiler anywhere till then. We insisted we could deliver within the time frame. There was a standoff, with our respective ministries (ministry of commerce and industry in the case of BHEL and ministry of chemicals and fertilizers in the case of Madras Fertilizers) backing our individual cases.

The matter reached the Union cabinet and I was summoned to appear before it. Morarji Desai, who was both finance minister and deputy prime minister, was quite curt with me. I told him that Trichy was in a position to supply the boiler at competitive rates and within the deadline. Desai said the public sector had never delivered anything on time and that a Rs 100 crore project would be delayed if we made a frivolous offer. I argued that if we were not given this opportunity, we would lose a chance to establish ourselves in this field. He asked me if I was willing to stake my job for this. I said I was.

It was a large and prestigious order, and the Trichy team went all out to execute it, coping with enormous difficulties. When we finished making the boiler and put it through the hydraulic test to see that all the tubes were in position, it was found to be leaking! My confidence was rattled, and I was sure I would lose my job. It was one thing to cockily say I was prepared to lose my job but quite another to actually face the prospect, especially with the responsibility of a wife and two children. But the engineers and workers rose to the challenge and worked hard to fix the problem. Finally, we managed to deliver the boiler two weeks ahead of time. AMOCO not only praised us but also agreed to give us a bonus. It was a big boost to the image of BHEL Trichy, and people began to sit up and take notice of us.

Desai's jibe that the public sector could not deliver on time rankled in my mind. I then quietly removed one line that was a must at the bottom of the letterhead of every public sector company—'A Government of India Enterprise'. I didn't want that line to prejudice customers even before they started negotiating with us. The tag had its own advantages and disadvantages. While public sector companies were given a price and purchase preference and many used it to their advantage, some foreign customers saw the public sector as a symbol of inefficiency. My objective at that time was to bring about a customer orientation in the organization and run it as a customer-oriented private organization. Hence this move.

By and large, we achieved the objective. Many foreign visitors expressed publicly that they never knew that the Trichy unit of BHEL was owned by the government. On the other hand, the Bureau of Public Enterprises in the Government of India, at a later stage, insisted that the words 'A Government of India Enterprise' be prominently displayed on the letterhead. But by then, the Trichy unit had established a reputation for itself.

With Madras Fertilizers in the bag, we adopted the same pushy attitude in going after international business. Tapping the export market was a part of my strategy to overcome the lack of confidence on the part of customers. I believed that domestic customers would accept us only if they saw that our products were being accepted in other countries. We started participating in international tenders floated for World Bank-aided projects. It was an audacious move, since the boilers supplied by us had not started working.

Our first big pitch was in 1969 for the supply of two 60 MW boilers for the Port Dickson power plant under the National Electricity Board (NEB) of Malaysia. Malaysia had a history of buying boilers only from Japan. It also had a Crown Agent—a British firm of consulting engineers, Preece, Cardew and Rider—which would help in assessing quotations and deciding on the supplier. Our tender had many deficiencies, and we were not called for negotiations. One problem related to the design of our boilers. By then, boiler design globally had changed significantly, and boilers made to the new designs were far more cost efficient. We, however, were still following the Czech technology, while the Malaysians wanted the new one. Hence we lost the order due to technological inadequacy.

Soon after, however, NEB floated another tender, and this time we prepared ourselves thoroughly. Through our own efforts, we modified the design we were following and came up with a design that met the Malaysian specifications. No one could pick holes in our tender, and we were called for negotiations with the Crown Agent in London. Despite my best efforts in trying to convince the Crown Agent, our offer was rejected on the grounds of inexperience, and the Crown Agent recommended that the order be given to the Japanese firm again. The Crown Agent said it would not want NEB to be a guinea pig to test BHEL's capabilities.

I could have left it at that, but I did not. I took the fight to NEB, making repeated visits to Malaysia, and represented our case. I did not plead, but marshalled facts and logic to try and persuade NEB that BHEL Trichy was in a better position to give them good service, and that there was no reason for it to reject our offer. I said we were prepared to give all the guarantees they wanted and even agreed to a heavy penalty if we were not able to deliver. However, the Crown Agent again discouraged the Malaysian government, saying they would not like it to board a plane with an ill-trained pilot.

Those words hurt deeply, but they only served to strengthen my resolve to fight back. We invited the general manager of NEB, Raja Zainal bin Raja Sulaiman (the first Malaysian to head NEB after the country became independent), and persuaded him to visit the plant at Trichy. He agreed and spent three days there. When he returned, he wrote a recommendation saying BHEL Trichy might be a young organization but seeing the men behind it, he did not believe that they would ever let a customer down. The Malaysian government then rejected the advice of the Crown Agent and placed the order with BHEL. It had never happened before in Malaysia. The Crown Agent was very upset. Dire predictions were made that NEB would realize the follies of going with BHEL at great cost.

There was jubilation among all the executives in Trichy when they got the news of the contract being bagged. I called a meeting to make a formal announcement and told the executives not to become complacent because we had won the contract. They had to prepare for bigger challenges ahead—the need to ensure global standards of quality and timely delivery. It was no easy task to get the order completed. For a young organization which had no record of achievement within the country or a foreign collaborator for this project, and whose prestige (as well as mine) was at stake, the job was executed to the utmost satisfaction of NEB, and due credit must go to the managerial team at Trichy. The first order was executed on time and, to date, BHEL is supplying power plants to Malaysia.

After that, there was no looking back for BHEL Trichy. This single action of executing an order for a foreign customer increased the confidence of the worker, set global standards of production, and gave BHEL a brand image.

On a more personal note, it was during my repeated visits to Malaysia that I developed what was later to be my style statement. I found the safari suit was the most preferred office dress there, and I bought two of them. But I found those very ornate. Later, I got a tailor in Delhi's Connaught Place to modify the style to a simple but elegant design in white and started wearing it regularly to office. This later set a trend among the office-going executives in Delhi. I still wear my trademark white safari suits to office.

~

When I studied the problem of customer dissatisfaction, one of the reasons I identified was the lack of a quality culture. In the late sixties, Indian goods were not known for quality or reliability. So our customers, like many others, preferred to import equipment. I realized that it was not enough to get foreign quality certificates (though that was necessary as well). I wanted quality to be ingrained in the work ethic of the organization so that it would make the pursuit of quality a continuous effort.

The question then arose about how best to achieve this. This was not a subject that was taught with great rigour in management institutes at that time, nor were there very many books on the subject. I asked around and came to know that the only serious work that was being done in this area was in the Indian Statistical Institute (ISI), Kolkata, which had designed what was known as statistical quality control methods. I took the initiative of approaching the institute and got the person in charge of its Chennai branch, an outstanding technologist called S.M. Sundararaju, to come to Trichy. Sundararaju and his small team put all our executives through a series of training programmes based on the statistical quality control methods they were teaching. This was the beginning of a quality culture, certainly in the public sector but also perhaps in any industrial enterprise in the country.

This was another experiment that I scaled up to the national level when I later became chairman of BHEL. I found that the Department of Atomic Energy had done a lot of work on quality and that the Atomic Energy Commission had a strong quality assurance team. After all, atomic energy was one area where there could be no scope or tolerance for errors. P.N. Arumugam, a research- and analysis-oriented person from the Atomic Energy Commission, was good at training people, and I persuaded him to join BHEL as general manager, quality, reporting directly to me and through me to the board. The general manager's designation was the highest that could be offered at that time, and it sent out a message about the importance I attached to quality.

Arumugam's brief was to start a quality department, whose task was to train and certify executives and engineers in quality systems apart from designing and putting these systems in place. It was not easy, and they had to face some internal resistance. After all, when a factory manager who thinks he knows all that there is about maintaining quality is told by a bunch of outsiders that he should work in a particular way, keep certain records and follow certain procedures when a defect is detected, he is bound to resent it. There were several occasions when the quality team would complain that a particular division was not adhering to procedures. It required a lot of persuasion and some stern action on my part to convince the employees about the necessity to adhere to quality standards. Ultimately people began to see the logic of the move.

~

In the third year of production, the Trichy plant achieved its rated capacity of 30,000 tonnes. We could have been satisfied with this, but I thought of taking it to higher levels of production. I realized, however, that something would have to be done differently to achieve this. Achieving this objective would be difficult if the plant was caught up in a large spectrum of work—from high end to low end.

I believed that the only method to develop optimum levels of business through the limited resources available within the company was to leave the highly trained engineers and managerial staff of BHEL to concentrate on the high end of technology, leaving the medium and lower end technologies and products to smaller entrepreneurs. This would also make the organization cost competitive. Coincidentally, that was also the time that the government was propagating the concept of ancillarization in a major way in order to encourage self-employment and give a fillip to industrial development. I saw this as an opportunity to achieve our objectives.

As a first step, BHEL Trichy drew up a list of the low end technology products which were to be outsourced. Next we set about finding suitable suppliers. The whole process was transparent. We put out advertisements inviting expressions of intent. Young executives at the plant were encouraged to start out as entrepreneurs. I told them I would give them a sabbatical for two years—if the venture succeeded, they could continue with it; if not, they could come back. Some took up the offer and are now owners of large businesses. We then worked in association with the state government to provide them land and other infrastructure facilities. BHEL also provided these ancillaries with technical expertise and managerial services. I set up a separate ancillary development department, with highly competent managers who would assist the entrepreneurs in setting up and running the business, helping them choose the right machinery, the right processes and solving some of their problems. This gave the ancillaries the confidence that this was not a one-time effort and that BHEL was looking for a long-term partnership with them. Some of them started operations almost immediately, making it possible for BHEL to expand its core business. The initial success of these ancillaries prompted me to intensify this programme and make it a continuous process in the organization when I became chairman.

Since these ancillary units had lower overheads, the Trichy unit was able to keep its costs down. By 1972, the plant crossed the 30,000-tonne production mark and was well on the road to achieving production of 1,00,000 tonnes. I can quite proudly say this was one of the best examples of ancillarization in the public sector and that, over the years, this group of ancillaries has become one of the largest centres of manufacturing activity in India and is often cited as a model. The most gratifying experience of this ancillarization programme was that Trichy, which had no industrial development worth the name besides the railway workshop, was converted into an industrial hub with a large network of small and medium manufacturers undertaking diverse activities like welding, steel fabrication, manufacturing of industrial tools and components of windmills, etc., with BHEL as the driving force.

Other public sector undertakings also undertook ancillarization programmes but not so successfully. They approached them as if they were throwing crumbs to someone. I considered the ancillaries crucial to our plant—they were the best way of augmenting our own capacity; their success would accelerate our success. I always used the word 'partner' when talking about them and initiated several trust-building exercises. The hallmark of my management in BHEL Trichy was the high level of integrity which I ensured at all levels. I said that if a supplier's payment was delayed by more than fifteen days, he could come to my office and take up the matter. I selectively looked into cases of delayed payment to ensure that the system did not get vitiated. If a supplier didn't get orders from us for some time and had suffered some losses as a result, we would go out of our way to give him some extra help. There was a feeling among the entrepreneurs that BHEL Trichy would never let them down. More importantly, this built up tremendous goodwill for BHEL within the local community, which realized that the plant was helping to improve their economic status.

~

Simultaneously with all this, I was laying the foundation for a technological transformation of the Trichy plant, which would later become the springboard for the technological modernization of BHEL itself.

Even in the early days of planning for these projects, I had always known that we were not getting the best of technical expertise. At that time, there was no alternative but to accept the situation, since the government had gone in for the collaboration with the East European countries, largely because of its agreement with them for economic assistance. Soon after moving to Trichy, I realized that we could not go along with Czech technology for long. The collaboration was for ten years, so there were still six years to go. But I have always believed in working on parallel paths. Most people follow one path and start thinking of changing direction only after hitting a road block. I tended to anticipate problems and address them at the outset. So I had started identifying others who had better technology and established contact with two American firms which were the leaders in boiler engineering technology—Babcock and Wilcox, and Combustion Engineering.

Babcock and Wilcox was my first choice, but it was already collaborating with ACC on a boiler manufacturing project in Durgapur and so a relationship with BHEL was ruled out. On the other hand, the attitude of Combustion Engineering was very negative. The company's officials said they did not believe that a collaboration with BHEL could be successful and that we would never be able to design certain complex parts of the boiler like the economizer or super heater. They also pointed to the ACC-owned boiler manufacturing unit and said that no country could afford to have two boiler units. I was disappointed but had to leave it at that.

But soon we found that Czech-designed boilers were not meeting the changing requirements of the customers. The design assistance available from the Czechs was not on a par with the advances that had taken place in power generation equipment. But in spite of these limitations, the design team strived to meet the requirements through its own efforts and succeeded to a large extent by continuing supply to domestic and foreign customers. But it was clear that the need of the hour was to upgrade the technology as the Czechs could not help us any further, and going with them had limitations.

We continued scouting for other technology suppliers when Combustion Engineering, which had initially shown reluctance to associate with BHEL, suddenly approached me for a collaboration. I believe that the main reason for this change of stance was the progress shown by Trichy, demonstrating its capability both in India and abroad. A team from Combustion Engineering, led by Ted Dyke, one of the persons who had rejected our earlier offer, had come to India for a survey of the boiler manufacturing industry. The Directorate-General of Technical Development (DGTD) was taking the team around the country and brought it to Trichy as well. Dyke and the others found Trichy had progressed quite well since we met last. We had designed the boiler for export markets through our own efforts, and this must have impressed them. They were now willing to collaborate with us.

But this time we were able to talk like equals (though I respected their technical superiority), and the negotiations and agreement were on our terms. The only doubt in their minds related to our collaboration with the Czechs, as they feared that Combustion Engineering's knowhow would be passed on to them. However, we were not in a position to end the Czech partnership before the end of the ten-year period, as it covered products other than boilers (which was what the collaboration with Combustion Engineering would be confined to) and there were several ongoing projects to be completed. The American team understood the situation and agreed to BHEL continuing its relationship with the Czechs without in any way affecting their position.

There was another tricky situation to deal with—we had to go back to the Czechs and tell them that what they were offering was not good enough for our requirements and that we needed to update our technology, which really meant letting them know we were looking for another suitor. This had to be handled deftly. After all, we had never dealt with the Americans, and we didn't know how the relationship would proceed. More importantly, there was a sense of gratitude to the Czechs—they had trained us and put us in business. In fact, they were the reason why the Americans were now coming to us. If they had raised objections with the government, we could not have proceeded with our proposed collaboration with Combustion Engineering.

We had to convince the Czechs that the partnership with Combustion Engineering was in the interest of both of us. I told the Czechs that while the assistance they had given us was invaluable, it was not suitable for the changing market requirements or for the manufacture of large boilers. In essence what I meant was: what was best for the Czechs was not good enough for India. I pointed out that the Czechs, being part of the Soviet bloc, could not get American technology while India could, and suggested that the rest of the world would benefit if we updated our technology.

The Czechs were convinced by my arguments and acknowledged that they could not meet the requirements of the fast pace of growth of the Trichy plant. I thus averted a situation where the Czechs could have raised the issue at a diplomatic level. We then proceeded to conclude the agreement with Combustion Engineering. As a consequence of this, new technology had to be obtained for other parts of boilers like the pre-heaters and fans and, therefore, a number of subsidiary agreements with new collaborators were also entered into. With this, Trichy could now cover the entire requirement of a power plant rather than supplying a portion of it.

This was the first step towards moving away from the technology provided by the Communist bloc. Over the next few years, BHEL would move slowly towards more modern technology that had been developed in the western countries.

Over the years, the Trichy plant made the best use of its association with Combustion Engineering and other collaborators. It upgraded its facility and its technological status to become one of the world's leading boiler designers. The

Trichy unit could now manufacture a whole range of boilers at the most competitive prices. It was this bold step of upgrading the technology that led the plant to great success.

The technological modernization of Trichy had other elements as well. Even at that time, I realized the advantages of information technology (IT) and its impact on the efficiency of an organization. Computerization was nearly non-existent even in the best of enterprises at that time. We thought that the first thing that needed to be done was to sensitize the organization to the benefits of computerization. All efforts were made to make the best use of the existing, though poor, data processing facilities we had.

In those days, computer import was restricted to the Department of Electronics. In the late sixties, the department procured, with British aid, three large computers from International Computers India Manufacturing (ICIM). A committee was set up to allocate these. BHEL Trichy made a strong pitch and managed to secure one along with IIT Delhi. This triggered a massive application development effort at Trichy, making it perhaps the first industrial unit to use a large computer successfully. A number of software programmes were developed in-house under the leadership of A. Krishnan, and even ICIM was amazed at the progress Trichy made in computerization in comparison with IIT Delhi. This became the nucleus for a company-wide computerization programme when I became BHEL chairman.

~

With many public sector undertakings at that time being badly managed and making losses, the public sector had become synonymous with inefficiency and sloth and was seen as a drain on the resources of the country. I felt the negative perception was because of a lack of communication with the public regarding the role of this sector in public welfare. Public perception is important for any organization, as it has a bearing on the morale of employees as well. While the activities of BHEL Trichy had earned the appreciation and support of the local population, the general image of BHEL as a whole was very poor.

I tried to address this in a limited way in my individual capacity in Trichy through a national advertisement campaign that could explain the contribution of BHEL Trichy to the country's economic development. The objective of this campaign was to highlight not just the achievement of the Trichy unit but also the benefit that could accrue to a particular region through the products of BHEL. My brother suggested tapping one of the pioneers of the Indian advertising industry—R.K. Swamy—for this campaign. Swamy was then heading an American advertisement agency, J. Walter Thomson (JWT), and was in the process of setting up its Indian wing, Hindustan Thomson Associates, because of a government policy that foreign-owned agencies could not undertake work for the government or the public sector.*

I contacted Swamy and explained what I wanted. He came to Trichy, went around the plant and, after his return to Chennai, put out twelve advertisements, each related to a product and projecting its impact on the population of the area where it was supplied. One advertisement showcased the benefit that would accrue to western Uttar Pradesh when the Harduaganj power plant was commissioned with BHEL equipment. The campaign was an instant success. It was the first organized campaign by a

*JWT left India in the 1970s because of this policy. Its Indian employees, led by Swamy, took charge of the company and renamed it Hindustan Thomson Associates (HTA). In 2002, HTA reverted to its original name—JWT.

PSU, and the advertising world sat up and took notice. The brand image of the Trichy unit went up to great heights.

My small effort at image management for the Trichy power plant could not, however, do anything for the rest of BHEL, which also had come under fire. Among the three units, the largest investment had been made in Haridwar, which had not yet started operations due to various delays. Responding to criticism in the press, Murthy publicly stated that the investment was not likely to yield handsome results and raised doubts about whether BHEL should continue to invest more in the Haridwar plant. He suggested that the plant be mothballed, that is, investment in the plant be stopped for a while and the organization concentrate on the other plants. I remember this was the first time that I had heard the word 'mothballed'. It became quite an issue—that at a time when the country needed more of power equipment, people within the organization itself doubted its capacity to undertake its stated task.

It didn't help that HE(I)L, which had its only plant at Bhopal, was also in bad shape. Its production amounted to just about Rs 40-50 crore, and for such a low output, it had 19,000 employees. It took on a large number of projects without any focus, and its record of keeping customers satisfied was poor. HE(I)L was also running into heavy losses and, worse, it was projected by the British collaborator to be loss-making for another fifteen years.

With newspapers carrying negative articles about the public sector every day, Prime Minister Indira Gandhi was under pressure to demonstrate that her emphasis on a state-dominated economy was succeeding. The government decided that something drastic needed to be done to reform the public sector. It set up an Action Committee of Public Undertakings headed by M.S. Pathak, the managing director of Engineers India, along with Vasant Rajadhyaksha, a former chairman of

Hindustan Lever Ltd (now Hindustan Unilever), and Prof. Nitish De of the Indian Institute of Management (IIM) Calcutta. Its brief was to look into each public sector company and suggest what needed to be done with it. In the course of its work, the committee members met me and I exchanged a lot of ideas with them about how BHEL should be managed and the need to have a professional management rather than retired railway officers being posted to head it. Little did I know that this would lead to something very unexpected.

In mid-1972, I was travelling back from the United States, where I had gone for some meetings with Combustion Engineering. At London, the Air India staff brought a message that I should proceed straight to Delhi as the prime minister wanted to see me. My ticket to Trichy via Chennai had been booked and, not understanding the urgency, I replied that it would be difficult to change course now and that I would first go to Trichy. At Beirut airport, I got another message from Pathak that someone would be waiting at Mumbai airport with a ticket to Delhi. So from Mumbai, I flew directly to Delhi.

From the airport, I went straight to see Pathak. The two of us then met Subramaniam, who was minister of planning and deputy chairman of the Planning Commission. It was then that I was told that the Action Committee of Public Undertakings had recommended the integration of BHEL and HE(I)L under a common chairman and identified me as the person most suited to head the integrated organization.

In hindsight, the choice was perhaps natural. The committee thought the organization needed a younger, professional team. BHEL at that time had a large number of retired people at the board level. In addition, the performance of the Trichy plant stood out—it was the only profit-making unit of BHEL. However, the decision to appoint me as chairman came as a surprise to me at that point, and I was not mentally prepared for it. A few months earlier, I had been approached to manage a small car project in the public sector, and I had declined since there was a lot of unfinished work in Trichy.

I was engrossed in many experiments in Trichy and was reluctant to move out of that place in spite of being offered the chairmanship of BHEL. Making a success of the experiments started at Trichy seemed more important to me at that stage than heading BHEL. Besides, several of the top managers were way senior to me, and I was not sure how they would react to my elevation or whether they would give me the support I would need for an extremely challenging task. But Subramaniam, Mohan Kumaramangalam (who was minister for steel and mines and an ardent advocate of the public sector) and Pathak would not take 'no' for an answer. Their argument was that I could continue monitoring the projects at Trichy while being chairman, and accepting the chairmanship would not hamper my experiments. I, therefore, accepted the offer. I was told I would have to take over immediately. Since Murthy—the chairman—was retiring shortly thereafter, I was designated deputy chairman until his retirement. I had less than a week to wrap things up in Trichy and return to Delhi. All formalities relating to my appointment, including following established procedures, were done much later.

I was a bit sad at leaving Trichy because I had wanted to see some actions I had initiated carried through to their logical conclusion. But there was also a sense of satisfaction at what I had achieved. The achievements extended beyond just the plant. I made it a point to integrate BHEL with the local population and their aspirations. It is my strong belief that an organization, no matter how big it is, should learn to live amongst the local people if it is to succeed in the long run. In Trichy, I consciously worked towards this, and it has stood BHEL in good stead. I also got the state government to establish an Industrial Training Institute (ITI) for providing engineering skills to the local population, a polytechnic to train supervisory cadre for the industry, and a regional engineering college to train engineers and scientists. All worked in a coordinated manner, with BHEL providing the necessary infrastructure facilities. BHEL itself set up a strong training centre, which worked in conjunction with these teaching institutions. Over a period of time, Trichy developed into a strong engineering centre with several engineering colleges and polytechnics.

Whenever any natural calamity struck, I made sure that BHEL was always the first to extend assistance. The plant was always a part of the local festivals. On one occasion, BHEL provided an engineering solution to restore the temple chariot (weighing over 200 tonnes) and make it functional, enabling the resumption of the car festival at Tiruvaroor after many years. This gesture earned BHEL tremendous affection from the local people. When I left, I carried with me a key learning, which became an essential element of my management philosophy: that productivity can be achieved only through people. We were handicapped by the lack of access to modern technology as well as to capital. In spite of that, by sheer motivation, a group of people was able to achieve results far in excess of what organizations which possessed all that had achieved. I had also demonstrated that even a government organization can be result-oriented, customer-oriented and competitive.

Some time after I had taken over as chairman and managing director, in one of my informal meetings with the then chairman of the empowered selection committee which had to ratify my appointment, I was shown my file in which former chairman Mathur had written: 'Watch out for this boy; one day he will occupy my position.' He had written this despite the fact that I had differed with him on several matters. I was extremely moved when I read that. I knew that I had to strive to be a bit like him when I set out to discharge the duties he once had.

# 3

# RE-ENGINEERING BHEL

I took over as chairman and managing director of BHEL on 1 July 1972. I knew that the task at hand was an extremely daunting one. BHEL itself was a huge challenge, what with the Haridwar plant not having commenced operations, and I also had to integrate an ailing HE(I)L into it. Merging two entirely different organizations was a very complicated exercise.

I also knew that I would face some resentment both from HE(I)L and from within BHEL when I took over. After all, I was only forty-seven years old and the junior-most of the senior-level managers who could have qualified for the post. Besides, Murthy and his immediate deputy as well as the second-in-command at HE(I)L had been asked to leave. I also had to battle a lot of cynicism. Except for a handful of colleagues, most others were sceptical about whether I could revitalize the organization, and I could sense that they were just waiting for me to trip. None of them offered a word of encouragement but would only keep pointing out that this was a very difficult job.

What I did not bargain for was that the country's prime minister would be sceptical of the exercise to create a power equipment monolith. I had met Indira Gandhi soon after C. Subramaniam had broken the news to me that I was to head

BHEL. She was very brief. 'I think Pathak and Subramaniam must have briefed you,' she began. The government wanted to change the face of public enterprises and she expected me to do that, she indicated. At this and at a later meeting a month after taking over, she told me that she had no faith in the ability of Indian managers to manage large enterprises. She, therefore, wanted me to work towards splitting BHEL into a number of single-unit enterprises.

That unsettled me a bit. I believed that the strength of a power equipment manufacturing firm lay in providing composite service to the customer instead of different companies supplying different pieces of equipment separately. In fact, I had argued with Subramaniam on these lines when HE(I)L was split and BHEL formed in 1964. But how does one argue with a prime minister? So I told her that I should be given some time to study whether it would be more practical to split the organization or more advantageous to keep BHEL as a composite multi-divisional unit. I pointed out that General Electric and Siemens were very large organizations but were also strong because their multiple units could supply a wide range of power plant equipment that could meet every need of their customers. She, however, countered this by saying that India did not have that quality of managerial talent. I once again asked for a year's time to study the two options, and she reluctantly agreed to review the arrangement after a year.

Her opinion about Indian managerial talent rankled in my mind, and throughout my stint in BHEL, I did everything possible to demonstrate to her and the world that even Indian managers working under Indian conditions could manage large enterprises as efficiently as those in Western countries. That became, in a sense, my driving mission. Over the next five years, I not only retained BHEL as a multi-unit company but also merged several organizations with it and made it much larger than what it was. I also conclusively proved that Indian managers are capable of running behemoths efficiently, even in a public sector milieu.

~

There was no denying that the public perception of BHEL at that time was very poor. Doubts were raised about whether it would be wise to rely only on it to meet the growing demand for power plant equipment. Opinion was building up in favour of imports. Some of the criticism was justified—there was no denying that the Haridwar plant was way behind its completion schedule or that there were long delays in supply of equipment. I, however, felt it was unfair to put the entire blame for the poor power situation in the country on the domestic manufacturers alone. I noticed that there were several instances of power projects not being commissioned in spite of equipment being delivered on time, as well as instances where power projects were completed within a short time because of timely and coordinated deliveries. I realized I had a serious problem at hand and there was a need to change the way BHEL was managed.

The first year was spent almost entirely on fire-fighting, that too on several fronts among the four units at Haridwar, Hyderabad, Trichy and Bhopal, with almost every issue I took up being extremely complicated. There was not a single plant that did not require change in some form or another.

The Bhopal unit of the erstwhile HE(I)L was the most vexed. It was also the only plant whose every aspect—from the technology to the people—I was completely unfamiliar with. The plant's actual production fell short of the annual targets, which were anyway much lower than its installed capacity. Worse, delivery schedules were not being adhered to, resulting in a number of power projects being delayed. A Committee on

Public Undertakings of the Lok Sabha pointed out that in a large number of cases, equipment that had been produced by March 1969 had not been dispatched till February 1970.

The industrial relations scenario was also very hostile. Indiscipline was the order of the day and unions wanted extra benefits and facilities without a corresponding increase in productivity. There were multiple unions, and they expected the management to take sides in their battles. I realized that this was going to pose a huge challenge to my more participative approach to labour relations.

The hostility and resentment I faced from HE(I)L was more palpable than that from within BHEL. Quite a few of the senior managers had far more experience than I did. The employees were bitter about the fact that HE(I)L was being merged with a company that was born out of it, instead of the other way around. The fact that BHEL was a larger and more successful organization did not strike a chord with them. There was also a lot of insecurity and fear about loss of identity among all levels of employees, as is the case when any company is merged with a better performing one. There were concerns whether their aspirations could be fulfilled in a larger organization and whether BHEL employees would dominate the organization. In view of this insecurity prevailing in Bhopal, all the issues relating to integration had to be dealt with in a comprehensive manner. Issues relating to product mix were resolved by engineering reorganization under the corporate plan. Issues relating to systems and procedures took a little longer and were resolved in a phased manner. As far as employees were concerned, dealing with the workers was covered under the common policy being evolved for the organization, though Bhopal had a multiplicity of unions and a large workforce.

Employee morale had hit rock bottom. The insecurity in the minds of the technologists and executives was more serious and engaged our attention to a larger extent. At the first meeting I held at Bhopal after becoming chairman, several of the younger executives asked whether they should continue in the organization and whether it had a future at all. They were fine engineers and managers who had been trained abroad. If I had lost them, it would have been difficult for me to revive the organization. I had to create confidence in their minds that their future in BHEL was bright and motivate them to give their best. I assured them that, given time, I would ensure that each one of them was gainfully employed and that my vision for an integrated BHEL would throw up so many opportunities that the company would face a shortage of talent in the days to come. To fulfil their aspirations, HE(I)L executives were given senior positions in other units of BHEL. This movement was systematically monitored to see that at all plants there was a healthy representation of executives of other plants. This helped speedy integration and in developing a BHEL culture.

Morale was low in Hyderabad and Haridwar as well, but this had less to do with concerns over the merger and more with the peculiar situation of each plant. In Haridwar, Murthy's public statements questioning its viability and suggesting that the plant be mothballed had shaken the confidence of the employees. Among the earliest actions I took was to tell people that my priority would be to complete the project. Much of the first year was spent in motivating people and completing the construction of the plant.

In Hyderabad, ironically, I had to wrestle with a problem arising out of decisions to which I was also a party as project officer way back in the early sixties. The plant had been set up to manufacture turbines and generators at the lower end of the capacity spectrum—12 MW, 25 MW and 60 MW. These were the standard units available at that point of time in Czechoslovakia, which was providing the technical collaboration for the plant, and BHEL had little choice but to go along with it. By 1970, when the plant went into operation, the Indian power sector required larger sized units. So BHEL Hyderabad was stuck with a completely tooled factory and 6,000 employees (of which 300 were trained engineers) but practically no orders. Whatever little revenue the plant did make came from peripheral items and not from the core business. As a result, there was uncertainty in the minds of the employees about the future of the plant. Trichy, of course, was the only exception, and the unit progressed well under P.V.K. Achan, who had succeeded me as general manager. This was the only unit where I found the employees motivated and raring to go.

So as I started to settle in, I had three challenges facing me—motivating the employees, winning over customers, and making a government-owned organization work efficiently. There were three options before me. One was to let the various plants operate more or less as independent units, with little coordination among them, as was the case till then. That option was quickly ruled out, as I felt that this was one of the main causes for the problems that BHEL was facing. So independent were the three units that soon after I became chairman, the Haridwar plant found it did not have any balance in its bank accounts to pay salaries while the Trichy unit had surplus funds. The second option—and one which had some takers—was to let BHEL be a kind of holding company and let the four units work with a limited degree of autonomy. The third option was an integrated management of all the plants, centralizing the policy making and decentralizing the implementation. This would enable rationalizing the product mix and technology and providing more challenging and coordinated services to the customers. Such a reorganization would be more complicated, but I strongly felt that this was the only way to fast-track the country's self-reliance in the manufacture of heavy electrical equipment. It would also be more beneficial from the point of view of the customer, in line with my objective of making BHEL a customer-driven organization. This gamble was to prove right.

Irrespective of the model I followed, a multi-unit company like BHEL required a full-fledged corporate office at the headquarters—which was something I had always believed. Until then, BHEL did not have a corporate office but only a liaison office in Delhi. This was because of a government decision that public sector undertakings should locate their headquarters outside the capital. However, my predecessors preferred to stay in Delhi and therefore maintained only a liaison office there instead of developing a proper corporate office. Hence, the chairman of BHEL did not attend a corporate office but a liaison office. The chairman's office was, therefore, deliberately kept small. That perhaps would have been all right between 1964 and 1971 when this office was preoccupied more with getting the projects off the ground and liaising with government agencies and a bit of sales coordination. The challenges facing the power equipment industry in the early 1970s, however, required the chairman's office to be more proactive in preparing the organization for future challenges. The organization needed a more coordinated view and approach on personnel, financial, engineering and sales matters.

Some days after I took charge, the industry secretary called me and pointed out that I had not called on the minister, Moin ul Haq Chowdhury, which was what convention required. I then called the minister's office and sought an appointment. The special assistant to the minister called back and said the minister would visit me instead The next day, Chowdhury and minister of state Siddheshwar Prasad came to see me at the BHEL office, a dingy set of rooms in one of the buildings owned by the public sector insurance companies on Parliament Street.

We discussed BHEL and its future, and I pointed out that it needed a proper corporate office and that this could require a few hundred people. I said (with my heart in my mouth, I must confess) that if the government still felt that it should not be located in Delhi, I was willing to shift to any other place except where BHEL had a plant. Locating the corporate office at a place near a plant would have resulted in the chairman becoming the de facto head of that plant and the local management becoming weakened. Chowdhury immediately said the government had brought me to Delhi so that it could be in constant touch with me and so I must remain here. Relieved, I then asked for cabinet sanction to set up a corporate office in Delhi, which later came through.

But getting an office with 20,000 sq ft of space was not easy. Since BHEL was a PSU, it couldn't get an office in any of the government buildings housing the various ministries. Other buildings owned by the public sector insurance companies had been rented out to private sector and multinational companies. When we came to know that the USAID complex in what is now the Qutab Institutional Area was up for sale, I promptly sought sanction from the finance ministry to purchase it. But Subramaniam, who also held the science and technology portfolio, said he wanted that building for his ministry.

That was the time when the multi-storey Hindustan Times House on Kasturba Gandhi Marg, off Connaught Place, had just been completed, and we thought of renting space there. Our company secretary met his counterpart in the Hindustan Times, who said he would consult the proprietor, industrialist K.K. Birla. After doing so, he said they were not keen on renting out the place to BHEL, as it was a government organization and would not be able to maintain decorum or cleanliness. I was furious when I heard this. I knew that the building was constructed with a loan from government institutions. The Hindustan Times establishment was adamant on not having BHEL as a tenant, and so I went and complained to Subramaniam and sought his help in securing a proper office space. He directed me to minister of state for company affairs K.V. Raghunatha Reddy.

I pointed out to him that the Hindustan Times building stood on land owned by the government and was constructed with the help of loans from public sector banks but BHEL was being refused space there. Reddy promptly asked his secretary to tell Birla that the government would cancel the lease if his company continued the policy of discrimination against public sector undertakings. In no time at all, the Hindustan Times representative got back to us, saying we could take whatever space we needed. We took four floors, two of which we later gave to the Steel Authority of India, which had been set up in 1972. We maintained the office very well, belying the sloppy image that most public sector companies had. My personal office was done up so well that Chowdhury's successor T.A. Pai would schedule meetings with foreign delegates there instead of Udyog Bhavan, which housed the industry ministry.

I realized that the chairman's office did not have a holistic view of the organization and dealt with each unit as a separate entity. It is always important for all the departments of an organization to have a coordinated outlook, which was completely missing at that time in BHEL. For example, financial decisions were being taken without an assessment of their impact on other units and divisions or the company as a whole. Murthy had also been very regimental and centralized in his approach and rarely delegated authority to the general managers of the three units or gave them enough elbow room to function. As a result, the chairman's office had become a bottleneck. I had experienced this first hand and was determined to change this. I wanted to move to a more responsibility-oriented set-up, in which executive decisions would rarely come to the chairman or directors so long as they conformed to the broad policy and approved budget set by the board. Over time, we made the corporate office a policy making body and transferred all functional responsibility to the units. Centralized policy making and decentralized execution became our mantra. Over the years, we also set up several new divisions to enable managers to focus better on their responsibilities and fostered a coordinated functioning of the company as a whole.

The board of directors also needed to be revamped. Till then, it had comprised the chairman; representatives of the finance, heavy industries and power ministries; and one representative each from the Central Electricity Authority and a state electricity board (SEB). Each plant would bring its individual proposals to the board, and the chairman would take a decision after examining them. But the company was too large for any one person to have expertise in all areas. A large corporate organization needed specialized expertise in the headquarters for the board to take informed decisions.

I, therefore, decided to create four functional divisions and had a director head each of them. In line with the Pathak committee's suggestions, these were finance, human resources and engineering. I also set up a corporate planning division, which was important for the company to move away from the ad hoc decision making that was typical at that time and to develop a strategic vision, identifying growth opportunities, planning for the long term, constantly assessing the internal strengths and weaknesses of the organization and analyzing the changes in the external environment. What I did was nothing new—multinational companies were organized along these lines.

I put a core team in place, comprising S.V.S. Raghavan (who had headed the finance division in Trichy) as director, finance; R.N. Srivastava (the finance head at Haridwar with excellent inter-personal skills) as director, human resources; and K.R. Paramesvar (who had been my colleague in the Planning Commission and who was part of the turbo-generator division in Haridwar) as head of the corporate planning division. Given my technical background, the post of engineering director was not filled for some time. Later, I appointed H.N. Sharan, who had been with Swiss engineering firm Sulzer, to the post. It was an excellent team, and I doubt if I could have achieved all that I did without its backing.

Sharan's induction in 1974, initially as head of a new division, was a major departure from existing public sector practice and among my early attempts to get people from diverse fields into BHEL, thus enriching the organization. I also brought in P.N. Arumugam from the Atomic Energy Commission as general manager, quality, to give a thrust to quality consciousness in the organization.

I had met Sharan during a visit to Europe when I was general manager at Trichy. He was credited with a large number of patents related to boilers, and I had kept in touch with him. He had taken Swiss nationality, and I had to get special permission to get him into BHEL. I also had to get him some extra benefits, including a company-paid annual vacation abroad, since he had a British wife and children studying overseas, and an independent house while I myself lived in a flat. I made him director after some time because I wanted him to learn about the organization and for the organization to get to know him and also to overcome any resistance to an outsider being made a functional director immediately.

~

About six months after my taking over, having familiarized myself with the issues facing BHEL, work started on a corporate plan that would give a vision for the future of the company. I had heard about strategic plans prepared by large companies in other countries. Having been involved in planning since my early days in the Madras Electricity Board, I understood the importance of preparing and sticking to a plan of action rather than working in an ad hoc manner.

I also saw the corporate plan as a way to communicate to the employees the critical situation facing the company, what its goals were, how they were to be achieved and their role in achieving these goals. Every employee should understand and work to a common goal rather than groups of people working without any direction or understanding of the strategic vision of the company. It was just common sense logic, and there was no management jargon about corporate plans at that point of time.

A small group at the corporate headquarters, led by Paramesvar, worked on the plan. Initially, it looked a bit vague, and it was revised at least twice. When we had what appeared to be a more cogent and workable draft, we threw it open for discussion, circulating it to all employees, trade union leaders and also to the power ministry, which was our customer. A number of suggestions and comments came, but overall there was appreciation that BHEL was working on the right lines. Some of the suggestions were incorporated in the document, titled *Outline of a Corporate Plan*. Around a year after we started the exercise, the *Corporate Plan* was issued in March 1974 after the board gave its approval.

The broader vision of the document was to transform BHEL from a purely manufacturing company to an engineering organization of international repute. The plan set ambitious targets for the company in terms of profits, turnover and volumes of exports. In addition, it mentioned that the business should be enlarged from the narrow field of electric power to the broader field of energy, thereby opening up new opportunities in nuclear power engineering and non-conventional sources such as solar, geo thermal, and wind energy. Further, the plan envisaged graduation from just being a supplier of individual products for the energy sector to the supplier of total turnkey systems. This implied diversification into systems engineering and turnkey project management, both under-exploited opportunities at that time. The company adopted a slogan, 'Engineering to the fore', reflecting this goal. The plan also provided for the development of a new human resource management philosophy that would 'bring about an increased sense of belonging and team spirit among our employees'.

Among the key elements of the plan were functional orientation of the management, rationalizing and standardizing the product mix of different plants, and a limit of 10,000 for manpower in any plant. There was also an appeal to the government for more autonomy in BHEL's investment decisions and flexibility in operative functions. To develop a business of the magnitude BHEL was planning, the *Corporate Plan* pointed out that it 'requires a measure of understanding from the government, and faith that BHEL will deliver the goods'. It was perhaps the first openly declared call for more freedom from government control, something that was to be granted more than a decade later.

The *Corporate Plan* was a first for any public sector company and made BHEL stand out in the crowd. So impressed was the government with the plan that the Bureau of Public Enterprises circulated it among all public sector firms and exhorted them to prepare similar plans. The document even got international attention. When we started on the exercise, however, we never expected it to be such a revolutionary document. It was just meant to help BHEL focus on its goals better.

Even as we were working on the document, we had started

executing some of the ideas outlined in it. Over the next three years, we systematically went about implementing all that we had set out in the document and made BHEL a force to reckon with. There is no denying that the *Corporate Plan* galvanized the whole organization like never before.

I had been keeping the government constantly in the loop about the changes I was planning and the steps I was taking. Almost all of them started to show results very soon, and a year after I took over—the time I had sought from Mrs Gandhi—I had convinced the government that breaking up BHEL would not be a good idea.

~

One of my priorities on taking over was to win customers for BHEL and make it a customer-oriented organization. I found that BHEL was not the supplier of choice for most of its customers. There was a marked preference for imports and the only reason many of them bought equipment from BHEL was that the government gave it price preference and often did not sanction individual import requests (those were the days of import restrictions). There is no denying that the government gave price preference to the public sector enterprises in order to give them a boost. This was not unique to India. The bias towards imports was attributed to the fact that the domestic power equipment industry could not meet the requirements of its customers. When I went deeper into the reasons for this, I found that customers were ordering power equipment of odd specifications, which BHEL did not manufacture, to justify imports. They would say that their project needed a 66 MW turbine merely because some other country had this in surplus and they could get it cheap.

Once I identified this problem, I found a way to tackle it. BHEL worked closely with the power ministry and helped standardize the sizes of power equipment—60 MW, 110/120 MW, 200/210 MW and so on. We also indicated the time BHEL would take to supply that equipment—forty-eight months in the case of hydro projects, thirty-six in the case of thermal projects. Only if a customer needed equipment which was not of this standard size (which would have been rare since these specifications would meet 90 per cent of the domestic power plants' requirements) or if BHEL could not deliver within the time schedule (again a remote possibility since that was the minimum time for commissioning of power plants) could imports be justified. We also offered a price challenge—if the import price of standard-sized equipment was cheaper, then too the customer was welcome to import. I also daringly announced that BHEL was giving up the privilege of 15 per cent price preference for the public sector, which meant that it would compete on equal terms with other private or foreign suppliers. This was not liked by other public sector companies, which used this provision to shelter themselves from market competition. Some public sector chief executives openly expressed their annoyance with me. But BHEL did see an increase in orders, thanks to all this. In contrast, most of the companies that clung to the price preference regime later became sick units.

However, there was criticism that this was arm-twisting of a different kind and that the customers actually did not have a choice of supplier. After all, they did have to give BHEL a fair chance and could import only if it indicated that it would be unable to deliver. To a limited extent, this policy did restrict their choice, but unless there was some standardization, it would have been difficult later to maintain equipment of different sizes. Customers themselves later accepted that such standardization was in the larger interest of the power sector and was the need of the hour.

I cannot deny that the government decision did give BHEL a measure of protection. But the management did not rely on this protection alone to win customers, which it could have. Many public sector companies never move out of the comfort zone afforded by government patronage and protection. We at BHEL did not do this. Instead, we went the extra mile and identified the weaknesses within the organization and addressed them in order to keep customers happy.

In my first year as chairman, I took two initiatives which sowed the seeds of a customer-oriented culture in BHEL. One relates to advance payments. BHEL had hitherto followed the international norm for payment of power equipment—half the payment made in phases as advance and the balance paid after delivery. I brought this advance down to 10 per cent. It hurt our financial position, but it was a huge boon for the cash-strapped SEBs. The other relates to the setting up of a spare parts and service unit, with a nucleus of expert engineers, to provide SEBs with specialized service for maintenance. These two actions won them over completely.

In addition, we also set about identifying reasons for customer dissatisfaction and started addressing them one by one. One complaint related to the quality of equipment, and here I found myself up against a mindset problem within BHEL. We had to wage a major battle with what was known as the 'March Syndrome'. The production bonus paid in a particular financial year was based on the production of the previous financial year, that is, up to 31 March. Just in order to show increased production, anything that could be declared as produced was declared as such, even if it was not ready for use at the site and this often led to problems later. A case in point was a steam turbine—a very large order by itself—that was to be delivered to a customer. This type of turbine had been giving problems at sites in earlier cases. Sharan had looked into this and had specified certain tests that were to be carried out before the turbine was dispatched to this customer. However, he found this was not being done. When he insisted on the tests being completed, he came under severe pressure to let the turbine be delivered in spite of the tests not being carried out. We had to keep talking to employees and trying to convince them about the importance of not short-circuiting processes. I then realized that when it came to quality control, mere diktats would not work and it required a lot of persuasion to ensure strict quality compliance.

In the case of Bhopal, we found that while the plant as a whole fell behind in deliveries, individual groups showed 100 per cent achievement of production targets. It turned out that no one was taking the responsibility of putting the parts together and supplying composite equipment to the customer. I had to sit with each group, identify the problem and correct it. It was not the job of the chief executive but I had to do it, visiting Bhopal every month.

Another major complaint from customers related to delays in deliveries of equipment. When we studied the reasons for such delays, we found a complete lack of coordination among different units of the organization. A power plant requires boilers, turbines, generators, feed pumps, transformers and a number of other products. There is a sequence to be followed in installing and operationalizing each of these. The customers would usually source equipment from each of the plants and put it together themselves. Often the lack of coordination between the plants resulted in equipment arriving regardless of the sequence. Not only did this delay the project, it also meant that it was impossible to pin responsibility on someone when a problem surfaced. The Trichy team would take care of only the boiler, Hyderabad only of feed pumps, Bhopal only transformers or switch gears and Haridwar only turbines and generators.

Besides, there were other components sourced from different suppliers. The customer, however, blamed BHEL as a whole for any problem since, quite rightly, he was not concerned with the internal working of the organization.

This problem only gave weight to my argument that BHEL needed to be an integrated organization and that it would be a folly to break it up. A power equipment manufacturer could grow only if it kept its customers satisfied, offering everything from a boiler to a transformer yard. The parts might have to be manufactured in different units, but these units would have to work in a coordinated manner under a unified leadership. This is what large global companies did. This was what BHEL was not doing.

I realized the need to set up a formal structure to facilitate such coordination. In 1974, I set up a power projects division to provide an integrated service to the customer, including erection and commission of power plants. It initially had three centres—in Mumbai, Chennai and Kolkata. Later, in 1975, another organization—the Indian Consortium for Power Projects (ICPP)—was merged with BHEL and became the Delhi centre of the power projects division. The ICPP had been set up in the late sixties to take up power projects on a turnkey basis in India and abroad. BHEL and HE(I)L along with two other companies were its members. Unfortunately, it had not performed up to mark. In 1974, following HE(I)L's amalgamation with BHEL, the latter ended up owning 70 per cent of ICPP, making it a BHEL subsidiary. It did not make sense to keep it as a separate unit, and I recommended its merger with BHEL. One of the first assignments the power projects division took up was the revamping of the Ennore Thermal Power Plant in Tamil Nadu. Later, it took over the turnkey construction of the Badarpur Thermal Power Station from the Delhi administration. Neither of these two assignments would have been possible without the setting up of the power projects division. Later, it would enable BHEL to participate in and bag an international tender for a turnkey project.

~

I realized that BHEL had to be reorganized to achieve what was going to be its expanded mandate as outlined in the *Corporate Plan*. In fact, the existing operational set-up did not even allow it to carry out its present mandate efficiently. Such a comprehensive reorganization required augmentation of BHEL's engineering capabilities and quality control. The engineering reorganization exercise that BHEL undertook in 1975, spearheaded by Sharan, was an extremely ambitious one.

As a first step, there was a need to rationalize production. At that time, one product was being produced in different plants to different designs and standards drawn up by different collaborators. The Bhopal, Haridwar and Hyderabad plants all produced steam turbines but according to British, Soviet and Czech designs and standards respectively. Haridwar and Bhopal both manufactured water turbines but to Soviet and British designs and standards respectively. This was not a sustainable or efficient operation, as it did not allow the company to benefit from economies of scale. No company can afford to have this luxury of three different streams of technology, all operating at sub-optimal levels. It was also leading to problems at the customer's end, since a boiler produced in Trichy was not compatible with a turbine produced in Haridwar or Bhopal. Apart from addressing this, we also had to standardize and rationalize the various associated auxiliaries, materials and components. Based on discussions with engineering executives at all plants, a comprehensive document for reorganization of the engineering function was brought out.

We decided to streamline operations in such a way that each

unit concentrated on the design and engineering of some designated products and became an engineering development centre (EDC) for those products manufactured in other plants called the 'away centres'. Each centre was headed by an engineering development manager (EDM), whose responsibility was to integrate the designs of a product received from various licensors by different units of BHEL, take the best from each, and evolve a new design and a set of standards that would make the various products compatible with each other. Each EDC had a research and product development wing (for product improvement and development), a product engineering wing (to design and analyse tenders and prepare technical proposals) and a field engineering services wing (to solve operational and engineering problems during and after commissioning equipment and give feedback to the design groups).

Thus, Bhopal became the EDC for hydrosets, motors, switchgears, large transformers and traction equipment. Haridwar was made the EDC for turbosets and motors of higher ratings. Trichy was the EDC for boilers and components. Hyderabad became the EDC for industrial products.

Hyderabad, in fact, had shifted almost entirely from the low capacity turbines it was originally meant for to an entirely different range of products that were suited more for industrial applications. This was a business decision necessitated by the fact that it had become clear, around the time I took over, that there would be little demand for the equipment it was originally mandated to produce. The natural choice would have been to move to production of 120 MW turbines. But there seemed little point in spending on that once HE(I)L's Bhopal factory (which manufactured 120 MW turbines) joined the BHEL family.

A team from Hyderabad then went around different industries to see where the smaller turbines the unit produced could be used. It found that the fertilizers, petrochemicals and sugar industries could be potential customers with robust demand. Till then, these industries were importing their equipment or buying them from Triveni Engineering. We then entered into a limited collaboration agreement with Siemens for high-speed turbines, with Nuovo Pignone of Italy for ammonia synthesis compressors, and with General Electric for gas turbine components. The Hyderabad unit thus started manufacturing ammonia synthesis compressors (which are at the heart of fertilizer plants), high-speed drive turbines, gas turbines and feed water pumps (components that form part of a power plant) with the help of Siemens and General Electric (GE) as well as other Western firms. Under M.R. Naidu, the unit kept adding products to its portfolio, including parts for some equipment that the Trichy plant was producing, developing and mastering technology in the process. Over the next five years, we completely re-tooled the plant and re-trained the engineers. It was the shortest period in which a factory had been transformed to manufacture a product different from what it was originally slated to. It was a dramatic transformation and one which has stood the Hyderabad unit and BHEL in good stead.

As part of this rationalization, it was decided that no plant should have more than 10,000 people; once it crossed that level, a new unit should be set up close to the mother plant, with a minimum staff of 500. As the *Corporate Plan* had noted, production units with over 10,000 employees do become unmanageable. Siemens and GE, for example, rarely had production units of more than 5,000 people. Haridwar, Trichy and Hyderabad had between 7,000 and 10,000, so they did not pose any problems. Bhopal, however, presented a challenge, since it had 20,000 employees, and we realized that relocating 10,000 people would be fraught with problems. So we decided to keep the employee numbers there at 15,000. A part of Bhopal's transformer unit had already been transferred to a new unit in Jhansi, also in Madhya Pradesh, set up in 1974, and some people from the main plant had been shifted there. A few years later, when I was secretary, heavy industry, and also temporarily chairman of BHEL, I sanctioned a similar satellite unit for Trichy at Ranipet in Tamil Nadu.

The engineering reorganization exercise, by ending duplication and helping managers focus better, started showing results within a year of being put into effect. Earlier, the drawings that were to be supplied to our clients were invariably delayed. Now they were being released on time. The performance of the power plants improved as the engineers who designed products supplied to them also got directly involved in their performance in the field. The quality of products also improved, with rejection rates and instances of reworking at the sites both declining.

~

The *Corporate Plan* had suggested that BHEL diversify into a range of new products in order to maintain its pre-eminent position in the field of power equipment. Among the opportunities it identified was the development of know-how for non-traditional energy systems such as MHD (magneto hydro-dynamics), coal gasification, fluidized bed boilers and solar and geo-thermal energy. It was to spearhead this initiative that I got Sharan into the company to head a new division on energy systems and new products (ESNP). I gave him full freedom to formulate his programme and develop a team of his own. It was under his supervision that BHEL got the Rs 15 crore coal gasification research and development (R&D) centre sanctioned. Over time, the ESNP division, with which the EDCs were closely linked, helped BHEL develop capabilities in all the areas that the *Corporate*

*Plan* envisaged as well as components for nuclear energy systems. Sharan's contribution in this field was extremely valuable.

The diversification into lighter electronic products was a difficult move. There was a very strong view in the government that BHEL should continue to remain a heavy engineering company, but I knew that the shift to electronics was necessary for BHEL's future. The Bhopal plant already had an electronics division from its HE(I)L days, but it was working at sub-optimal levels since it had limited facilities. The Karnataka government was managing three companies in the power sector. Of these, the biggest of the three, New Government Electric Factory (NGEF), was operating reasonably well. I came to know that the other two, Radio and Electricals Manufacturing Company Ltd (Remco) and Mysore Porcelains, were sick companies. Seeing the potential of all these companies and the muscle it would give to BHEL's own electronics division, I offered to buy these companies. But Karnataka's then industry minister S.M. Krishna was reluctant to give up NGEF. But he took the bold step of agreeing to transfer REMCO and Mysore Porcelains to BHEL.

Thus REMCO was converted into a centre for electronics, control and instrumentation, while Mysore Porcelains was converted into a centre for electro-porcelain development, thus adding to BHEL's technological strength. The Department of Electronics opposed this strongly on the grounds that the public sector units under its jurisdiction, the largest of which was Bharat Electronics Ltd (BEL), would suffer. I had to spend a lot of time convincing Ashok Parthasarathi and the secretary of the ministry, M.G.K. Menon, that BHEL should also develop in-house knowledge and facilities for the manufacture of electronic components as they formed an integral part of the systems BHEL supplied.

Another important business strategy that the *Corporate Plan* had outlined was for BHEL to take its place in the global market for power equipment and set an export target of 20 to 25 per cent of its production. This was something I was personally very keen on. The *Corporate Plan*'s target seemed too ambitious at a time when BHEL was heavily dependent on foreign technology, and the export of manufactured goods from India, especially sophisticated machinery, was rare. But the Trichy plant had bagged a prestigious export order even before any of the boilers it had supplied were commissioned, so I saw no reason why BHEL as a whole could not make a bid for a slice of the world market.

My rationale for pushing for exports at a time when the domestic market was unhappy with BHEL was threefold. One, since BHEL aspired to be a global organization, it should be able to enlarge its activities beyond the country's frontiers. Two, unless the company tested itself in the international market, it would not be able to improve on its organizational and technological capability. Three, the unfortunate truth was that chances of acceptance from domestic consumers improved only when one proved oneself on a global scale.

We started participating in international tenders. Our target was mostly the West Asian countries, Africa and South Asia, where our chances of success were greater. Malaysia's NEB repeated its orders for boilers from Trichy. Bhopal started exporting transformers, motors and switchgears to Malaysia, West Asia and Africa. We bagged orders from New Zealand and Saudi Arabia. But the feather in our cap undoubtedly was winning a Rs 96 crore contract for a comprehensive 2 X 120 MW power plant in Tripoli, Libya, in 1976 on a turnkey basis in the face of stiff international competition.

We went after this contract with the same aggression that BHEL Trichy had exhibited when pitching for the Malaysian order. Our competitors in Libya were Western and Japanese companies, including General Electric Company, which had taken over AEI (the technological collaborator for HE(I)L, Bhopal) in 1967. The lobbying by these companies was vicious. Indian newspaper stories critical of BHEL were translated into Arabic and distributed to key ministers in the Libyan government. The Libyans were told that BHEL was a relatively young organization with no experience of turnkey projects and that it was relying on borrowed Western technology, the reference being to AEI being the collaborator for the Bhopal plant. If as general manager of one unit I had not let the Malaysian order slip out of our hands, as chairman, BHEL, I was hardly likely to lose the Libyan contract without putting up a stiff fight. Apart from numerous trips by me and my team to Tripoli, I got the Libyan prime minister and minister for energy to India and took them around our plants. Muralidhar Shukla, the marketing chief, did a remarkable job of building a relationship with the Libyan authorities. We did not rely on lobbying alone. We realized that the efficiency of our turbines needed to be improved and worked on it. The EDM for steam turbines, K.C. Vaishya, worked hard on it and redesigned the blades. The Trichy plant also redesigned the boilers to suit the Libyan requirements. Our efforts paid off, and we bagged the contract, which was then considered to be the largest thermal power station in northern Africa.

I knew that BHEL would not make any profit out of this deal. We were weak on the civil construction side and had outsourced the construction to Gammon India. Estimations on the earthwork and structural steel requirements went wrong, and we ended up paying more to Gammon than was contracted. But the order was a huge image boost for BHEL. This was the third turning point in BHEL's history, the bagging of the Madras Fertilizers order and the Malaysian contract being the other two. BHEL may not have reached the 20 per cent export target that was set in the *Corporate Plan* within the time frame fixed but no one could now question the fact that it had emerged as a serious player, not just in the country but globally.

~

The underlying theme of the *Corporate Plan* was to transform BHEL from a purely manufacturing organization into an engineering organization, a point I had often raised with both Mathur and Baijal. I was now getting the chance to put this idea to work.

I strongly believe that unless engineers know the philosophy behind a technology or the design of a particular product, they will not be able to improve upon it or solve a problem when it arises. BHEL, until then, was only manufacturing products as per a design provided by a foreign collaborator. Our engineers were very conversant with the manufacturing processes, but few had any understanding of the design philosophy behind a product and the assumptions behind something being done in a particular way. Whenever the power plants that we set up had problems, they were not able to solve them effectively due to gaps in design knowledge. The knowledge base was, thus, inadequate for what BHEL was supposed to deliver for the country. I wanted BHEL to be an independent engineering organization, where engineers understood why a particular product was designed in a particular way so that they could also improve upon or modify a design when needed, and also develop engineering design and standards that would help the company be self-reliant in the long run. My aim was to help BHEL become a technology provider instead of a technology buyer.

Towards this end, I set up a corporate R&D centre at Hyderabad in 1973 to provide research support to engineering activities in the plants and also think of new projects. It was also meant to bring about overall economy by formulating designs that were more efficient and reducing problems that occurred at the sites. Another responsibility was continuous research in material sciences. Those were days when domestic R&D had not taken off in any other field. The finance ministry whose financial sanction was necessary was very reluctant and seriously objected to our proposal for the specialized R&D centre. The *Corporate Plan* had provided for this, but the finance secretary thought it was money down the drain. Eventually, I got the secretaries of the departments of atomic energy, science and technology, electronics, and space, apart from the director general of the Council for Scientific and Industrial Research (CSIR) to support my proposal. The government finally relented and sanctioned my proposal for the R&D centre. T.V. Balakrishnan was put in charge, and the centre took off to a flying start. Later, the Research and Development Organization for Electrical Industry (RDOEI), which had been set up by the government as part of HE(I)L to prepare project reports and take up consultancy work, was merged with the Hyderabad centre. The research and technical work being done at the R&D centre at Hyderabad improved over a period of time and is of outstanding quality today.

Over time, the centre secured a large number of patents, and it is this concerted research effort that is keeping BHEL on top even today. When I look back, I feel that some of the best organizations like Heavy Engineering Corporation (HEC) and even organizations like Hindustan Machine Tools (HMT) and Indian Telephone Industries (ITI) have all failed to make the grade only because they did not pay attention to in-house R&D and engineering to upgrade their technology. It is because of this research focus that BHEL was able to later upgrade to turbines of higher capacity as well as come to the nation's rescue in areas that had nothing to do with power.

There are two examples of this. Around the time of the global oil crisis, the Oil and Natural Gas Commission (ONGC) had invited bids for deep drilling rigs to augment production. Only one offer was received from an American company with unacceptable conditions—delivery would be made as and when the rig was available and at prices ruling at the time of dispatch. Mrs Gandhi and Subramaniam called me and asked if BHEL could help in any way. I visited the United States along with the ONGC chairman and met several companies. Unfortunately, all of them behaved in a high and mighty manner. We then decided that BHEL would, acting discreetly, source the technology required for individual items of oil rigs and manufacture the deep drilling rigs itself. Through a combination of sourcing some parts of oil rigs and taking assistance to develop the mast within BHEL, we created the systems capability of putting them all together and manufactured a complete deep drilling rig in Hyderabad and supplied it to ONGC in 1977.

We met the requirements of ONGC, though this was not our core business. Once the capability was demonstrated, the foreign suppliers conducted themselves well in their future dealings with ONGC.

Yet another more important example of BHEL's engineering and technology capability was the assistance it rendered to the Department of Atomic Energy. India's fledgling nuclear power programme was put in jeopardy after the first nuclear tests in Pokhran in 1974. Following sanctions imposed by Western countries on India, Canada, which was collaborating on the Rana Pratap Sagar and Kalpakkam nuclear plants, stopped all assistance. The government turned to BHEL and Larsen & Toubro to help complete the plants. The Bhopal and Trichy plants were already producing components for nuclear plants, and the *Corporate Plan* had highlighted the need to create an engineering group to study India's nuclear power programme. This request gave BHEL the opportunity to expand its work in this area.

Partly through its own capability and with some support from Kraftwerk Union (KWU, a subsidiary of Siemens specializing in nuclear power plants), BHEL helped these nuclear power projects come up despite the withdrawal of foreign collaborators. The association of KWU was kept completely under wraps because it was a sensitive issue. We could do this only because Siemens was already assisting us in technological upgrade of our plants, and the KWU engineers could come here without arousing any suspicion.

~

By 1976, BHEL had expanded immensely, having got into a number of new areas, and had a large number of new divisions, including a consultancy services division, an exports division, oil rigs division and marketing and sales division, to name just a few. In order to integrate their operations better, BHEL had also invested heavily in setting up two new projects to strengthen their material base. The critical material that goes into a boiler is the seamless steel tube which was available from limited international suppliers. The suppliers dictated the time of supplies, thereby making it difficult for BHEL to meet its delivery commitments. To overcome this, we designed and set up a seamless steel tube manufacturing facility as a part of the boiler plant at Trichy. Still more complex was the problem of securing on-time delivery of heavy castings and forgings needed for turbines and generators. The availability of such components was again very limited internationally, and delays in procurement affected the delivery schedules of BHEL. With our own limited resources and taking help from Creusot–Lloyre of France, we designed a new Central Foundry Forge plant, located it at Haridwar and got Col S.P. Wahi from Bokaro Steel Plant to head it. Col Wahi turned out to be a good addition to the cadre of managers and did an outstanding job of establishing and operationalizing this plant.

All this was throwing up huge organizational challenges. I had nearly twenty divisional heads reporting to me, and this would only increase as the organization grew. The general managers of plants were also over-burdened, with their involvement in the day-to-day management of the plants and townships leaving them little time to plan for the future of the products their plants manufactured or focus on improving the quality of working. Given the wide product range of BHEL, the corporate planning cell could not devote the kind of attention to product development that was needed to keep the company competitive. Failure to address this would have proved Mrs Gandhi's view that Indians lacked the capability to manage large organizations.

A special unit had been set up under the corporate planning division to study how contemporary multi-division, multi-disciplinary organizations are managed and keep abreast of latest global developments. Our two favourite subjects of study were Siemens and GE. Our studies confirmed that organization design is contextual and influenced by markets, technology and strategies of an enterprise. Our attempt was to create a nimble flexible organization that was result-oriented. We judiciously adopted temporary structures like task forces, committees and project management techniques to supplement organizational capabilities. Every six months, the organizational structure of BHEL was reviewed to assess if it was commensurate with the tasks it was mandated to carry out. Sometimes small changes were effected and sometimes a more thorough overhaul. The *Corporate Plan* had also talked about the need to give the integrated structure of BHEL a more functional orientation. It was now time to put this into action.

The first step I took was at the board level. The general managers of the plants and of the various divisions were very senior people but not members of the board. Their voices needed some representation at the board level and they needed to be involved in overall policy decisions. But inducting them into the board would have made it unwieldy and proved counter-productive. I then thought of structuring BHEL on the lines of German companies, which had a two-tier supervision—a supervisory board which looked into broad policy issues and an executive board, presided over by the chief executive, which looked into operational issues. So the general managers were re-designated executive directors and made part of an executive committee, which also had a representative from the union. Any proposal being put up to the supervisory board would have to go through the executive committee, which would discuss the proposal with a more holistic perspective, and only then go before the board for clearance. In addition, any policy issues the board decided would be sent to the executive committee, which would then discuss and work out the operational details and then pass them on for implementation. This was taking the concept of centralized policy making and decentralized implementation a step further.

Executive directors of plants were also designated group general managers, who would take care of a group of activities formed either on the basis of locational proximities or allied technologies. Thus, the person heading a plant would be an executive director for the outside world and group general manager for different activities related to his plant. He would be in overall charge of the plant and its satellite unit, assist the chairman and board in formulating long-term strategy for the products and systems that his plant was the EDC for, and be part of various committees he was assigned to. The gamut of activities relating to the day-to-day management of the plant—engineering, operations and administration—was put under different general managers, leaving the executive director free to focus on playing a leadership and coordinating role. Decision making within the organization became faster, and managers got a lot more operational freedom. This arrangement, no doubt, went a long way in making BHEL a nimble organization despite its huge size.

~

The *Corporate Plan* had highlighted the need for a new style of personnel management which would foster team spirit among the employees and bring about a sense of involvement. Given the low morale among employees when I took over, people management was to pose as tough a challenge to me as a chief executive as the engineering challenges. I realized that it would not do to focus on maintaining machines alone; maintaining men was equally important. My appointment as chairman gave me an opportunity to implement some of the ideas I had as general manager, Trichy, but could not implement.

The engineering reorganization exercise threw up what has been called 'the human side of engineering'. It was one thing to decide on rationalizing and streamlining production across plants but quite another to implement it. It was not easy for an engineer who had trained for two years in Czechoslovakia in technology for small turbines to be suddenly told that there was no use for his knowledge and that he should now get trained to manufacture a totally new product. Or for someone who had been comfortably settled in Bhopal and was looking forward to retiring there to be told that he would now have to move, along with his family, to Bengaluru. We had to be extremely sensitive in this exercise, taking care to ensure that no employee was inconvenienced or felt insecure. If a person trained in a particular function was not in a position to shift when the function was transferred to another unit, we did not force him to go if he could do something else in the place where he wanted to remain. As far as possible, we tried to ensure that people got promotions when they were transferred.

When I took over, there was some apprehension in the minds of engineers in Haridwar over the merger of HE(I)L's Bhopal unit with BHEL. Both were producing turbines, and it was acknowledged that the British technology in the Bhopal unit was superior to the Soviet technology in the Haridwar unit. Engineers in Haridwar were naturally insecure about their importance in the organization. This was addressed when Bhopal and Haridwar both became EDCs for different kinds of turbines.

Taking a leaf from my stint in Trichy, where I found that communicating with employees helped win their trust, I constantly explained the logic of our actions to all the employees, pointing out how each action would benefit the organization as a whole. I made it a point to visit every plant frequently and interact with as many people as possible, impressing upon them the fact that individual excellence, while necessary, was not sufficient, and each individual action should benefit the organization as a whole. I drove home the point that wherever an organization succeeded, individuals also prospered. This was in addition to circulars and periodical newsletters, the drafting of which was usually done by Paramesvar. Sharan used to spend a lot of time in the plants talking to engineers and explaining the rationale behind the reorganization. Both were of immense help to me during this exercise, and I doubt whether I could have pulled this off if it were not for them.

In spite of this effort to reach out, affected people accepted these changes grudgingly. Some managers proved very difficult, and I had to let them go. In the case of the Bhopal plant, when I shifted the electronic operations to Bengaluru and transferred people there, some officers approached Shankar Dayal Sharma, a former Madhya Pradesh chief minister, who was then the communications minister at the Centre (and who later became President). He saw the move to shift some operations to Bengaluru as a conspiracy against the state. Rejecting the logic of keeping the number of employees in a plant at 10,000, he argued that when Nehru had inaugurated the plant in 1956, it was supposed to have a strength of 30,000. The fact that I had kept the transformer division in the state at Jhansi did not seem to count for much in his eyes, and he complained to Mrs Gandhi that I was trying to reduce the importance of the Bhopal unit. Fortunately, neither Mrs Gandhi nor Pai interfered in my decisions.

I realized that it was important to address the career aspirations of employees in order to keep motivation levels high and get them to be more accepting of the changes that were being proposed. But there were limits to what I could do, given the hidebound public sector style of personnel management, with seniority counting for everything and talent for very little. I could not change rules unilaterally nor could BHEL pay more than public sector scales. So we had to work around this by giving people higher increments or out-of-turn promotions, wherever it was possible to use my discretion.

BHEL faced a unique problem in going by the seniority principle. It was not a very old organization at that time, and most people at the senior levels were not only of the same batch of 1963 but were also of roughly the same age—in their early thirties. Fortunately, the expanding scope of BHEL's activities provided numerous growth opportunities as people became heads of new divisions or got other important responsibilities. The re-designation of general managers and executive directors and group general managers also created more promotion avenues for those below them in the hierarchy.

On the one hand, the executives, by virtue of their proximity to the top management, and the workers, because of the trade union, always had their interests taken care of. It was the supervisors who were invariably neglected, as they were not members of the union nor were they close to the top management. One way of addressing this problem was the creation of specialist cadres at not only the senior scientist levels but also at the supervisory levels. We found that often a senior scientist may reach a point in his career where he would need to be given the designation of a general manager but may not have the administrative acumen to become a good general manager. Similarly, there were supervisors who earned the same as an executive but were denied the designation only because they were not graduates (executives had to be graduates). I believed that just because a person had joined at the lower level, or did not possess an academic qualification, he should not be denied the opportunity for upward mobility if he is meritorious. When we made such people general managers or executives, however, there were complaints that the organization was losing a good scientist or supervisor and getting an average general manager or executive, as the case may be. So we gave both the senior scientist and the supervisory cadres two options. They could continue to be in the positions they were in and be re-designated as specialists with the pay and perks of a general manager or executive. Or, if they wanted to become general managers and executives (and were found to have the requisite capability), they could move into the managerial cadre. This worked extremely well, and the potential of middle level managers was ably harnessed.

As BHEL grew in size and strength, I noticed that whenever a vacancy arose in a senior managerial position, we were always scurrying around to find a replacement. There was a lot of talk of succession planning in those days, and I realized the need to have an advance plan to identify and groom BHEL's future leaders from within the company.

Sharan, Paramesvar and I carefully observed the middle level managers and selected around forty who showed leadership qualities. Apart from us, this list was known only to Raghavan and Srivastava. We decided to put these people on a fast track and rotate them through different functions and departments. Each was also given some important assignment. I used to keep in touch with them, find excuses to identify myself with their work and ensure that their motivation levels were kept high. One or two fell by the wayside, but by and large the experiment was successful. Over ten years later, when I was heading SAIL, I found that not less than twenty-five chief executives of different public and private sector companies were from among the high fliers we had identified and groomed in BHEL. To date, BHEL has also never had to look outside the organization for its top leadership.

The nurturing of these high fliers did not mean that the average performers were ignored. That would have negated my efforts to create a highly motivated organization. We consciously worked towards getting these ordinary people do extraordinary things and to compete for the top slot. They were closely watched and counselled to identify the reasons for their average performance. Sometimes it was because they were in the wrong job; in that case, we tried to identify their aptitude and put them in the right place. In other cases, they did not have a good equation with their immediate seniors, so we put them in a different division to see if that would help. There were several cases in which we found that someone who was performing below par started to shine and exhibited the potential of a high flier merely with a change in job profile or division. A few did not improve despite all this, and they had to be discarded. On the whole, however, the average performer in BHEL did better than his counterparts in other organizations. I was once told that BHEL representatives outshone everyone else at meetings where people from other companies were present. The difference was that in BHEL we instilled a sense of pride in them; they never worked as if they were there only to earn their salary but as if they were part of a larger mission for the economic development of the country.

Another area on which I laid great emphasis was training. I would start every visit to a plant with a visit to the training centre to interact with the trainees. One of the good features of the public sector in India is the importance it attaches to in-house training of employees at all levels. Consistent with this philosophy while designing the plants, I had lain emphasis on each having a strong training centre, imparting skills at all three levels of personnel. At any given time, around 5,000 personnel would be under training at these centres.

~

The continuous training of executives also received due importance. Training programmes were conducted on their areas of technical specialization and general management. A very important component of executive training was financial management. Raghavan and his team spearheaded this effort. The spread of financial literacy across the organization was an important step and helped attain sustained profitability.

As part of this effort to create an internal management development capability, I was very keen to set up an in-house Management Development Institute. Engineering organizations always laid emphasis on continuous education to keep technological capability up to date, but I believed it was necessary to do the same for managerial capability. However, this did not materialize during my stint as chairman.

An interesting fallout of all this was that BHEL soon became a destination of choice for students passing out of our top management institutes, even as the public sector in general was shunned by most of them, who largely preferred private sector jobs, especially with the Tata Group, Hindustan Lever and Larsen & Toubro. Technocrat Lovraj Kumar, who was then in the Planning Commission, and I had often spoken of the need to attract some of these bright youngsters to the public sector. Soon after becoming chairman, I had also become a member of the governing board of the Indian Institute of Management Ahmedabad (IIM-A), and I arranged for Paramesvar to make a presentation about BHEL and the prospects it held out. In the first year, there was not a single response.

The following year, instead of waiting for the annual placement drive, Paramesvar got a few students from IIM Ahmedabad and Calcutta to do summer internships at BHEL. We chalked out a programme to best utilize their time. That turned out to be such a success that they went back with glowing reports about BHEL. Some of them expressed interest in working for BHEL after they graduated. The peer review worked better than all our presentations, and for three consecutive years, the gold medallists from IIM-A opted to join BHEL.

~

Dealing with trade unions was another problem that tested my managerial capabilities. Militant trade unionism was the order of the day in the seventies, especially in the public sector. I had wrestled with this when in Trichy but, as the general manager of a plant, could do little to bring about a systemic change across the organization. As chief executive of the whole organization, I now had a chance to test some of the solutions I had thought of.

Just before I took over, there had been serious labour unrest in Bhopal, Hyderabad and Haridwar. Discipline was a major problem in Bhopal, where people were working at sub-optimal levels. When production was stepped up, the unions complained about being subject to pressure and demanded more facilities without a corresponding increase in productivity. The management was expected to take sides in inter-union rivalries. I shunned the adversarial attitude that the earlier management of HE(I)L had adopted and continued my participatory approach that I had adopted in Trichy.

I knew that a large part of the industrial relations challenge could be met by dealing with the problem of multiple unions owing allegiance to different parties—the bane of industrial relations management in those days. I had seen how the works committee in Trichy had resulted in different factions getting represented, and I decided to apply the principle to a different mechanism at the centre. In 1973, an apex bipartite forum—called a joint management committee, consisting of representatives from the management and workers of all BHEL units—was set up. Since it was not possible to have only one representative of a plant with a few thousand workers, elections to the joint management committee were organized in each plant. Whichever group got 10 per cent or more of the votes would get a proportionate representation on the committee. This ensured that all political formations were represented on the committee, and this led to more fruitful discussions and negotiations.

I had had another idea in Trichy, and I managed to implement it now as chairman. During the periodic wage revisions, trade unions used to demand uniform salary increases for all employees, whether unskilled or skilled workers or supervisors. I had always argued that this was not correct—that if a foreman and an unskilled worker both got a uniform Rs 50 increase, we would be disrespecting the responsibilities and skills that a more experienced or educated person has. So when a wage revision was due in 1969, I had suggested a graded increase, depending on the skills, responsibilities and performance of a category of employees. While everyone saw the logic of this and the matter was being discussed rationally, the desire among the unions to placate the lowest level of workers—the bulk of the employees—stopped them from supporting the idea openly. We were the first to devise a wage structure and implement a wage revision based on skills and responsibilities. I was not able to implement this graded increase when I was in Trichy because of the reluctance of the then top management of BHEL to break the norm and convince the union leaders. The next wage revision was due in 1974 when I was chairman, and I decided to push this proposal through. Fortunately, I was able to convince the more progressive union leaders like G. Ramanujam and proceed with this. BHEL became the first public sector company to adopt this approach.

I regard the changes we made in BHEL in dealing with people and their problems at all three levels—executive, supervisory and workers—as unique. They established new standards in dealing with a new breed of skilled workers in a complex engineering organization. For me, it was great education in people management, and it stood me in good stead in my subsequent assignments in Maruti and SAIL.

~

Another major task I set to work on was continuing the technological upgrading work I had started in Trichy. At that time, the country was manufacturing only 210 MW steam turbines, and we at BHEL decided to gear ourselves up to manufacture 500 MW steam turbines, skipping the next higher 300 MW steam turbines offered by the Russians for the Haridwar plant. I recommended this to the government, pointing out that this was necessary for an accelerated power development programme to meet the country's growing power needs. The government then asked BHEL to find the technology and a suitable collaborator. A search committee was appointed with Sharan, Paramesvar and Balakrishnan as members, and it identified around a dozen potential collaborators.

Initially, the terms of reference for collaborations were similar to the existing ones, with the collaborators giving us drawings which we would follow. But later, the committee decided to move away from this and push for a collaboration in which BHEL would get not just the know-how but also the know-why which could enable its engineers to both produce to print as well as develop the capability to design steam turbines. We reframed the terms of reference accordingly and made it clear that we wanted our designers to work with the collaborator's designers in designing turbines. We were not prepared to go by drawings alone.

Around ten potential licensors had applied on the basis of our first terms of reference. Some lost interest after the revised ones. After a process of weeding out, we finally zeroed in on three firms—General Electric, Siemens and Brown Boveri & Cie*—for the last round of negotiations relating to the transfer of know-why, financial implications and a buyback clause (part of the royalty that BHEL was to pay was to be taken as components from us).

The GE turbines were the best, but the company refused to give our engineers access to its laboratories; it was only willing to share drawings. Brown Boveri was willing to share the know-why but was not in a position to buy back components. Siemens alone accepted all the three conditions.

When the Soviet Union came to know that BHEL was going to use Siemens technology in Haridwar, it lodged a strong protest with the Indian government, and the then Soviet deputy prime minister flew down to India to stop the deal. The Soviets claimed that the Haridwar factory was their fiefdom and that we should be content with the 300 MW technology offered by

*In 1988, Brown Boveri & Cie merged with Swedish firm ASEA to form ASEA Brown Boveri (ABB)

them. When I drew the government's attention to the fact that the Soviet Union was upgrading its own steel plants with the help of Siemens, and the Soviets were confronted with this, they acknowledged that to be correct but said that they had the political and managerial strength to deal with multinational companies which a young nation like India did not. They mocked at our ability to get the best out of a partnership with Siemens. The government, however, stood firmly behind BHEL and approved our proposal to take technology from Siemens. The agreement was approved and signed. With this agreement, the Haridwar plant gradually moved away from Soviet bloc technology to Western technology. It was a very successful agreement.

The decision to move away from the Soviet Union gave Indian engineers the right opportunity at the right time to get familiar with the more advanced and more acceptable development in the Western world, notably from Siemens and GE. The insistence of BHEL on gaining the know-why through intensive training and interaction of Indian engineers with the chosen partner has helped them absorb the technology, and they are today in a position to design these products on their own.

Having selected Siemens as the collaborator for the 500 MW steam turbine, it was logical for BHEL to deepen its relationship with the Siemens group of companies to upgrade all its other products, as it did not make sense for a company to have different streams of technology for the same products. The government appreciated this point and gave BHEL the go-ahead to start negotiations with Siemens. Once again, the Soviet Union protested, but we went ahead with the negotiations. We identified several areas in electrical engineering where BHEL was weak and started negotiations in all of them.

This time the agreement, which came to be called an omnibus

agreement, was a more broad-based technological and managerial assistance agreement. It involved extending the licensing agreement to cover anything Siemens had in its manufacturing units, BHEL engineers being associated with some Siemens research projects, and assistance in techniques to manage large enterprises in high technology areas. BHEL was to pay a certain lump sum over ten years and pay a royalty of 1.8 per cent of its turnover. Even as we were negotiating this agreement, there was a change of government. Shortly thereafter, the new Janata Party government shifted me to the higher post of secretary, heavy industries, which was the administrative department for BHEL. Raghavan was appointed BHEL chairman.

Taking advantage of these developments, the Communist Party of India (Marxist) launched a scathing attack on me, accusing me of falling into the hands of Western multinationals. The draft agreement thus ran into a major political storm. There was a vituperative attack on me as well. A CITU leader, P. Ramamurti, wrote a book titled *Stop BHEL's Truck with Siemens: An investigative analysis of the process of mortgaging a core public sector undertaking to a West German multinational and of its impact on other industries.* CITU was the trade union arm of the CPI(M), which was an ally of the ruling Janata Party. I am sure it was the Communists, by themselves or instigated by others, who led this campaign as they were not reconciled to BHEL moving towards Western organizations for more modern technology. The issue was raised in parliament and a parliamentary committee on public undertakings also examined the agreement. Some people from within BHEL trained in Soviet technology deposed before the committee, saying that the agreement would be detrimental to BHEL and that it would go against the ideals of self-reliance set out in the *Corporate Plan*. I pointed out the hollowness of these arguments, considering the Soviets themselves had sought assistance of Siemens. Morarji Desai, who was then the prime minister, tore into me for a clause that suggested assistance from Siemens on the management of large enterprises in high technology areas. Management is not something we do not know, why do we need managerial assistance, he wanted to know.

This attack on me suited certain people close to Desai who agreed that BHEL needed to move away from Soviet bloc technology but wanted it to collaborate with Brown Boveri. So I was attacked on all fronts by both those who did not favour Western technology and those who did. George Fernandes was the industry minister at that time and was supportive of the umbrella agreement. As the minister concerned, he could have seen it through, but for some reason he did not throw his full weight behind it. All he offered by way of support were some public statements that BHEL was going in the right direction. Unfortunately for me, Raghavan, who had been a party to all my negotiations with Siemens, changed his stand to such an extent that the contents of the agreement received a setback.

The agreement that was finally cleared after much delay was a truncated one, with the government omitting the managerial component and the technology upgrade of some products that I had negotiated. Moreover, against a negotiated royalty of 1.8 per cent, BHEL now had to pay 4 per cent, in effect paying more for less. If the agreement as conceived during my time had gone through, BHEL today would have been in a much stronger position.

I was deeply disappointed that the very purpose for which I supported Raghavan's choice as my successor—that he would continue the unfinished agenda of BHEL's technology upgrade—did not happen. When I took over as secretary, heavy industries, there was no decision about my successor, and I was overseeing BHEL till one was appointed. When the question of my successor was discussed, I thought it would be best to recommend one of the serving directors—Raghavan, Srivastava and Sharan—for the post to ensure continuity. I could have considered the next rung of leaders at the level of executive directors such as A.K. Khosla (who headed Haridwar), Deenadayalu (who headed Trichy), M.R. Naidu (who headed Hyderabad) or Paramesvar (who headed the corporate planning division) who were equally deserving, but I confined my selection to the top three. Of the three, Raghavan, by virtue of his overarching responsibility as director, finance, was more familiar with all areas of organization and had greater chances of success. Hence, I recommended his name. The proposal went through the routine process. Doubts were expressed at various stages in the government regarding his capability to measure up to my performance, but I stood firmly behind his candidature along with Mantosh Sondhi, who had been secretary, heavy industry, and had become secretary, steel, as well as Vasant Rajadhyaksha in the Planning Commission. I also assured Fernandes about Raghavan's suitability for the top job. This open expression of doubts by sections of the government, in spite of my very positive support both in writing and in discussions, perhaps hurt Raghavan's pride.

When I think of BHEL today, my only regret is that such an opportunity provided by the proposed omnibus agreement with Siemens—one that would have strengthened the company immensely and benefited the country as well—was missed due to petty personal and political considerations.

~

My stint at BHEL earned me some prestigious awards. In 1973, a year after becoming chairman, I was conferred the Padma Shri. The following year, the Madras Management Association honoured me with the Business Leadership Award, making me the first public sector chief to be awarded. The other three who had been given this award were stalwarts like Lala Shriram, J.R.D. Tata and Arvind Mafatlal.

I felt honoured to have received those awards but, when I left BHEL, far more precious to me was the satisfaction of knowing that, in five years, it had become a strong and viable multi-unit, multi-disciplinary organization which not only established itself within India but competed with large Western firms in the African and South Asian markets. Moreover, the transformation of BHEL was a matter of envy for someone like Arnold Weinstock, the managing director of General Electric Company. He was particularly impressed by the smooth integration of HE(I)L with BHEL in just five years. General Electric Company, incorporated in 1869, became a huge conglomerate by first taking over AEI (the collaborator for the Bhopal plant) in 1967 and then English Electric in 1968—four years before HE(I)L and BHEL had merged—and in the late seventies, he was still struggling with issues relating to the merger, and he wondered how we had achieved such levels of integration which he could not in fifteen years.

Moreover, BHEL had become a showpiece for the government. When Robert McNamara, who was the president of the World Bank, visited India in the seventies, the government chose BHEL to showcase how India was progressing on the economic front. I took him to Hyderabad, where we organized a slide presentation that R.K. Swamy had put together for us. The slides and colour pictures, beamed through four projectors, took him through what different units of BHEL were doing, how skills were being developed, the setting up of power plants, and the way in which these were transforming the regions they were in. In the discussions that followed, McNamara grilled us on how managerial capabilities were being built up, how skill development was being done, and what we were doing in order to remain ahead in an increasingly competitive world. He was so engrossed in the discussions that he overshot his time with us. His protocol officials reminded him about a luncheon appointment with the Andhra Pradesh governor, but he did not leave and kept the governor waiting.

Apart from this compliment, there was a more substantial gain for BHEL from this visit. World Bank-funded projects selected suppliers through the international competitive bid process, in which bids would be entertained only from companies that had supplied similar equipment for three years. That often precluded BHEL from bidding for some projects. At that meeting, I convinced McNamara to waive that stipulation for BHEL, and he agreed.

The McNamara visit also had an interesting personal story. As he was leaving, he asked me whether I had ever served abroad and if I would like to. I said I had not and that I was enjoying my job. Later I was told by Pai that McNamara had told Mrs Gandhi that he was impressed by what BHEL had done and asked if my services could be spared for an assignment with the World Bank. The bank was grappling with some problems in Brazil and Pakistan, and he wanted me as a trouble-shooter. He also pointed out that this would be a good exposure for me. Mrs Gandhi had then told him that she was not sure if India was in a position to relieve me just yet.

For any business to succeed, the support of its customers is crucial. In the case of BHEL, I had the good fortune of earning the support of K.C. Pant, the then minister for energy who did an outstanding job in many areas, notably in brining a better understanding between the state electricity boards and BHEL. For any public sector organization to succeed, there should be a coordinated approach based on mutual trust and respect among the minister, the secretary of the ministry and the head of the company. For the best part of my stint at BHEL, I had the benefit of Pai and Sondhi as minister and secretary respectively. We got along well and the result manifested itself in BHEL.

Within a few years, BHEL's strength became a national asset, and BHEL executives played important roles in many national tasks. BHEL had become an important instrument in formulating national level policies in the industrial and energy sectors. It was also the favourite source for future CEOs. I also felt the need for ensuring that this work in BHEL was documented for the benefit of the future generations. Hence I encouraged all divisions at the corporate office and all plants to develop case studies, to document proposals, to prepare project reports, and to undertake organizational studies. An enormous amount of documentation got generated in the process on each of the subjects, a treasure for serious students of management.

How did I succeed in doing all that I did? I did not have the luxury of engaging consulting firms or the explosion of books on management, as is the case today. BHEL couldn't even get sanction from the Reserve Bank of India to subscribe to membership of the Stanford Research Institute. Nor were there organizations that had gone through a similar exercise for me to use as a model. Whatever I did was a practical, common sense approach to problems. It succeeded because it was implemented honestly and with conviction.

In the early 1990s, long after I left BHEL, I was invited to inaugurate a seminar in Chennai on change management and business process reengineering conducted by two eminent professors of the Kellogg School of Management. These were new terms in business at that time. I took Paramesvar along and, as part of the inaugural keynote address, we explained to the audience all that happened in BHEL during my tenure as chairman. When we completed our presentation, the visiting professors said that they had nothing more to add on this subject. They were surprised that we were able to achieve all that we had without any formal training or education in the subject and that we had done in the seventies what was becoming a subject of study in the nineties.

# 4

# ENGAGING WITH POLICY

In the general elections held in 1977, the Congress suffered a defeat and Mrs Gandhi was no longer the prime minister. When the Janata Party assumed charge with Morarji Desai as prime minister, the late Biju Patnaik, the stalwart of Odisha politics, was appointed steel minister. That was the time BHEL was pitching for revamping the power systems and electrical controls required by steel plants with the help of Siemens technology, and I met him on a couple of occasions to discuss this matter. He once casually asked if I would like to become secretary, steel. I declined and did not think much of it. But he still seemed to have proposed my name for the office of secretary, steel.

The new government was in the process of reshuffling top bureaucrats across ministries. Desai had apparently expressed the view that some well-qualified professionals and technocrats should be brought in at the secretary level. Suddenly one day, I got a posting order at home saying I was to be the new secretary, heavy industries. I was not keen on the shift; there was still a lot to be done at BHEL, especially seeing the omnibus agreement with Siemens through. I, therefore, did not respond immediately. The next day, the cabinet secretary, Nirmal Mukarji, called me and asked why I had not taken up my new assignment. Rather than telling him on phone that I was not interested, I sought an appointment with him. When I met him, I pointed out that there was still a lot that needed to be done at BHEL and that I should be allowed to continue there.

Mukarji was very forthright in his reply. 'Look Krishnamurthy, there are some things you should keep in mind,' he said. 'If you don't join now, you will be unnecessarily giving an impression that you don't want to work for this government.' He said that the Janata government genuinely wanted to try out a few technocrats in high positions, and that is why I was transferred. He thought that would be a great opportunity for me to demonstrate my capabilities. He said he understood my desire to continue my work in BHEL and that they had found a way for me to do that. That is when I came to know that my name had initially been proposed for the post of secretary, steel. But Mantosh Sondhi, who had already spent four years as secretary, heavy industries, had expressed a desire to move to the steel ministry. Sondhi was a steel man—he had been general manager of the Bokaro Steel Plant. Mukarji felt both our interests would be served by posting Sondhi as secretary, steel, and me as secretary, heavy industries. As secretary of the administrative ministry of BHEL, I would get to oversee the company and complete my unfinished agenda. Mukarji's arguments were quite convincing, and I joined as secretary.

The heavy industries department and the issues it dealt with were not uncharted territory for me. When I was chairman, BHEL, former industries minister, Pai, Sondhi and I formed a triumvirate of sorts. We would meet two or three times a week and discuss a range of issues relating to improving the performance of the public sector, sometimes general and at other times specific to a particular company. Pai, a banker before he joined politics, wanted to introduce a lot of new practices in the public sector. We also used to brainstorm on the future of industrial development.

Within a few weeks of my joining, Brijlal Verma, who had been the industry minister, was replaced by George Fernandes, who had been minister for communications. We got off to a somewhat rocky start. The change happened at a time when ministers are normally not changed—during the budget session of parliament, which had got delayed that year because the new government took charge only in March.

Soon after taking over, Fernandes called the secretaries of the three departments under the ministry. The first department was industrial development, dealing with policy matters under S.S. Marathe; the second one, under me, dealt with heavy industry; and the third, dealing with technical development, was under a director general of technical development, Brigadier Sawhney. Dr Bimal Jalan was our economic advisor. Fernandes said he wanted to make a statement on the floor of the House, distancing the ministry from the actions of the previous government. After consulting with us over two days, he told us, on the day before he was to make his statement, what he was planning to say—that the Nehruvian model of economic development, with its emphasis on large industry, was wrong and had resulted in the country not progressing in the past thirty years and that there should have been greater emphasis on small and medium industry.

It was a typical political statement by a politician dismissing everything previous governments of a different political persuasion had done, but I was very disturbed. I asked him, 'Do you have to make this statement?'

He was a bit taken aback and said, 'Yes. I am convinced about this'.

I then responded, 'In that case, let me have my say.' I said, 'If as an education minister or health minister you say that all that has been done in the last thirty years has not produced results, I will agree with you. But as an industry minister, for you to stand in parliament in 1977 and say that the country has not achieved anything in industrial development, it will not be appreciated.' I pointed out that India was self-reliant in all consumer goods, had 200 engineering colleges against five when the British left, that it had the capability to set up cement and power plants and maintain the railway and communication networks on its own. The country, I added, had even conducted a nuclear explosion entirely on its own. Then I said something which could have got me into serious trouble if it was some other minister. 'If you had been an industry minister long enough and made this statement, people would have attributed it entirely to you. But you have come here just a few days back, so people will think we have briefed you. I cannot be a party to that.'

There was shocked silence in the room. Fernandes ended the meeting. As we left his room, my colleagues told me I would not last in the ministry. But they were wrong. Much to the relief of the three of us, Fernandes refrained from making any controversial statement. Though my colleagues had warned me after my initial spat with Fernandes, over the next two years we developed a good working relationship. He gave me a lot of freedom. Though we did have differences of opinion on several issues, he always let me have my say. Once the rationale of some action was explained to him, he did not put up unnecessary roadblocks that stemmed from his political ideology. His public image was that of a difficult man with a closed mind, and his stint in the ministry will always be associated with IBM and Coca-Cola having to shut their operations in India. However, in the years I worked with him, I did not see him doing anything any sensible minister would not. Not once did he ask me to do anything that was wrong.

~

My discussions with Pai and Sondhi when they were in the ministry and I was in BHEL had lain a good foundation of ideas and concepts to carry out the ministry's mandate. My stint in the ministry helped me give shape to some of these and bring in some fresh ideas into the bureaucratic machine.

The heavy industries department's mandate was to look after four sectors—automobiles, capital goods, heavy engineering and heavy electricals—which formed the core economic strength of India. I wanted to make these industries more result-oriented. I decided to structure the ministry on business lines, moving away from the existing system in which officers dealt with unrelated subjects. I divided the departments into four major groups—power equipments and construction, heavy engineering and mining equipment, machine tools and automobiles, and other capital goods. This lent a degree of specialization within the department, resulting in more focused and faster decision making.

I had three outstanding officers—two joint secretaries (Naresh Chandra and Alban Couto) and a technical adviser of the rank of joint secretary (Hari Bhushan)—under me. While Chandra concentrated on power equipment and construction, Couto looked after machine tools and automobiles. Hari Bhushan was put in charge of heavy engineering, mining equipment, etc. The other capital goods industries were looked after by T. S. Vijayaraghavan and N. Mohanty, both of whom later became secretaries in the same ministry. I had also taken five bright management executives from BHEL—R.K.D. Shah, P.K. Sardana, Bharat Krishnan, H.K. Agarwal and A.P. Agnihotri. They continued to remain on BHEL's rolls but were assisting us in the ministry in research and analysis.

I had been brought into the ministry because of my demonstrated managerial ability to get a public sector undertaking to perform. The government naturally expected me to do the same for other public sector undertakings that fell within the administrative control of the department. There were thirty-odd companies, and they were a mixed bag. These included BHEL, Heavy Engineering Corporation (HEC), Mining and Allied Machinery Corporation (MAMC), Hindustan Machine Tools (HMT), Scooters India, Triveni Structurals, Bharat Pumps and Compressors, Bharat Heavy Plates and Vessels, Engineering Projects (India) Ltd (EPIL), and a clutch of sick units which had been taken over by the government from the private sector, such as Jessops, Burn Standard, Braithwaite and Richardson & Cruddas. Each had problems of its own and required a different strategy and approach.

BHEL was the most successful among them and was seen as a role model, but what was suitable for BHEL would not have suited other organizations. HMT was doing exceedingly well and had a good image, but I found it very insular and it showed no great enterprise to assume leadership in the public sector. Being one of the early public sector companies, it encouraged inbreeding and lacked new talent from outside. HEC and MAMC were not faring well despite the fact that they were meant to service the two important sectors of steel and coal. These suffered from technological obsolescence and lack of rapport with customers. Scooters India had its own peculiar problem. This was a case where a second hand plant was transplanted from Italy and, though the product was good, the organization was not able to overcome teething troubles and market it in the wake of stiff competition from a private sector brand, Bajaj. EPIL, originally designed to construct factories in India and overseas, had changed course and was engaged in the construction of townships abroad. I had my doubts whether a government agency was suited for this kind of activity, and I was proved right later on.

I initiated a review of all the public sector companies under the ministry. Each of the four vertical divisions would go through the programmes, budgets and balance sheets of the companies under its jurisdiction with a fine toothcomb, identifying the problems and working out solutions. Every month, the companies would provide information in a prescribed format on what they had achieved in the previous month vis-à-vis what they had proposed to do, and this was publicized. The formats for the monthly information system (MIS) were similar to those of BHEL but were modified by the management executives to suit the different enterprises. This MIS that I initiated was unique and a first for any government department.

In doing this, the ministry did not function in a bureaucratic fashion, trying to micro-manage the enterprises. Instead, it provided managerial and consultancy support to them. This constructive approach by the ministry was the first of its kind and evoked varying reactions from the chief executives of these companies. Many resented the review exercise and felt the ministry was interfering in their working. From their perspective, that was probably right, but we could not allow things to continue as they were. The review would then have been pointless.

One of the early—and ticklish—problems I was confronted with was that of BHEL. Raghavan, who had succeeded me as chairman, did not welcome the ministry's initiatives and did a few things that were against the tradition of BHEL. Normally, I would have left Raghavan alone to pursue his own path so long as he was able to carry his top team along with him. Unfortunately, all the directors and other members of the top management—notably Sharan, Deenadayalu and Srivastava—were constantly representing to me and the minister that BHEL was losing direction. I tried my best to bring about an understanding between Raghavan and the others, but he was just not willing to cooperate. The reversal of his stand on the terms of the omnibus agreement with Siemens after having been with me in all negotiations and decisions also left me in doubt about his intentions regarding BHEL. Eventually, Fernandes asked Chandra for a report on the whole issue. Chandra submitted a confidential report, which broadly made the point that the other senior members of the BHEL management did not accept Raghavan's leadership and that there was a genuine apprehension that the organization would soon lose direction. On the basis of this report, Fernandes terminated Raghavan's services as chairman, BHEL.

Although the decision to remove him was that of the minister, an impression unfortunately gained ground that I was responsible for his ouster. Having personally recommended him for the post, this episode weakened my position to suggest some other name as a replacement and was a huge setback to my efforts to take BHEL to greater heights. Unable to find a suitable candidate within the organization in the changed circumstances, the government resorted to the extreme step of inviting a former chairman of the Railway Board to hold fort.

The review of public sector enterprises was useful because sometimes an outsider's perspective highlights issues that insiders fail to see. In some cases, the product mix of companies had to be changed. For example, Jessop, Braithwaite and Burn Standard—all based in Kolkata—had overlapping product portfolios. Two of them manufactured railway wagons, and all three produced overhead cranes. The ministry worked out a product rationalization exercise, which resulted in only one manufacturing wagons; of the other two, one concentrated on small cranes and the other on large cranes. There was resistance from within these companies, as there had been at BHEL during the engineering reorganization. Managers were apprehensive that their fiefdoms were being reduced. They lobbied with the minister, but Fernandes did not interfere.

HEC blamed its poor performance on the fact that the steel plants were not placing orders with it. The ministry's review revealed that this was because of a lack of coordination between the steel plants and HEC, which was not marketing itself to the former. I identified S.R. Jain, who was the managing director of the Bhilai Steel Plant, to head HEC as I felt he would be able to make a difference to the organization. Jain, however, was reluctant to move, as the shift to HEC, even as the chief executive, from the Bhilai Steel Plant was seen as a comedown. I had to do a lot of convincing, pointing out that the HEC assignment would be a challenging one, that he could be a good bridge between HEC and the steel plants and that this was in the national interest before he agreed to take over. I bypassed the Public Enterprises Selection Board and got him appointed as head of HEC. I believe that HEC was resurrected to a large extent because of Jain coming on board. Later, it went into a decline again.

The monthly review exercise of EPIL put me in a situation where I came under political pressure for the second time after the BHEL-Siemens agreement. EPIL, one of our seemingly successful organizations, had taken on a large housing project in Kuwait and had earned a lot of praise. There was much chest-thumping in the country at that time about a public sector undertaking setting up housing colonies abroad. However, not many knew that EPIL was incurring huge losses on the project. This remained unnoticed because EPIL kept moving from one phase to another without assessing the financial performance of each phase. The money that it got in the later phase hid the fact that the earlier one was losing money. It was the review that revealed this problem.

When EPIL proposed a new project in Iran, we put a stop to it. I was subjected to a lot of political pressure not to block this by a powerful Indian business group based overseas and the powers-that-be in India at that time. A large number of contractors and sub-contractors stood to benefit from this project. But we in the ministry saw no reason why the Indian tax payer should lose money on something that would benefit private parties in another country. The pressure on me came from different sources. Nobody came and asked me directly why I was stopping the project. But the EPIL chief executive made public statements about how the project would be in India's interests. I was told that the Indian business group had said that it would ensure my tenure was cut short. But Chandra and I stood firm, and fortunately for me, Fernandes did not put any pressure on me to change my stance, and the project was stopped and the losses curtailed.

The changes that I initiated with regard to the public sector did begin to show some results, with companies starting to post better results.

~

The government at that time believed in the philosophy of promoting small and medium enterprises and gave less importance to building large and heavy industry. However, I was an ardent advocate and practitioner of the Nehruvian model of development and believed that both were complementary and not exclusive of each other. The deriding of the previous model, I believe, was essentially out of political compulsion. On more than one occasion, Desai made light of my assertions of India's achievements on the economic front, saying that all the emphasis on high technology and heavy industry would not solve the problem of improving water supply. I would point out that providing clean drinking water was not a low technology solution and required the application of high technology and support of heavy industry. My position that knocking large industry all the time would not be in India's best interests was vindicated when, consistent with government policy, we introduced certain new technologies for mini cement plants—a distributed method of producing cement. Though initially successful, economies of scale forced the closure of these plants, thereby giving credence to my theory that certain items are better manufactured in high volume by large units in order to keep costs down.

The approach to the private sector in the areas the ministry looked after had to be different. That was the time of stifling controls on industry. While in BHEL, I had sought greater freedom for the public sector. As secretary of the department, I could hardly continue with the control mindset, and the department passed up no opportunity it got to make forceful pleas for relaxation of controls.

The relationship between the department and the private sector changed during my tenure. I was the second secretary, heavy industries, after Sondhi. Before the department was created in 1973, private sector companies dealt with the DGTD, which was the regulatory arm of the industry ministry, either individually or through their industry associations. But because of the personality and standing of Sondhi and me, they gradually started looking to the heavy industries department for support and guidance.

The automobile sector threw up several issues while I was in the heavy industries ministry. Little did I know then that I would become part of the industry in a few years.

On one occasion, Fernandes decided that Hindustan Motors, which manufactured the Ambassador car, be nationalized. The automobile sector at that time was not known for quality consciousness, even though automobile firms were making huge profits. I do not know whether his decision was prompted by this larger issue or whether he had something specifically against Hindustan Motors. He wanted industrialist Rahul Bajaj of Bajaj Auto to head the nationalized venture and spoke to him about it. Couto and I pointed out that it would not be possible to nationalize one company and that the government would have to nationalize the entire automobile industry. Bajaj also pointed out the folly of the action and refused to be a party to it. Fortunately, Fernandes heeded our views and dropped the idea.

B.M. Birla, proprietor of Hindustan Motors, had expressed a desire to see me whenever I was in Kolkata. On one visit, I dropped in to see him. That was not generally done. The culture of that time dictated that I should have asked him to drop in to my office, as I was a secretary to the government. But I took this unprecedented step because he was, after all, a very senior industrialist and I was in Kolkata where I had visited the Hindustan Motors factory. When I met him over tea, I mentioned that Hindustan Motors was doing a disservice to the country by not updating its technology and not addressing the needs of the Indian customer. He said that the government has never been supportive of Hindustan Motors and that its policies were to blame for the company not being able to be of greater service to the public. I told him to bring to my notice any specific assistance that he needed in order to ensure that Hindustan Motors functioned more efficiently and was more responsive to public needs. Those were the days when a company could not change the model of a vehicle or manufacture another vehicle or get technological assistance without the government's permission.

When I told Fernandes about this meeting, he was not amused. I tried to explain that if the government kept blocking Hindustan Motors' technological improvement plans which would improve the Ambassador car's fuel efficiency, it would not affect the company or Birla (who would continue to earn profits) but hurt the Indian public and the nation as a whole, since the Ambassador car would continue to guzzle precious fuel. Therefore, allowing Hindustan Motors to upgrade its technology would be in the interest of the consumers and the country. I was not sure if I convinced him, but he did not prevent me from continuing my dialogue with Hindustan Motors. Hindustan Motors was finally permitted to introduce the Contessa car and upgrade the Ambassador.

Soon after my meeting with Birla, Hindustan Motors came forward with a proposal. The company had put up a facility for the manufacture of Bedford trucks in collaboration with General Motors but these had failed in the market. Hindustan Motors now wanted to use this facility to manufacture another truck, using a new design which would be more acceptable to the customers. I saw no problem with the request; after all, a facility had been created and not letting it be put to use was a national waste. I, therefore, supported the proposal when it came to the ministry. Under the erstwhile Monopolies and Restrictive Trade Practices (MRTP) Act, the matter was referred to the Department of Company Affairs, which opposed it on the grounds that it would not be desirable to allow an already large company to expand its business further.

I could not understand this logic—here was a facility that could be put to use in a way that would benefit the national economy, and it was being allowed to go waste only because of a mindset against large companies. The matter went back and forth between the joint secretaries of the heavy industries and company affairs departments, but there was no solution in sight. I then called another meeting at which company affairs secretary P. Krishnamurthy and I were present. Again, there was no meeting point. In the course of the discussions, it emerged that Krishnamurthy's objection stemmed from his feeling that if the proposal went through, both of us would be accused of favouring the Birlas. I got my trump card.

I then said that his apprehension was genuine, and we should analyse who would benefit if Hindustan Motors was refused this permission. It turned out that only Telco (Tata Engineering and Locomotive Co, which is now Tata Motors) would stand to gain, since it was the closest competitor. I pointed out that the same logic could be reversed and both of us could be charged with protecting the interests of the Tatas. Krishnamurthy saw the point, and the Hindustan Motors proposal went through.

A similar issue arose with regard to Bajaj Auto, which was producing 1,00,000 scooters and wanted to increase production to 3,00,000. At that point of time, the scooter was the only personalized transport a young executive could afford. I was keen on increasing the numbers manufactured and thereby improve mobility. There was an eight-year waiting list for Bajaj scooters, which was ridiculous when the company had the means to increase production. I moved the proposal through the ministry. However, the MRTP Commission as well as the departments of company affairs and industrial development raised strong objections. The objection was the same as in the Hindustan Motors case—that it would give rise to a monopoly. I had to argue a great deal with all of them, pointing out that this was a volume-sensitive industry, and that unless production was ramped up, the manufacturers would not be able to introduce new technology or bring down prices. Risking the accusation that I was favouring Bajaj Auto, I finally convinced them to give the necessary permissions to the company to increase production. This was a breakthrough decision not only for Bajaj Auto but also for the automobile industry in India. I dare say that this was a turning point in the history of Bajaj Auto.

The automobile industry threw up a few more absurdities. Any change in the selling price of a passenger car needed the ministry's approval. I felt that this was a luxury segment where government interference was not required. Hence, with the approval of the minister, I had this dismantled. The ministry also had a discretionary scooter allotment quota, using which a certain number of scooters manufactured could be allotted to people decided by the ministry. It was entirely to the credit of the minister that this practice was also discontinued during my tenure.

~

Sondhi and I had on various occasions discussed the need for a strong body to project the problems of industry in general. Though there was an apex chamber of commerce in the Federation of Indian Chambers of Commerce and Industry (FICCI) and some sectoral associations like the Textile Manufacturers' Association, the Association of Indian Automobile Manufactures and Automobile Components Manufacturers Association, there was none which was projecting the problems of the entire engineering industry effectively. In the case of a majority of the capital goods industry, a relatively new organization, the Association of Indian Engineering Industry (AIEI), was operating out of Kolkata and was able to establish frequent consultations with the ministry, thanks to its enterprising director, Tarun Das. Between Sondhi in the steel ministry and I in the heavy industry department, we actively encouraged Das and brought AIEI to the centre stage, making it more or less the representative of the engineering industry. AIEI later moved from a sectoral association to an apex chamber and became the Confederation of Indian Industry, covering both the public and private sectors.

My tenure as secretary enabled me to do my bit for the technological modernization of Indian industry. Given my experience in BHEL, I knew that organizations needed to upgrade their technology to stay ahead in the race. This is the reason why BHEL became a success, and HEC, which was created at the same cabinet meeting as BHEL, fell by the wayside. The department under me played a proactive role in pushing industry to take the necessary steps to modernize and be competitive.

Often industries, especially the textile and machine tool industries, in those days recognized the need for technological improvement but could not pursue this for lack of funds. I mooted the idea of a Technological Development Fund and got money sanctioned for it. The fund provided financial assistance at moderate rates of interest, and this did help a large number of small and medium industrial units to upgrade their technology.

The policy environment prevailing at that time helped a large number of small and medium entrepreneurs attempting to produce components achieve varying degrees of success. We had some outstanding success stories of high technology components produced within the country. For example, almost all the components of textile manufacturing machinery were manufactured by over forty discrete manufacturers, each doing one component. However, none of them had developed the capability to put a system together. In other words, they would manufacture all the components required to set up a spinning wheel but would not be able to design and offer a spinning wheel as a whole to the customer. This is called 'systems capability', and I always laid great stress on the need to develop this capability.

Similarly, in the automobile industry, there were outstanding manufacturers of individual components, but few could offer to put up a manufacturing plant. Though it was not really part of my brief, I tried my best to get these industries to develop systems capability, pointing out to them that the future lay in turnkey solutions; and if they did not address this, they would lose their competitive edge. Only one company, Lakshmi Machine Works from Coimbatore, heeded my words and is one of the few surviving textile machinery manufacturing companies. The rest did not take my recommendations seriously. It needed sustained long-term efforts, and I did not stay long enough.

As secretary, heavy industries, I was also involved in the country's foreign economic relations programme. This was also the period when the government started placing emphasis on economic and industrial cooperation in the foreign policy agenda. The external affairs ministry was the nodal agency for this, with other ministries being responsible for some activities or a group of countries. The department of heavy industries dealt with programmes on industry-related cooperation and was also the secretariat when the industry minister was the leader of any inter-governmental cooperation effort. I had got a team from BHEL to survey the hydro potential of Nepal and found that India could harness power from the water resources of that country. Hence, I mooted a collaboration plan in which India would set up a cement plant in Nepal, in return for which that country would allow us to use its water resources for power generation. This would benefit Bihar as well as northern and eastern Uttar Pradesh. The then prime minister of Nepal was very keen on the cement plant near his constituency. However, decision making in India was very slow, and the external affairs ministry did not pick up the thread. We failed to take advantage of this opportunity. We thus not only lost an arrangement that would have benefited Bihar and eastern Uttar Pradesh but also a very good opportunity on water sharing with Nepal.

In a similar effort, I also tried to open up the railway route from Kolkata to Assam through Bangladesh. This would have enabled a less expensive movement of goods and services to the northeastern part of the country from West Bengal, avoiding a circuitous route. I almost convinced the Bangladesh government on the advantage of this arrangement flowing to Bangladesh in the form of employment generation. This proposal, however, did not have the support of the then political leadership in India and hence did not take off.

Much of my efforts relating to international economic cooperation were indirectly aimed at supporting the efforts of the ministry of petroleum in securing additional quantities of crude from Iraq, Saudi Arabia and Libya. The discussions with these countries helped demonstrate to them the technological capabilities of India and our ability to support their industrial economy, and thereby strengthened the industrial ties between India and them.

The high watermark of my stint as secretary, heavy industries, was organizing the Commonwealth industry ministers' conference in India, at Bengaluru, and the awareness it created in the Commonwealth countries of India's potential as a developing industrial nation and a reliable trade partner.

~

Even as I was initiating changes and preparing to follow them through, things changed in the ministry. In the general elections of 1980, the Congress returned to power with Mrs Gandhi as prime minister. Charanjit Chanana, considered close to Sanjay Gandhi, became the industry minister.

Though I had not been troubled in any way during the Emergency when Sanjay Gandhi ruled the roost, he had never been comfortable with me. I do not know if this was because I was close to Pai, whom he did not trust very much. My relationship with Mrs Gandhi was very formal, and she trusted me as a technocrat, but I could sense that Sanjay Gandhi was wary of me, especially because I had shared an excellent working relationship with Fernandes. I did not give this much importance since, as a professional, I was expected to work with whoever my political bosses were. But in what was probably a reflection of Sanjay's mistrust of me, I could sense that Chanana did not like me. We had an extremely rocky relationship, marked by clashes on several matters.

In those days, scarce raw materials and inputs for the engineering industry were distributed by the department of heavy industries under a prescribed formula. One of these inputs was hot rolled coils. The steel ministry would place a certain percentage of the domestic hot rolled coils production at the disposal of the heavy industries department, and we would allot these to various steel tube manufacturers. The formula by which these were allocated to different tube manufacturers had been fixed by my predecessor, Sondhi, and I had left this unchanged.

One of the first things that Chanana did after assuming office was to take an interest in the allotment process. A business house known to him wanted a higher allocation than what the formula entitled it to and had approached the minister. One day, Chanana called me and said that Hari Bhushan, one of my joint secretaries, was not following his orders. When I asked Bhushan what the matter was, he told me that the minister had wanted him to change the formula to give a higher allocation to a particular business house and that he had said he did not have the authority to do so.

I went back to the minister and explained that these principles of allocation were an established practice which I had inherited. If he felt the formula was wrong, I would put up a file, and he could change the policy or formula in whichever way he thought fit; but once a policy/formula had been issued, it had to be adopted uniformly for all. As long as the current policy/formula remained, the joint secretary would not be able to make any changes or use his discretion. He did not expect this kind of a reply from me. I knew from experience that it was not easy to change the policy/formula, and Chanana had sensed it too.

Chanana was also furious with me on another issue. One of the development officers in the ministry had told me that the minister was asking him to collect money from industrialists for advance licences. I mentioned this to K.S. Rajan, under whom the development officer was working, and asked him to put a stop to this. Instead of doing so, Rajan informed the minister.

I also strongly opposed Chanana's decision to abruptly transfer Chandra to the department of official languages and to place his own nominee as joint secretary in the heavy industries department. Convention required that I be kept informed. Chandra was undoubtedly the best and most contributing officer in my department, and I protested his transfer. The surprising part of it was that Chanana tried to convince me, saying that this transfer would actually benefit Chandra. Finding it difficult to quell my protest and meet my objections, he had to reverse his decision and Chandra was retained. Chandra later went on to become cabinet secretary.

These were just a few instances where I differed with Chanana, and it became evident that I did not get along with him. These instances must have induced him to complain to Mrs Gandhi that his secretaries were not cooperating with him.

One day, Marathe, secretary in the industrial development department, and I were summoned to meet Mrs Gandhi at Parliament House. She hauled us over the coals and said that, as secretaries, we were expected to cooperate with our minister and that the minister had complained we were not doing so. I asked her if there was any specific instance the minister had complained about, and she mentioned the allocation of hot rolled coils. I explained the details to her and told her that the minister was free to change the policy/formula entirely but he should not ask the joint secretary to use his discretion to favour certain people when the policy did not allow it. She was not amused but did not say anything and dismissed us. As we were leaving the room, I stayed back and told her that every minister was entitled to have a secretary of his choice and that I did not have any objection to moving out of the ministry if the minister so desired. I do not know what prompted me to say it but I did. She seemed to have conveyed this to Chanana.

Chanana was quick to act and I was relieved immediately. I was not from the IAS but was on a five-year contract with the Government of India, so in effect I was without a job. I took my three months' salary and came home.

I was in the ministry for only three years, and this was too short a period to have a dramatic impact. If I had a longer stint, or the public sector review exercise had continued even after I left the ministry, the story of the Indian public sector would perhaps have been different. I had taken up this assignment with the hope of continuing the good work done by Pai and Sondhi in terms of better management of industry in both the public and private sectors. Unfortunately, the government comprised a heterogeneous group of people who concentrated more on political issues arising out of the Emergency rather than on the development of the nation.

K.C. Khanna, who was then chairman of SAIL, was chosen to succeed me as secretary, heavy industries, to avoid the criticism that a technocrat was unceremoniously ousted from the post. But, interestingly, Khanna refused to accept the post and later confided in me that he would not have been comfortable joining the ministry given the circumstances under which I left. For quite some time after that, K.S. Rajan held additional charge of the office until Abid Hussain joined.

I had no idea what lay ahead of me. Little did I know another challenge was waiting just around the corner.

# 5

# STEERING MARUTI

Some time after I was relieved of my job as secretary, heavy industries, I went to meet Mrs Gandhi. I asked her if she had any objection to my taking up any other assignment. In fact, I was hoping to find a place in the World Bank following its former president Robert McNamara's earlier invitation. I was also curious to find out why I was removed so unceremoniously from the ministry. My services had been terminated—I had not been shifted to another ministry or a public sector undertaking.

She was surprised at the turn of events and said that she had assumed I would be shifted to another ministry. She was under the impression that I was from the IAS and could be transferred. She had not known that I was on contract from the Central Engineering Services. Chanana, of course, had known this, and when she had told him he could get a new secretary, he had moved quickly to terminate my services.

I later learnt from Rajiv Gandhi that around the same time when I approached Mrs Gandhi, he had told her that she had made a mistake by letting me go. He had learnt about what had happened from the chairman of ENI, an Italian multinational company that was setting up fertilizer plants and gas pipelines in India. The chairman used to meet me frequently when I was secretary, heavy industries. Soon after I left the ministry, he had met Rajiv Gandhi, who had told him that his mother had many good ideas but lacked good people who could implement them. The chairman had then told him that India had good people like Krishnamurthy but they were treated shabbily. Rajiv Gandhi had then taken the matter up with his mother.

Mrs Gandhi told me that she would try and find a place for me in the Planning Commission. Later, she suggested that I become member, energy, in the Planning Commission. Even as the paperwork for my appointment was being processed, N.D. Tiwari, who was the deputy chairman of the Planning Commission, suggested that I start attending meetings informally and also preparing for a meeting of state level power ministers. As I was doing that, I got a call from L.K. Jha, who was the principal adviser to the prime minister, asking me to go along with him to meet her. I went and was in for a surprise. Mrs Gandhi asked me if I would take charge of Maruti Udyog Limited, the public sector car manufacturing company formed following the nationalization of Maruti Motors that her younger son, Sanjay, had started in the early 1970s. The company had gone into liquidation in 1978 and nationalized in June 1980 after his death. Mrs Gandhi was keen to ensure that her son's dream of making a people's car was fulfilled.

My instinctive reaction was to decline. Taking up the offer would have meant that I would once again have to interact closely with Chanana, since Maruti came under the administrative control of the heavy industries department. Besides, heading a public sector undertaking after having been secretary of a ministry would have amounted to being put in a lower position. But I could not cite these as reasons. So I thanked her for thinking of me for the assignment but said that the papers for my appointment as member, Planning Commission, were being processed and I would like to opt for a less demanding job there. She said, 'I can get any number of advisers for the Planning Commission, but I can't get a good manager. L.K. tells me you are among the few people who can make Maruti a success.' It was important for her to make Maruti a success, she said, because the party was being ridiculed and her family was under attack. Allegations were flying thick and fast at that time that the nationalization was a cover for the Gandhi family and for some of the original shareholders to get their money out of the company. She told me to get the project started, stay with it for two years, after which we could discuss what I wanted to do.

I was still not comfortable with the idea, and she sensed it. She asked if there was some other problem. I then had to tell her that this would involve my going back to the same place that I had left on such an unhappy note and, given my equation with Chanana, I was not sure if I would succeed in my task. She said she would address this problem separately and that it should not be the reason for my refusal. At that stage, Jha took me aside and said she was very keen on this and that I should not make a fuss. I, too, realized that it would be churlish to refuse because of my ego when the prime minister herself was giving the assignment so much importance and saying she was under attack. I, therefore, agreed. I asked her what the time frame to launch the first car was, and she asked if it could be done in eighteen months. I said it would be difficult but that I would make an honest effort.

I couldn't but wonder at the quirks of fate. When I was general manager in Trichy, the then industry secretary, B.D. Pande, had asked me if I would head a public sector small car project that the government had decided on in November 1970, much before Sanjay Gandhi came into the picture. It later dropped the idea after holding discussions with foreign automobile majors, as it was found to require huge investments which the government could not afford, especially for a non-priority item like cars. It was then that private players were given licences to manufacture small cars, and Sanjay Gandhi's company was one of them. I had then turned down Pande's offer, since I was enjoying my stint at BHEL Trichy. Ten years later, under completely different circumstances, I was going to be doing exactly what I was not inclined to do then.

My appointment was put on the fast track. Mrs Gandhi asked C.R. Krishnaswamy Raosaheb, the cabinet secretary, to speed up my appointment. I did not understand why she did this but later came to know that she wanted it formalized before P.C. Alexander joined as principal secretary to the prime minister. Alexander and I had a private misunderstanding when I was secretary, heavy industries, and it was well known that we did not get along. In fact, later, too, Mrs Gandhi told Tiwari, when he became industry minister, to send all files relating to me or Maruti directly to her and not to route them through her secretariat.

My family and friends were convinced that I should not have taken up this assignment. The project was seen as being born in sin, and so negative was the image of Maruti at that time that my wife stopped socializing, except when it was absolutely unavoidable, because she was hesitant to face remarks about my wisdom, or lack thereof, in accepting the assignment.

A few days after our first meeting, I met Mrs Gandhi to discuss my new assignment, and she asked me if we could make this project a good example of public private partnership and whether I could develop it along with S. Moolgaokar, chairman of the Tata Engineering and Locomotive Company, or Telco, as Tata Motors was then known. It unsettled me a bit. I had met Moolgaokar a few times when I was secretary, heavy industries, and knew that he was an undisputed authority on the automobile sector. But I had presumed that I was to be in charge of the project. I told her I had a lot of respect for Moolgaokar and would be prepared to work with him but that it should be consistent with my own dignity. She said Moolgaokar would be the non-executive chairman and I the executive vice-chairman. It could, she said, be an excellent example of two leaders from the private and public sectors working together on a national project. I had no objection to this kind of an arrangement, particularly considering my inexperience in creating and running an automobile manufacturing company. I also believed that my managerial capabilities combined with Moolgaokar's deep knowledge and experience in the automobile industry could make Maruti a success.

The decision to bring Moolgaokar on board was perhaps to impart some respectability to the project, which was getting a bad name. Chanana had made some questionable appointments to the company; French automobile firm Renault had been identified by him as a technology partner. Renault had opened a liaison office in Delhi. Though Renault had been identified after the ministry had gone through a particular process, there were still all kinds of rumours about this arrangement.

Between the time of my first meeting with Mrs Gandhi and my joining Maruti Udyog as vice-chairman and managing director, I tried to learn more about the automobile industry and the ground realities associated with it in general and the Maruti project in particular. I read up anything on the industry and cars that I could lay my hands on and passed no opportunity that would help me understand the sector. I met Mrs Gandhi immediately after taking over on 22 April 1981. Though she had initially dismissed my apprehensions about reporting to Chanana, I was not sure what she had in mind when she had assured me operational freedom. Political interference in public sector companies was quite common, and I had realized that there would be much more of it in Maruti, given its history. I raised the issue again at this meeting, and once again she assured me that she would take care of it.

I then suggested that she should nominate to the board of Maruti such persons in whom she had absolute confidence and whose capabilities and decision making she trusted. This was to ensure that decisions taken by the Maruti board would not be subject to second guessing by the different government departments, leading to delay in project execution. This was also to ensure that certain critical decisions of the board which might invoke criticism or require a change in government policy had her support through her nominee. Some months later, she nominated Arun Nehru, a close relative who had become a member of parliament (MP), to the board. It turned out to be a boon for Maruti. With his corporate background, Nehru enriched boardroom discussions vastly. Mrs Gandhi also agreed to my suggestion to appoint secretaries of the heavy industries and finance departments to the board. In the appointment of Nehru and the secretaries to the board, she deviated from the conventional practice of not nominating MPs or secretaries to the government to public sector boards. These actions instantly gave a status to the Maruti board and sent out a message in government circles about the seriousness of the project.

Mrs Gandhi also kept her promise of insulating me from Chanana by having Rajiv Gandhi informally oversee the project. I met Rajiv Gandhi around a week after I had agreed to Mrs Gandhi's proposal and we had discussed the project extensively. While for Mrs Gandhi the project was about fulfilling her dead son's dream, for Rajiv Gandhi it was only about setting up a good automobile company that would serve as a catalyst for modernizing the Indian automobile sector and changing its image. We discussed the technological trends in the sector and developments in the Western markets. He suggested that I work towards developing a concept car.

I had met Rajiv Gandhi for the first time when I was secretary, heavy industries, and he was still a pilot in Indian Airlines, staying well away from politics. I had gone to Kashmir on the invitation of then chief minister, the late Sheikh Abdullah, who wanted to discuss prospects for industrial development in the state. Rajiv Gandhi also happened to be there on assignment, and we met at a dinner to which we were both invited. We talked about the public sector, and Rajiv Gandhi, being a public sector employee himself, was disturbed by the way it was being managed and had suggestions about how it could be made more efficient. I had met him on a couple of occasions after that, but it was only after I took up the Maruti assignment that I had extensive interactions with him. This was to be the beginning of a long and intellectually nourishing relationship, in which we would often discuss a range of issues from technology to management to governance. I never came away from a conversation with him without learning something new. At our first meeting on Maruti, he, too, repeated Mrs Gandhi's assurance that I should not bother about the minister. Indeed, I never had to meet Chanana even once during the time he stayed on as industry minister.

It was because of Rajiv Gandhi and Arun Nehru that I went about my task with complete confidence. Both of them understood what I was trying to do and backed me completely. They never interfered in my work but were always there for me when I hit a wall and needed them to weigh in on Maruti's behalf. It was not often that I went to them for advice, but I kept them periodically informed of my actions, and their immense trust in my capabilities helped.

~

As I got started on my assignment, there was a feeling of déjà vu. Once again, I found myself taking over as head of an organization with a credibility crisis. In the case of BHEL, people doubted the capacity of Indian managers to manage large organizations. Here, they doubted the capacity of an Indian firm—and a public sector one at that—to produce a quality car and that too in the volumes that the project was targeted to achieve.

The government had set ambitious targets for the project—that it should set up a capacity to manufacture 1,00,000 passenger cars and 40,000 light commercial vehicles a year. Nobody believed this was possible, since Premier Automobiles and Hindustan Motors together were selling less than 40,000 cars a year. In fact, that was one reason for the Maruti project being ridiculed and seen as a cover for the Gandhi family and some of the original shareholders to siphon out money. At the most, people felt, Maruti would produce a few thousand cars similar in quality to the Ambassador or the Fiat and then close down, or that it would import a few thousand cars and sell them.

When we later produced a quality car, people were sure that Hindustan Motors and Premier Automobiles would close down, since the market was not large enough to accommodate so many cars. I constantly pointed out that Indians wanted value for money and had the means to buy cars. It was just that no one had been able to give them a car that was affordable, convenient and fuel-efficient and tap into the latent demand. Hindustan Motors and Premier Automobiles, I pointed out, were run by shrewd business families and were not likely to shut down only because Maruti was producing a few thousand cars more.

I was faced with a humongous task—building up a new company in a sector that was meant to serve as a catalyst to improve the Indian automobile industry. At least I knew the industry in the case of BHEL and had also been with the company from the start. At Maruti, I had to do everything from scratch—from creating infrastructure to identifying and training people, putting in place new practices, systems and standards of operations and creating a customer-oriented organization, to manufacturing a world-class car at affordable prices. Even as I went about building all this, I tried to understand the larger ecosystem in which Maruti would have to function, meeting automobile dealers and auto component manufacturers.

My first priority was to select my team. This was the only organization where I created my own team. Whether it was earlier as general manager at BHEL Trichy and then chairman and managing director of BHEL, or later as chairman and managing director of Steel Authority of India Ltd (SAIL), I had always inherited a team. Though I never made significant changes and believed in taking people along with me, getting the chance to build my own team was a major advantage.

At Maruti, I deliberately did not choose people from the automobile industry, though that may have helped me with domain knowledge. There were two reasons for this. One, I strongly believe that the top management of any large organization should be a composite one, with expertise in different areas—technology, finance, administration and the like. Just because Maruti was an automobile company, there was little point in having only automobile engineers in top positions. In BHEL, too, I had brought people in from different backgrounds. Two, I could only have drawn on people from Hindustan Motors and Premier Automobiles, and I was worried that they would bring along with them the work culture of those organizations and that would certainly not have helped the objective of Maruti—which was to change the face of the industry. I did think of tapping Telco, which had a more professional ethos. Moolgaokar had recommended someone from Telco's truck division, but that person backed out when it was decided that Maruti's priority would be a small car. I, therefore, took most of the top management from either BHEL or the railways.

I invited D.S. Gupta from BHEL to join Maruti. He had been one of those youngsters we had managed to woo from the IIMs and was among the high fliers I had identified and encouraged there. He had been trained in planning at BHEL and also had an engineering background, talents that I needed in this project. Gupta dealt with all aspects of planning and designing this project and excelled in it.

I felt that a large project like this which involved a lot of government procedures required someone who knew the government machinery well and had an extensive network within the bureaucracy. R.C. Bhargava, an IAS officer whom I had earlier brought in as director, marketing, in BHEL, had just finished a two-year deputation there and was available. I felt that he fitted the bill and could take this liaisoning burden off me, leaving me free for long-term planning. More importantly, he had a flair for marketing, something that would be crucial in the automobile industry. Hence I proposed his name for the post of whole-time director. But I encountered resistance from Chanana, who had already got his person appointed for marketing and did not want him replaced. This was one area where I could not bypass the minister, since not only was Bhargava an IAS officer but the position of a whole-time director also required the ministry's approval. The ministry took its own time to sanction this post, so Bhargava joined as officer on special duty in the meantime and started working on his responsibilities. When it eventually did sanction the post, it raised questions about his suitability to hold it. However, with Nehru's backing, I was able to get Bhargava's appointment cleared by the Cabinet Committee for Appointments. Gupta and Bhargava became the two key officials who assisted me throughout my tenure in Maruti.

Another equally important appointment was that of R.D. Deshpande, who was chief design engineer at Faridabad-based engineering firm K.G. Khosla Compressors and was brought on board as the first head of the engineering division. His contribution to the project on the technology front was immense. I could have somehow muddled through on marketing or planning or human resource development even if I had not got the right persons (which, fortunately, I did). But I was clueless on technology and could not have done a lot of what we did at Maruti without Deshpande. Other key appointments were V.K. Mathur, an Indian Railways engineer who had worked with me in the heavy industries department, to look after project engineering and supply chain management, R.S.S.L.N. Bhaskarudu from BHEL to look after production and production engineering, and S. Natarajan from the Indian Audit and Accounts Service to look after finance.

~

Our first task was to look for a collaborator for the car project. Though our mandate was to manufacture a people's car, there was no specific instruction on the size of the car. The heavy industries ministry had sent out requests for offers to several global automobile firms and had selected Renault from among the three firms that had sent detailed proposals. Renault had offered the R-18, a family sedan, as a car Maruti Udyog could manufacture. Going ahead with the choice of Renault already identified by Chanana might have saved us time. But we felt there was need to study more options before proceeding further with Renault.

As we got down to work, I realized that I was being subject

to different demands and pressures. On the one hand, there was the government mandate that Maruti Udyog should manufacture a people's car. On the other hand, there was a lot of lobbying to prevent us from doing so, with influential people dropping hints to me and my team that the Renault R-18 was the chosen car and Maruti should pursue the collaboration with Renault. On the third front was my chairman, Moolgaokar, who strongly felt that the company should produce a light commercial vehicle and not a small car. But I was in a position to ignore these.

Soon after I had been appointed and had heard whispers about the Renault deal, I had asked both Mrs Gandhi and Rajiv Gandhi as to whether I was bound by any decision that had already been taken with regard to a collaborator. Both of them assured me that I was not and could apply my mind afresh. At one of my interactions with Rajiv Gandhi, he had said, 'I will send a couple of my friends to you; they will tell you that something has already been decided on, but listen with one ear and throw it out of the other.' One of them was an earlier associate of Sanjay Gandhi, an investor in the erstwhile Maruti Motors, who told me precisely what Rajiv Gandhi said he would! Armed with the knowledge that I was not bound to go with Renault, I could ignore pressures in this regard, and we went ahead with pursuing other collaboration opportunities.

The Maruti team approached potential collaborators again and, on receiving their replies, re-evaluated the Renault proposal. That exercise convinced us that the collaboration with Renault would not be in the interest of either Maruti or of the country, essentially because the car that Renault was offering was a family sedan and we were not sure whether it was the right choice for the Indian market at that time. Besides this, we felt that the commercial terms offered by Renault were also very unattractive. One of the conditions for foreign collaboration that the government had set was that the collaborator should buy back 50 per cent of the production of the plant. This was done to offset a part of the foreign exchange outflow that any foreign collaboration would entail. Going by the Renault proposal, Maruti would have paid more for the completely knocked down (CKD) kits that would have to be imported than it would get for the complete vehicles it would export to Renault under the buyback clause. Thus Maruti would lose on every sale.

While this established the unsuitability of the Renault car, we were not certain what should take its place. At that point, Bhargava suggested that we should get a sense of what the Indian consumers wanted through a market survey. I thought it was a good idea and immediately gave the green signal. Many wondered whether this survey was first of all required and, if required, would serve any purpose. The ministry, too, opposed the survey, saying that large Indian families needed big cars. But we went ahead and commissioned the Indian Market Research Bureau (IMRB) to conduct the survey. This was a path-breaking exercise by a public sector company at a time when such surveys were rare even in the private sector, except in the case of fast moving consumer goods. The findings of the survey were revealing. It showed that 90 per cent of car usage in India was with four or less people, within city limits, and that the consumers were keen on fuel efficiency, reliability and low initial cost. This broke the earlier myth (on the basis of which the R-18 was chosen) that the market wanted a family car similar to or larger than the Ambassador car with adequate luggage room. Thus the survey sealed the fate of Renault and gave us the courage to change the earlier decision. We now had to find another collaborator.

What also helped me move away from the earlier preference for Renault was that Chanana (who was in favour of the Renault collaboration) was replaced by N.D. Tiwari as industry minister and K.S. Rajan was replaced by D.V. Kapur as secretary, heavy industries. Kapur had worked with me at BHEL and later became the first chairman and managing director of the National Thermal Power Corporation (NTPC). With these changes, we at Maruti were free to pursue other collaboration possibilities with an open mind, and working with the ministry became much easier.

Bhargava and Gupta did a lot of research on small cars and realized that Europe and Japan merited serious attention. Based on a literature survey, we contacted almost all manufacturers of small cars in Europe. We then went to Europe for the Frankfurt Motor Show and then visited Volkswagen and Daimler-Benz of Germany, Renault and Peugeot in France, Fiat in Italy and British Leyland in the United Kingdom. I was greatly impressed by the pioneering efforts of Italy in introducing the concept of a small car, the size and variety of operations of Volkswagen, the efficiency of a government organization like Renault, and the levels of automation which I saw in the Long Bridge plant of British Leyland. In Italy, I made it a point to visit automotive design firm I.D.E.A. in Turin (where the Fiat headquarters was also located). Rajiv Gandhi had been very keen that we design a concept car and had mentioned I.D.E.A. to me during one of our interactions. We had extensive discussions with the I.D.E.A. team and were able to evolve a concept car but did not pursue it as we were told that the tooling itself would take close to four years. As we had only eighteen months to get a car out on the roads, we decided to go for a model that was already in existence.

All the European manufacturers we met showed lukewarm interest and were uniformly sceptical about the viability of a car project in India. They had very little knowledge of the Indian market and some were wary of working with a government department. We looked at the Fiat model 125 developed by them for Poland, Golf model of Volkswagen, R5 of Renault, and the Mini Metro of British Leyland. None of them came close to our expectations, and almost all of them would have been expensive to manufacture in India. Hence, we did not list any of them for consideration.

Besides, the European manufacturers were also not comfortable with the buyback requirement that the government insisted on. Fundamentally, I was also opposed to the clause, as I believed that it placed the Indian operations on a weak wicket. Taking advantage of the export compulsion, foreign collaborators tended to misuse this clause and buy the product at a price much lower than the market price. I favoured foreign equity participation and building an industry that is competitive rather than insisting on the buyback clause. I believed that equity participation by a collaborator enhanced its commitment to the project and would serve the project better than a buyback clause. The ministry guidelines at that time did not permit foreign equity participation in the automobile sector. I was, however, able to convince the prime minister and the government to withdraw the buyback clause and allow foreign equity participation in the automobile sector on a case-to-case basis. In the case of Maruti, the terms of reference were changed to allow foreign equity participation of 40 per cent.

After exhausting all our options in Europe, we decided to pursue other alternatives in Japan. The Japanese car industry, which had a sizeable production of small cars, was creating inroads into the European market. The Japanese government was also encouraging the concept of small, fuel-efficient cars. Bhargava, Gupta, Kapur and I visited Japan, and the range of small cars that we saw there convinced us that we should pursue collaborations with Japanese companies more seriously. We met representatives from all the leading car manufacturers—Daihatsu Motors, Toyota Motors, Nissan Motors, Mitsubishi

Motor Company, Honda Motors and Suzuki Motor Company. It is very difficult to get doors to open in Japan unless you go with an introduction. My earlier associations with Sumitomo Corporation, a leading trading house, and Hitachi Ltd, during my days in BHEL and the ministry, helped. The then president of Sumitomo Corporation introduced us to many people and had deputed a senior general manager to help us in making contacts with these manufacturers. Another person who helped enormously was N.K. Singh, who was then the economic minister in the Indian embassy in Tokyo.

We got a mixed response in Japan and returned with only three offers in hand—the Minica from Mitsubishi, the Sunny from Nissan and the Cuore and Charade from Daihatsu. Some European firms also continued their discussions with us—Peugeot, Fiat and British Leyland.

As we were evaluating these possibilities, I met Moolgaokar to update him on our progress. From the outset, he had been strongly in favour of Maruti producing a light commercial vehicle. He believed that a small car was not a priority for India, that private transportation had no place in the country, and therefore public transport was more important. He would tell me every time we met that I should convince the government to drop the idea of a small car. We spent a lot of time in Pune, where Telco was headquartered, looking at various kinds of public transportation vehicles. In the few months that I interacted with him, I learnt more about light commercial vehicles than I did about cars! When we went to Europe in September 1981, he was focused more on commercial vehicles. Even after I briefed him on the outcome of the Japan visit, he was still not convinced about the logic of going in for the manufacture of a small car.

It was already late 1981, and we were running out of time. I had some firm offers and could not let opposition from

Moolgaokar jeopardize the project. I, therefore, informed Rajiv Gandhi and Nehru about his strong views on the small car project. Rajiv Gandhi and I, after a lot of discussion on the subject, decided that we would inform Moolgaokar about the government's firm resolve to go ahead with the small car. Rajiv Gandhi then wanted me to explain to Mrs Gandhi the strong views held by Moolgaokar and our decision to go ahead with a small car, which I did. She agreed with our views and left it to me to explain the government's decision to Moolgaokar. I then met him and told him that while the government respected his views and experience, it was determined to go ahead with the small car project and that commercial vehicles would come later. At that stage, Moolgaokar said that he would like to withdraw from the project. In December 1981, he resigned as chairman.

It was not as if Moolgaokar did not have a point when he said that public interest demanded greater attention to mass transportation, but he failed to appreciate the government's oft-repeated commitment to develop a small car at affordable prices to supplement public transportation. Nor was he alone in holding this view of private transport. Sukhamoy Chakravarty, the eminent economist who was economic adviser to the prime minister at that time, and a band of economists were constantly harping on the wastefulness of the Maruti project, saying precious foreign exchange was being squandered on something that was not a national priority. I, on the other hand, argued that in a modern society, personalized transport has an important role to play in economic development.

I was saddened by Moolgaokar's resignation. What could have been a very early experiment of public private partnership ended abruptly. In order to avoid adverse publicity about the failure of this experiment, the government left the post of chairman vacant for some time. To be fair to Moolgaokar, he recognized my role in liaising with the government and political establishment and never tried to take up matters directly with Mrs Gandhi or Rajiv Gandhi. He confined himself to an advisory role and never interfered in the day-to-day functioning of Maruti.

~

Negotiations, meanwhile, continued. Of the Japanese firms, the prospects of collaborating with Daihatsu appeared bright, and we came very close to signing a deal. But there was a sudden upset. We chanced upon a telex sent by Daihatsu to Escorts, the Delhi-based commercial vehicles firm. In that, Daihatsu had said it was talking to Maruti only to understand how the Indian automobile industry worked and that it intended to collaborate only with Escorts. Even before our visit to Japan, Daihatsu had written to us about its 500cc and 1000cc cars, and H.P. Nanda, the chairman and managing director of Escorts, had also written to me saying Escorts would represent Daihatsu in India and assist it in negotiations with Maruti. So we thought that Escorts was representing Daihatsu in India. The telex, therefore, came as a complete shock to us. It also contained some derogatory references to working with a public sector undertaking.

Nanda came to know that we had got a copy of the telex and wrote a very apologetic letter to me clarifying the misunderstanding. He said he had made it clear to Daihatsu that Maruti should get the first right of refusal to a collaboration on both a car as well as a light commercial vehicle and that Escorts would step in only if Maruti went in for a different collaboration. Daihatsu's decision not to go with Maruti, he said, was not a good decision. He advised me not to give up on Daihatsu and that he had told the company that it should not withdraw from Maruti in order to partner with Escorts. 'I hope … it is amply clear to you that we have not at any stage encouraged Daihatsu to drop off and withdraw their collaboration with MUL,' he said at the end of the letter. He also enclosed a copy of the letter he wrote to Daihatsu saying Escorts would start detailed discussions with the company only after Maruti finalizes its collaborator. Despite all the clarification by Escorts, we decided not to go with Daihatsu because it would have been very difficult to collaborate with an organization where there was a lack of mutual trust and respect right from the very beginning.

We then decided to resume talks with Mitsubishi, Nissan and a new potential collaborator—Suzuki Motor Corporation (SMC). SMC had not expressed much interest during our first visit to Japan due to a miscommunication between the marketing and engineering departments within the organization. But around the time that the Daihatsu collaboration was being negotiated, a director of SMC on a business trip to India had seen an article in *India Today* about the Maruti project and informed SMC's headquarters. Soon after we got the Daihatsu telex, we got another one from SMC wanting to know if it could still pitch for a collaboration. We immediately said 'yes', and SMC was very prompt in following up the matter with us.

Bhargava, Gupta, Kapur and I returned to Japan in March 1982 for another round of talks with the Japanese car makers. We met Osamu Suzuki, the SMC president, for discussions. He was due to leave for the United States that day but had a meeting with us. As the discussions were incomplete till the time he had to leave to catch his flight, he requested us to wait till he returned. He seemed a very down-to-earth and straightforward person, and we hit it off right from the start.

We also met with the top management of Mitsubishi and Nissan. Mitsubishi was headed by a very high class of technologists, and we were overwhelmed by its size. At our first meeting, the company was represented by forty executives seated across the four of us. Mitsubishi offered us its three-door model, Minica. We then met Nissan, which had offered the Sunny, which was too big for our needs. Nissan had, by that time, acquired Subaru, a highly respected technological organization, and Subaru's small car was also available to us. Though Subaru might have been acceptable to us, Nissan's reluctance to invest in India was a concern.

We met Suzuki after his return from the United States at the SMC headquarters in Hammamatsu. This meeting was more relaxed. Suzuki was accompanied by only three executives. I was very impressed by his quick grasp of issues and his decisiveness. I had engaged in several complicated negotiations while at BHEL, but I had not seen very many chief executives coming to such quick decisions in one or two meetings. SMC offered the four-door SS80 with the 800cc engine, which was the fastest selling small car in Japan at that time.

As we headed back to India, we evaluated the three serious proposals we had in hand—Mitsubishi's Minica, Nissan's Subaru and SMC's SS80. Each had its merits, and choosing between them was tough. We could have struck a deal with Nissan but for its reluctance to invest in India and its doubts about the success of the venture. We also had to drop Mitsubishi, because it did not have a four-door version of the Minica readily available and wanted some time to develop it for us. As a compromise with the concept of the family car prevalent in India and keeping passenger comfort in mind, we had decided to have a four-door version of the small car instead of the more prevalent two- or three-door versions. I was also sceptical about a fledgling organization like Maruti collaborating with a giant corporation like Mitsubishi, as it would have become a collaboration of unequals, with fewer chances of optimum results.

On the other hand, the discussions with SMC were more

purposeful. SMC was not risk averse, and it agreed to invest in India despite the fact that it had not made such large investments outside Japan and its experience in Pakistan, where it had a factory, was not all that good. Besides, it offered us the SS80, the 800cc four-door car which was the largest selling small car in Japan at that time. Along with this, it also offered us the 800cc van, which later came to be called the Omni, and the pick-up truck in the light commercial vehicle segment. Many of the parts for all the three products were common. Also in the SMC stable was a 1000cc four-wheel drive vehicle which we thought would be useful for India, and the company agreed to offer this as well. SMC's completely knocked down (CKD) kits were reasonably priced compared to what we had seen in Europe. It also offered the best training facilities for our personnel.

All this convinced us that SMC would be the best choice for collaboration. I reported this to the board and the government and got the green signal to proceed with further discussions on the agreement. Mrs Gandhi was curious to know why I placed SMC above Mitsubishi, since it was known more as a motorcycle manufacturer in India at that time. I told her that Mitsubishi may be a prestigious partner but its size and the inaccessibility of its top management was a negative point and that I was keen to collaborate with an organization where there could be close interactions at all levels, including the top management. This, I felt, was possible only with SMC, which was comparatively a smaller organization, whose president was easily accessible and would be a more cooperating partner than a formidable Mitsubishi, from my point of view.

~

The tedious process of negotiations on the joint venture agreement now began. Bhargava and Gupta handled these very ably. A certain amount of trust had built up between Suzuki and me as we negotiated the finer points of the collaboration. He was extremely reluctant to take 40 per cent equity in Maruti Udyog, which is what we wanted, and was unwilling to invest beyond 25 per cent. Even that was too much for SMC, which had never invested such a large sum in a foreign venture. Suzuki said he was doing this only because of the commitment of the Indian team. It was then agreed between us that he would increase his stake to 26 per cent, instead of 25 per cent, so that certain critical decisions would have to be taken jointly by us as per the provisions of the Companies Act 1956. It was also agreed that SMC will not rule out 40 per cent participation entirely but would retain the option of increasing its stake at a later date.

I was not being altruistic when I suggested all this. Getting SMC to take a 26 per cent stake was a way of insulating Maruti from political interference. I knew Maruti was more vulnerable than other public sector undertakings since it was identified with the Gandhi family. I would not be there permanently, and even if I was, the political bosses could change. In times of fluctuating political fortunes, Maruti would be a target since it would be seen as a way of hurting Mrs Gandhi. I could not say this then. How could I have said that I was trying to protect the organization from political interference? Mrs Gandhi may not have liked it. Telling Suzuki to retain the option of increasing the stake to 40 per cent was also to ensure that SMC always stayed with Maruti.

I also put a condition in the contract that Maruti could not do certain things unilaterally without the acquiescence of SMC. One of them was that every component produced in India by Maruti vendors must be homologated or approved by SMC. Suzuki thought I did this because I was not confident about Indian vendors being able to supply quality products. Indeed, that is the impression everyone reading the contract would have got. But a lot of what was seen as capitulation to SMC at that time was actually a reflection of my own apprehensions about the way the public sector was managed as well as my desire to protect the long-term interests of Maruti. The company would have built up a particular supplier only to find that it would be forced to shift to another supplier with a change of minister or chief executive. This clause came in handy later when we started developing the vendor base, as it helped allay apprehensions in the minds of the vendors who were hesitant to make the huge investments required. I also believed that this was the best way to ensure that there was no compromise on the quality of components.

All this was against my pride. Earlier in BHEL, I had fought similar conditions that collaborators wanted to impose. However, in Maruti, I myself had to suggest such conditions only because of the nature of the project. What was remarkable was that no one from the government objected to these decisions. Finally, the agreement was concluded with SMC agreeing to offer all the four models we had zeroed in on.

Other approvals and a host of sanctions for investment did not come easy to us. The Planning Commission's Project Appraisal Division (PAD) red-flagged the project, questioning various assumptions and estimates made in the project report. Bhargava and Maruti executives had several meetings with Planning Commission officials to explain things to them but in vain. Bhargava came to me one day saying he was not able to convince them and that they were raising all kinds of objections. Normally, a negative report from the PAD would spell the end of a project. Apprehending this and consequential delays, I mentioned the problem to Rajiv Gandhi. He and Nehru took a verbal assurance from me that the project would not seek any financial assistance from the government other than the initial capital cost and that this would turn out to be a viable project. Once assured about the viability of the project, Nehru helped us in getting the project cleared by the PAD.

It was not an easy assurance to give. I had to create a model automobile factory with the latest technology but with a limited investment of Rs 200 crore. But we silenced all sceptics by completing the project within the specified time and in Rs 180 crore—90 per cent of the estimated cost. To Maruti's credit, from the first year itself, it never showed losses. For over eighteen years, it posted profits, something that has never happened in most other public sector undertakings.

Rolling out a car by December 1983 was not going to be an easy task. Immediately on signing of the agreement, on 2 October 1982, SMC sent its team of people to help design the project, identify the machinery, and finalize the layout and estimate of the plant.

The cost of the project was something Suzuki fretted about as well. I found that SMC was avoiding the introduction of some automated processes that were in use in Japan in order to keep the cost low. These included a multi-spot welding machine in the body shop, automatic painting guns and industrial robots that did some repetitive tasks. When I took up the matter with Suzuki, he said it did not make sense to deploy these technologies in India, since Indian labour was cheap. It would be cheaper, he argued, to use thirteen welders instead of one multi-spot welding machine (which would fix all welds in one shot).

I pointed out that if welding was done manually, the first and last weld would not be of the same quality. Nor did I want to expose my workers to poisonous paint fumes. I said I would not brook any delay in the introduction of new technology in three scenarios—where consistently good quality was important (as in the case of welds), where the work was hazardous (as in manual painting), and where the work was below a worker's dignity. By this I did not mean menial jobs but work that was of a routine, repetitive nature like standing in one place and picking and sorting items. That was something that did not require any application of mind, and I felt this was not consistent with a worker's dignity.

I also had to keep in mind the stated objective of nationalization of Maruti Motors—modernization of the automobile industry. I wanted new technology, even if it was in limited numbers, so that the new generation of engineers and workers could keep up to date with technological developments and learn. As and when our financial position improved, we would scale it up. Suzuki made the cardinal mistake of arguing that the other two car manufacturers were not using these technologies. I was furious and retorted that I did not need SMC if I was to merely replicate the factories of Hindustan Motors and Premier Automobiles. Indeed, for me the real value of any joint venture was the flow of high technology from one partner to the other. The desire to get cutting edge technology had prompted me to move BHEL from its collaborations with the Eastern bloc countries to Western companies. I was hardly likely to give up that approach in the case of Maruti. Finally, I managed to get the multi-spot welding equipment, six industrial robots as well as introduce automation in painting.

A similar argument arose between Suzuki and me with regard to the overhead storage of painted car bodies. I had observed this in Japan and thought that this should be introduced in Maruti as well. This new technology would result in the effective use of space at the factory and facilitate flexibility in operations. Once again Suzuki argued that this would increase the initial cost, but I was firm and got it installed. A conveyer belt was also installed to end the practice of workers moving components by trolleys. Because of limitations of keeping the initial capital cost low, large scale automation was not attempted in Maruti, but we did succeed in introducing the essential elements of automation in the plant.

Whenever Suzuki used to worry about costs because of the introduction of new technology, I would tell him not to be concerned about it and that we would not exceed the project cost of Rs 200 crore under any circumstances. He, however, always doubted this. In the end, the project was completed in Rs 180 crore. We showed SMC that we could beat them at their own game, and that too one that we learnt from them. It was made possible in spite of introducing more expensive new technology, mainly by an efficient Indian team which we had organized by that time and which ensured utmost economy and efficiency in the execution of the project.

Apart from technology, training was another area where I was keen on getting the most from a technology partner. When I was at BHEL, it was Siemens' willingness to transfer know-why and train our engineers that had swung the collaboration deal in its favour. In the case of SMC, too, I was not disappointed. A limited number of managers, executives and supervisors were sent to Japan and put through rigorous training, which was closely monitored by us. This was later extended to the workers as well. In addition, SMC deputed Japanese supervisors to train Maruti workers at the factory in the operation and maintenance of machines as well as shop floor culture. Such on-the-job training by experts ensured that productivity levels were high and 100 per cent capacity utilization achieved in a very short time.

There was also an Indian effort to inculcate the right type of work culture in the employee, in the areas of punctuality, discipline, work ethics, etc. We made sure every employee knew exactly what was expected of him and the dos and don'ts of achieving it. I always believe that once a person knows what is expected of him by the management, half the battle is won. It is in this area of communication that Maruti excelled.

~

One of the unique features of the Maruti project was planning and designing for the production of 1,40,000 vehicles a year at the initial stage itself, when the domestic sales at that time were only 40,000 a year. In fact, Ratan Tata publicly acknowledged later that even if Tata Motors had been assigned this project at that time, he would have planned for an output of only 40,000 cars.

The immediate task was to get the factory up and running. When I had asked Mrs Gandhi whether I was bound by any decision taken earlier about a collaborator, she had said the only thing she was particular about was that the Maruti plant should come up in the original Maruti Motors location at Gurgaon and that the car should bear the name Maruti. Little did Mrs Gandhi know that her emotional request would prove to be an advantage for Maruti. The government had already taken over 300 acres of prime land at the time of nationalization and if this land had not been readily available, the search for and acquisition of a new site would have delayed the project by at least two years. Besides, the site was right next to the Haryana-Delhi border, enabling Maruti to attract the best of talent. It also made liaising with the government easier and helped us give concerted attention to the project. For the collaborator, too, the proximity to Delhi was an attraction.

But there was also a disadvantage in using the old location. The factory building was constructed in such a shoddy manner that even an ounce of concrete on the roof would have seen the whole structure collapsing. The roof itself used to leak like a sieve during the monsoon. There was no time to raze the building and construct a new one. I hired a structural engineer

Explaining a hydroelectric project to Prime Minister Jawaharlal Nehru in 1952

Receiving the Padma Shri from President V.V. Giri in 1973

Receiving the Business Leadership Award from the Madras Management Association in Chennai in 1975

With Prime Minister Indira Gandhi at BHEL's Haridwar plant in 1976

At the sigining of the agreement with Suzuki in New Delhi in 1982

With wife Rajam in 1980

With Indira Gandhi at the Maruti factory in 1983

With Osamu Suzuki, president of the Suzuki Motor Corporation, at the Maruti launch in New Delhi in 1983

Receiving the Padma Bhushan from President Zail Singh in 1986

With Prime Minister Rajiv Gandhi at the Padma Bhushan award function at the Rashtrapati Bhavan in 1986

With Rajiv Gandhi at the first auto expo in New Delhi in 1986

Receiving the Steelman of the Year Award instituted by The Indian and Eastern Engineer in Mumbai in 1989

Receiving the Lifetime Achievement Award from the All India Management Association from President A.P.J. Abdul Kalam in New Delhi in 2005

At the launch of the 'Visionary Leaders for Manufacturing' Programme in New Delhi in 2007

With Prof. Shoji Shiba, an international expert in Total Quality Management and Breakthrough Management, at the 'Visionary Leaders for Manufacturing' Programme in New Delhi in 2007

Receiving the Padma Vibhushan from President A.P.J. Abdul Kalam in 2007

Presenting the 'National Strategy for Manufacturing' to Prime Minister Manmohan Singh at 7 Race Course Road, New Delhi, in 2006

With industry leaders and Commerce and Industry Minister Anand Sharma at a meeting of the National Manufacturing Competitiveness Council

Receiving the Grand Cordon of the Order of the Rising Sun Award from the Emperor of Japan in Tokyo in 2009

With Prime Minister Manmohan Singh, senior ministers and industry leaders at a Trade & Indus Council meeting

Greeting Pranab Mukherjee at the Rashtrapati Bhavan after his election as President in 2012

With Rahul Gandhi at a Rajiv Gandhi Foundation meeting in New Delhi

With Congress president Sonia Gandhi and Prime Minister Manmohan Singh at a meeting of the Rajiv Gandhi Foundation

from the Indian Institute of Technology Delhi as a consultant and got extensive renovation work done, which itself was hampered by the absence of building plans or other details.

Normally, in those days, project managers attended to the different aspects of setting up a plant sequentially. In Maruti, we did not have the luxury of time. There was a compulsion to get the factory in operation within fourteen months of identifying the collaborator. It is here that I resorted to parallel processing. Simultaneous with the construction of the plant, we took care of recruitment, training and placement of people, vendor development, establishment of a marketing and dealership network and road shows to familiarize consumers with the Maruti 800—which was the name we had decided for the car. These road shows helped to demonstrably prove to onlookers the suitability of the car for Indian road conditions and dispelled many of the doubts they had in their minds about the size of the car.

Given my experience in HE(I)L when the three new plants that later came under BHEL were coming up, I was aware of the problems that could occur in public sector projects and set in place processes to ensure that there were no delays and consequent cost escalations.

The capital equipment was installed and commissioned, starting with the assembly and testing sections followed by paint and weld shops and then the decoiling and slitting facilities. This resulted in full utilization of the facilities as and when they were installed and the capacity was increased step by step to ensure that no capital equipment remained unutilized at any point of time.

The above sequence of installation of facilities and the gradual build up of the production capacity to manufacture 1,00,000 cars was meticulously planned and was a unique feature of this project. A project implementation schedule was drawn up, and

I formed a project review committee to take stock of the progress of the project every week. I was strict about punctuality and discipline at these meetings that were held every Tuesday. The committee monitored the project to ensure that no cost overruns happened and that the project execution was on time.

~

Even as we prepared to roll out the car, I was faced with the ticklish issue of pricing.

The only directive we had from the government was that the car would have to be affordable, since it was pitched as a people's car. Apart from this, we also realized that the price would have to be on the lower side—costing much less than the Ambassador and the Premier Padmini—for the car to sell in large numbers, enabling Maruti to attain the large volumes that would make the introduction of new technology viable. We did a literature survey and found that when the Buck Fiat and the Volkswagen Beetle had been introduced in the Western markets, they had been priced at around twelve to fifteen times the entry level salaries of executives. I took the outer limit of fifteen times, and since the average entry level salary then was around Rs 3,000, the board decided on a selling price of around Rs 45,000. The IMRB survey had also indicated a price of Rs 50,000 as what customers would be comfortable with. I publicly committed to this price. It was a bad habit with me—to make a public commitment and then go around finding ways to meet it. I had done the same in BHEL Trichy when I announced a bonus for workers without consulting with the headquarters. But having made a commitment, I make sure that I stick to it.

When I looked at the costing of the car, however, it was well beyond Rs 45,000. A closer analysis showed that taxes were a huge component of this. The import duty on components was 120 per cent! I then laid down some principles for the pricing strategy. One, the cost of operations within the Maruti factory in India should not be more than that in Japan. Two, Maruti would buy components from Indian manufacturers at a price no higher than the landed price of an imported product. This was to discipline the domestic manufacturers to factor in cost and price into their operations.

I then went to see the finance minister, Pranab Mukherjee. I told him that the final price of the car could not be more than Rs 45,000 and explained the two disciplines that Maruti was going to stick to in order to keep the cost down. But the government, I said, also needed to chip in. I sought a reduction of the customs duty to 25 per cent and suggested a fixed excise duty against the prevailing ad valorem one. I argued that Maruti was seeking these measures not to cover up its inefficiencies but to help it bring in new technology which was more fuel-efficient and would result in huge savings on foreign exchange being spent on importing petrol. The fact that Maruti was going to pass on any tax benefit to the consumer in the form of a cheaper car appealed to the finance minister, and he agreed to our proposals. Implementing it, however, was a bit of a challenge.

Since a blanket cut in customs duty for all automobile components would have played havoc with government finances and hit the local component manufacturers, it was decided that the concession would be available only for components of cars that met certain fuel efficiency norms. These norms were worked out with the help of the Pune-based Automotive Research Association of India (ARAI), which would also certify the vehicles. Customs duty on components for such cars was fixed at 40 per cent (25 per cent customs duty and 15 per cent special customs duty) while excise was fixed at Rs 5906.25 per car. The ex-factory price of the car came to Rs 47,500, and the final price came to Rs 52,000 (around $ 3,000 at that time) after adding sales tax, transport costs and dealer's margin. This was the best we could do at that time.

Both C.K. Birla of Hindustan Motors and Vinod Doshi of Premier Automobiles raised a hue and cry about this concession. I met both of them and tried to explain the logic behind the tax concession given to Maruti. However, they wanted similar tax benefits for themselves and that I—the head of their rival—should convince the finance minister accordingly! I went along with them to meet Mukherjee and argued their case. Mukherjee heard me out and then asked them, 'If I give you the same benefit that I gave Maruti, how much will you reduce your price by?' They could not give a convincing reply. They had not expected this question and had expected the tax cut to be an additional benefit to them. They did not, obviously, get the benefit.

The fuel efficiency norms worked out with ARAI once again subjected me to the charge of manipulating the government system to keep rivals out that I faced in BHEL when we worked with the power ministry to standardize the sizes of power equipment. Once again it was an unfair charge. If I wanted the government to move away from its earlier position, I had to bring a fresh line of argument. The only compelling new argument was fuel efficiency. Besides, the difference in mileage between the Maruti 800 and the Ambassador and Premier Padmini was so marked that this charge of manipulation is not valid. The 800 was offering a mileage of 14.5 km against 6 or 7 km that the Ambassador and Premier Padmini gave. If either of the two manufacturers had been prepared to change its technology to meet these norms, it would have got the tax benefit. The two manufacturers did not until much later. In any case, Maruti was not asking for anything that was unheard of. When small cars were introduced in Germany, the government gave various concessions to popularize them. Even in Japan, small cars did get a lower excise duty.

Once we got the tax benefit, we maintained the price for three years till an increase in taxes and duties forced a price hike in 1986-87. Unfortunately, even as we were pleading for a tax benefit on behalf of the consumer and operating with stringent cost controls, the buyer was using the low price as an arbitrage opportunity.

During the early months, when construction was in full swing and the equipments and machineries were ordered and we were working towards delivering the first car in December, doubts were expressed over what the market reaction would be. Many including Suzuki felt that the response would be muted. On the other hand, I strongly believed that the response that the road shows had evoked would certainly yield results. Few cars had been imported from Japan and were exhibited and demonstrated in different parts of the country. These model cars were in the public eye for quite some time, and people had seen their performance in Indian conditions. Besides, I felt that the affordability factor would be the game changer.

Sensing that we would get an overwhelming response, we decided to use this opportunity to mop up finances in the form of deposits at the time of booking to meet the working capital requirements. These booking deposits carried an interest of 7 per cent and were to be adjusted against the price of the car at the time of delivery.

The first car was assembled, and we noticed a few glitches. These were set right, and one principle I followed right from the first car was that whenever an error was rectified, it should never happen again. I frequently visited the shop floor unannounced and at odd timings to review the progress directly with the engineers. This also enabled me to get to know the workers personally and to learn the processes.

Not many people know that the first car produced at the factory was actually donated to Lord Balaji at Tirupati. In the initial stages, when we faced innumerable obstacles, which I thought were beyond human endeavour, in the execution of the project, I realized that divine dispensation was required. Besides organizing multi-religious poojas, I publicly announced that the first car would be offered for the service of the Lord at Tirupati. Realizing that none of us had the authority to donate company property, I requested those of the believers amongst the employees, vendors and dealers to contribute towards the price of the car.

Finally, commercial production did begin in December 1983. Mrs Gandhi inaugurated the factory on 14 December 1983. She was very emotional during the function, and in her address recalled the efforts Sanjay Gandhi had put in towards developing a small car. She handed over the keys of the first Maruti 800 to a Harpal Singh, an Indian Airlines employee, whose name had been thrown up by a computer generated random number allotment system.

The Maruti 800 was a runaway hit. Bookings opened in April 1983 and crossed 1,35,000 within two months. True to my belief, we garnered Rs 135 crore through bookings and invested the amount in public sector companies at 14 per cent interest. This was one major factor—apart from strict cost control—that enabled Maruti to be profitable from the beginning. The demand increased by the day, and there was pressure on us to ramp up the output, which we did in record time and to the extent possible. Such a rapid rate of increase in production was unprecedented in the automobile industry until then.

A serious clash occurred between Suzuki and me over the model of the Maruti 800 itself. Soon after the commercial launch, one of our executives, who was in Japan for training, discovered that SMC had introduced a newer version of the car there. This one had a contemporary look and was more suited to Indian conditions, with extra cabin space and leg space at the back. When I checked, SMC confirmed this but said it was too early to introduce this car in the Indian market. They said they would observe it for two years and bring it to India once all the glitches had been ironed out. They probably planned to sell the tools and dies after they had discarded the model.

I was initially upset with SMC that it had not, throughout our negotiations, mentioned that it would be going in for a newer and better version of the 800. I was not going to accept this and insisted that this new model also be introduced in India right away. Suzuki argued that having spent money on tooling the factory for the old model, we should continue with that. Retooling the factory would admittedly involve considerable additional expenses. Vendors, too, would have to write off their tooling for the components of the old model and invest afresh and would have to be compensated for that. But I had to keep the image and interest of the country in mind. The introduction of a newer model in Japan would become public sooner or later, and when it did, it would only reinforce the belief that India was just a dumping ground for old technology. As it is, people had been sneering that we would only get a discard from Japan and were wondering how serious we were about introducing a car of international quality. The government and Maruti would have lost face. I convinced the board that Maruti should take the hit head on and go in for the newer version and thereby establish a tradition that Maruti would always be contemporary in its products.

I had a rather stormy meeting with Suzuki on this issue. I said quite emphatically that if this was the attitude of SMC, I would have no difficulty in advising the government to call off the collaboration. Suzuki agreed very reluctantly, and the new model was introduced in June 1986. I then insisted that in future, within six months of any new model being introduced in Japan, SMC must transfer the technology to India if the model was found suitable. SMC agreed. The underlying management philosophy behind this decision was that, in a joint venture, there should be no time lag between the introduction of new technology or models between the two partners.

The Maruti van was launched in December 1984 in two models, one with a flat roof and one with a high roof. Initially it was promoted as a commercial vehicle and not a passenger car and did not take off because the design did not go well with the Indian idea of driver safety. It was later renamed as the Omni and pitched as a passenger vehicle, after which demand picked up for the flat roof model. The production of the high roof model was called off as sales did not pick up. As for the pick-up truck, the fourth vehicle that we were to get from the SMC stable, Maruti decided not to manufacture it as we were unsure of the market.

Then came the launch of the four-wheel drive Gypsy in 1985. The Gypsy was an instant hit with the Delhi Police and the army. It was released by Rajiv Gandhi in a specially organized function at the factory. During the course of the function, I suggested to Rajiv Gandhi that he should personally see the latest technological features that had been introduced in the factory for the production of this vehicle. Having encouraged and helped me in the early stages, I thought he would be happy to see this facility, but his security staff would not permit him to visit factories. Defying his security staff, he came with me into the factory and took a good look at the new facility.

In 1986-87, due to extraneous factors like increase in taxes and duties, the prices of Maruti vehicles went up. But the demand for the vehicles continued to grow, and Maruti had become a market leader in the automobile industry in India.

Encouraged by the success, SMC increased its stake in Maruti to the originally agreed 40 per cent.

~

If there is one organization which can claim to have been a catalyst for a different kind of work culture, it is Maruti. It was something that private sector organizations started to emulate. Sushil Poddar of Gillette India once told me that he had drawn heavily from the management practices at Maruti, and this helped him counter the scepticism on the part of Gillette's global management that their India venture could ever be successful.

I used to talk about the Maruti culture at every interaction with the staff. At one staff meeting, one of my executive assistants asked: 'You keep talking about a Maruti culture. What is this Maruti culture?' I could not articulate the answer immediately. He asked if it was a mere imitation of SMC practices. I said 'no'. He asked if it was something that I did in BHEL. I said 'no'. 'So what is it?' he asked.

It took me a week to frame an adequate answer. I knew it was not just what we borrowed from the Japanese nor was it only an adaptation of my management principles. It was a blend of the best of both and also a little bit more. I then issued a circular setting out what this Maruti culture was. It began with the words: 'We may be owned by the government, but we have no intention of running this like a government company.' This could have got me into trouble and was one step further than what I did in BHEL, Trichy, when I quietly got the line 'A Government of India Enterprise' removed from all letterheads! The underlying philosophy of the Maruti culture was that there would be no compromise on discipline, punctuality, productivity, cost and quality consciousness.

I could not, however, have established this Maruti culture

without devising new methods and systems of human resource management as well as industrial relations. Contrary to popular belief, a large part of the people management policies in Maruti was an extension of the policies I had initiated in BHEL. It helped, of course, that Maruti was a new organization, with no history of bad practices that needed to be eliminated. I built upon this advantage by putting in certain filters at the recruitment stage itself to ensure that there was no room for undesirable practices and elements to come in.

I had given thought to principles governing recruitment even as we were searching for collaborators. I had decided to apply the same thumb rules that had governed the selection of my core team—avoid taking people from other automobile manufacturers (though we did recruit a few from Tata Motors, commercial vehicles manufacturer Eicher Motors, and the public sector Scooters India).

From the outset, I ensured that Maruti had a very stringent selection procedure that gave no room for favouritism. The number of people for each job was clearly estimated in consultation with SMC, and the intake was as per the estimate. Nobody had the sanction to exceed the estimate. An engineer had to be a first class engineering graduate, pass a written exam and then clear a personal interview. Only those with a two years' diploma from an Industrial Training Institute (ITI) were considered for the post of operators, and they, too, had to clear a written examination and an interview. We did get requests from politicians to take in someone they recommended, but I made it very clear that there would be no relaxation in these criteria for them. Since most of the people recruited had no previous work experience, they had no set notions about hours of work, overtime and other hang-ups that were so common to the blue collar workers of that time. I converted this to my advantage and introduced a range of good practices relating to discipline and professionalism.

Among the first issues I addressed was absenteeism, which was almost 15 per cent in the case of public sector companies because of various leave entitlements. We wanted to bring this down to 4 per cent. So we rewarded people with high attendance records with an attendance bonus, through public appreciation at the annual Independence Day function, by giving them opportunities for training in Japan as well as by making attendance a criterion in determining promotions. In addition, we departed from the leave policy of public sector undertakings and allowed encashment of unused casual leave and accumulation of sick leave and earned leave for a maximum of 240 days. Workers were encouraged to go on leave during plant closures for preventive maintenance. We also put the onus of ensuring that absenteeism did not affect operations on the supervisors. If a particular work station was not manned because someone had taken leave, the supervisor would have to man it. This ensured that the supervisors took care while sanctioning leaves.

Another matter that I was very concerned about was that of effective working hours. From the outset, we insisted that an eight-hour shift meant that the machine had to operate effectively for that time and not just the time a worker clocked in and clocked out. Time clocks were introduced for perhaps the first time in a public sector company. It took time to develop the habit of punctuality among workers, but eventually it became a way of life at Maruti. We made sure that the senior employees also reached the office on time. Once an employee sees senior managers coming on time, he will automatically be enthused to do so himself. Another practice which was introduced perhaps for the first time in Indian shop floors was the physical exercises workers had to do before commencing shift operations. This was made mandatory, and the philosophy behind it was that it helped workers warm up and be productive right through the shift.

We then set about doing away with the difference between workers and managers. My own approach of treating people with dignity and the Japanese way of management were very similar in this respect. As a result of this confluence of ideas, the philosophy at Maruti was 'everyone is equal'. If a rule applied to a worker, it applied to everybody, including me as well. There was no class distinction at Maruti. The hours of work, number of holidays, medical benefits and comforts at the workplace were the same for all categories of employees.

There were three other areas where my philosophy of treating everybody as equal was reflected. This was seen as a radical departure from the practice prevalent in Indian workspaces.

I had seen that all levels of employees in Japanese companies wore uniforms. This was to drive home the fact that they were all equals. I liked this concept and believed that this would create a sense of belonging and pride in the organization. I, therefore, introduced a uniform at Maruti. Everybody, including me, wore it. The uniform bore the company logo, and the material and design were the same for all. If you were an employee of Maruti, you wore the uniform. I was strict in enforcing this rule. For people who had objections to wearing the uniform outside the factory, a change room was provided on the premises. As Maruti grew in stature, the uniform became a status symbol. People started identifying employees on the roads with the help of the uniform. The uniform achieved what I believed every worker in an organization should feel—a sense of pride about working in that organization.

Next came the issue of the canteen. I issued strict instructions to all the officers in charge of the canteen that there should not be any compromise with the quality of food and that it would be same for all, as would the plates and cutlery. Everyone had to follow the queue system. The seating area, too, was common, and there were no separate enclosures for managers. I once found some senior managers eating food brought from home separately in a room. I ordered the room to be locked and ensured that they ate in the common dining hall. Status-conscious Indians had a tendency to sit with their peers. I directed each general manager to sit at a separate table and converse with supervisors and workers, and I would do the same. The Japanese followed a practice that the person who finished eating last cleaned the table. At the table where I sat, I would invariably be the last to finish since I was busy talking. So I often ended up cleaning the table. There was some embarrassment initially, but I insisted on following the custom. That sent a powerful message across that there is nothing infra dig about doing menial tasks.

In India, there is a tendency to have separate toilets for workers and managers; while the toilets for mangers are invariably clean, those for the workers are generally not maintained that well. At Maruti, the toilets were all made common, and there was strict supervision of cleanliness and hygiene.

If I could enforce higher standards of discipline and productivity among the workers, it was because they saw that the same rules applied to everyone in the organization. In some cases, I even ensured that the workers got a better deal. Promotions, for example, were first announced for the workers and then for the executives.

I also took steps to ensure that the workers felt their views mattered. I realized early on that the people working on machines were best placed to provide solutions to problems that occurred. Workers were encouraged to constantly come up with new ideas to improve quality and productivity. A suggestion scheme was launched under which workers were paid for every suggestion made, irrespective of whether it could be implemented or not. This was to encourage them to participate in the improvement process and keep it a continuous happening in the company. This encouraged workers to think about improvements constantly.

Every action of mine conveyed to the worker that he was very important for the success of the company but I would not compromise with punctuality, discipline, productivity and quality.

Next was the introduction of open offices. The Indian tendency of hierarchy at the workplace would have defeated our objective of creating an environment of 'all are equal'. I believed that an open office enhanced the communication between employees and improved the quality of decision making. I had seen this in Japan, and I implemented it at Maruti. This arrangement enabled faster communication with the superiors and avoided loss of time.

I realized that if there was one thing that could spoil the work culture that I was trying to promote, it would be the militant trade unionism that was endemic in the public sector. I had experienced its debilitating influence in BHEL and was determined to nip it in the bud in Maruti.

But I also realized that if workers did not have a forum to air their grievances, it would provide scope for a union to emerge. Rather than waiting for such a situation to develop and then reacting to it, I decided to be proactive and encourage the formation of a union. We took in K.K. Datta—a member of the INTUC, who had been in BHEL and was now looking for a job—and got him to form a union, the Maruti Udyog Employees Union, which everyone was encouraged to join. To avoid the pitfalls of multiple unions, I told the workers that they could join this union and work their way up to leadership positions but they should not form another union.

I then tried to replicate the consultative mechanism that I had initiated at BHEL. It was far easier to do that here since there was only one union. Union representatives were involved in all decisions and policies relating to workers, from shift timings to the selection of uniforms to the management of the canteen and even transport for employees. At every official function, the president and general secretary of the union sat on the dais and greeted the dignitaries. The union was briefed on important developments in the company in monthly meetings. Before every meeting, a note was distributed, listing the tasks ahead and the problems being faced. These were discussed in detail, and the union felt that it was part of the decision making process in the company. I did not leave the interaction with the leaders of the union to others because I believed that, as CEO, I should be in constant touch with all employees and their leaders.

As a result, we got the full support of the union in our attempts to usher in a more professional work culture. An added bonus was a resolution passed by the union that it would not raise any demand for five years. It kept to its promise, and it was only in 1988 that there was some unrest over housing. By then, I was only non-executive chairman of Maruti, and Bhargava was in the driver's seat. He took a firm stand on the strike, which I still believe was the right thing to do.

Constant communication had been one pillar of my management style, as I genuinely believe that this helps companies avoid a lot of problems they tend to encounter. To this end, I also initiated the setting up of a Sahyog Samiti, which was a kind of inner parliament, comprising representatives of the senior management, managers and supervisors. This met every month and discussed a range of issues related to work and welfare. These representatives then communicated with their individual groups. Through these initiatives, all Maruti employees got a sense that they were involved in the running of the company and were not mere cogs in the wheel. The effectiveness of the human resource management policies in

Maruti can be gauged from the fact that, right from the initial stages, the commitment levels of employees was very high.

Cost consciousness and quality were two other essential elements of the Maruti culture. There was a significant Japanese influence in both of these. SMC was known for keeping a tight leash on costs. The belief that the organization would suffer unless there was a control on costs had seeped into every employee. At BHEL, I did not exactly encourage wastefulness, but the kind of attention that the Japanese gave to the cost structure was an eye-opener for me. It was particularly important to me for two reasons. I had to battle the cynicism in the government that Maruti was sure to be a drain on public resources and had to prove the Planning Commission's PAD report wrong. I also had to keep my promise to the finance minister that if he gave us the tax concessions we wanted, we would do our best to keep costs and the price of the car down. To this end, we had a tight budget for each item of expenditure and worked within this. The productivity of employees was higher than that of employees in similar plants in Europe though we could not match the productivity of the Japanese. I constantly told executives and workers' representatives at every interaction I had with them that there was no room for sloppiness and waste; that we could not expect any subsidy from the government and that we had to earn our keep; that we could not raise the price of the car further. So deep did this sentiment seep that at the end of one meeting in which Bhargava listed out a lot of things he was planning to do, the finance head sent me a note saying all this would increase the price of the car by Rs 24.

The lack of a quality culture in India was something I had always been concerned about, and I had attempted to address this at BHEL through the introduction of the statistical quality control methods at Trichy and then by appointing a general manager, quality. But the Japanese took the obsession with quality to another level altogether. Quality, for them, was not something to be checked after production but was to be built into the production process itself. It was also about being disciplined in following systems. I was very clear that whenever an error occurred, it should not just be rectified but steps had to be taken to ensure that it never occurred again. For the first time, process sheets were introduced at work stations, detailing what each worker should do.

It took us quite a while to get this attitude to permeate through the organization, given the Indian tendency to be casual about systems and procedures. Indeed, managers resisted the quality circle scheme, under which groups of workers involved in a particular activity identify problems and work out solutions. However, with the support of SMC, we were able to introduce it in 1985.

What struck me the most was the belief that ensuring quality does not increase costs; cutting corners, in fact, does. This learning was something I put to good use in my next assignment. Thus the 'Maruti culture' as defined by me was a new work ethos in Indian industry, with productivity, quality and cost as its main pillars.

~

To Maruti goes the credit of ushering in the concept of customer satisfaction in the Indian automobile industry, especially in the case of personal vehicles. In a seller's market that existed till then, where people waited for years to get the cars and two-wheelers that they had booked, there was no customer culture worth the name. Manufacturers never bothered to woo customers or to keep them happy once the car was sold. Maruti, too, could have continued with that attitude since it was operating in the same landscape. But I had ushered in a customer focus even in

BHEL, which operated in a near-monopoly market with inefficient public sector state electricity boards as its clients; I was hardly likely to allow Maruti to deal with its customers, who were individuals wanting value for money, in the same way as its competitors. The market survey that we commissioned was itself a major customer-focused step. Even private sector manufacturers had not bothered to understand what the customer really wanted. I knew that a satisfied and happy consumer would be the key to higher sales and production volumes that the automobile industry needed at that point of time. I summed up my approach to customer relations in my chairman's address in 1987: '...we are not in the business of selling cars. We are selling to our customers a long-term commitment to take care of their needs for transport efficiently and economically.' Fortunately for me, all my colleagues in Maruti thought similarly, and together we changed the way automobile companies and their dealers treated customers.

One prevailing practice that I wanted to put an end to was that of cars being driven to the dealers' end. This meant that they had already gone through some wear and tear when they were finally delivered to the customer, who was not actually getting a brand new car. Maruti had no railway siding either. While discussions were on with the railways for the design of special wagons to transport cars, I had a visitor called K. Rangaswamy, a former employee of General Motors in Detroit, who had returned to India and was looking for something to do. I had no specific assignment for him in Maruti, but I still explored through discussions the ways in which I could use his experience and expertise in assisting Maruti. It was through these discussions that we stumbled upon an idea of developing a trailer to carry five to eight cars by road to various destinations. I gave him the assignment to develop this and provided him with the necessary financial assistance. No such arrangement had been in existence in India for the transport of cars. Rangaswamy designed a trailer to suit Maruti specifications, and it changed forever the way new cars were transported to their destinations. There was no compulsion on us to do this, but I felt it was unfair to let the customers believe that they were getting a new car when in fact it had already done a few thousand kilometres.

I had learnt during my visits to Europe that sales of a particular brand of car are influenced more by the reach of the dealers and the ability to keep the customer satisfied. Dealers are the public face of any car company and we, therefore, went about drafting a sound dealer policy.

The first decision that we had to take was whether Maruti should take care of its sales or whether we should sell through private dealers. I believed that a public sector organization would not be able to implement a service function efficiently since it was bound by various rules and regulations. Besides, the public sector did not possess the kind of service orientation that this would require, and government employees were not known for treating customers with respect. So we decided to go with private dealerships.

At the same time, I was very keen on one outlet of our own in Delhi, to be run as a model dealership and service station and to also provide training for the dealers. There was a vacant area near the Delhi airport on the way to Gurgaon. It was a highly visible spot for people coming into Delhi as well as for those going towards the Maruti factory in Gurgaon. The land belonged to the civil aviation ministry, and I asked Bhargava to get in touch with the ministry to see if the land could be leased to Maruti. The minister initially agreed, and we started getting our plans ready. However, by the time we finalized our plans, the ministry changed its mind, and the idea of a model company-owned outlet could not materialize.

Since we wanted to usher in a new customer culture, we decided to avoid, as far as possible, appointing existing dealers of Hindustan Motors or Premier Automobiles as Maruti dealers. Dealerships were activated in a phased manner, keeping the production of cars in mind, as it was important for dealers to make reasonable profits. Advertisements inviting interested persons were issued. Selected candidates were issued letters of intent and contracts with them signed only after they had created the proper infrastructure as per our specifications. Showroom sizes, methods of display and the lighting to be used were all clearly specified. All models were to be displayed in one showroom, and the staff was trained to explain their features.

We ensured that the catchment area provided to the dealer had a minimum market which would make his operations profitable. I decided that all dealer appointments would be approved by the board to avoid allegations of favouritism. We allowed a little bit of extraneous influence in the case of dealerships. A few businessmen who had invested in the erstwhile Maruti Motors and had suffered losses needed to be compensated in some manner and some of them wanted dealerships. This is the only consideration we gave them. Other than this, the process of dealer selection was extremely fair. This could be gauged from the fact that at least two of the dealers did not expect to be selected.

One of them was from Kerala. I had sought the help of the state's chief secretary to help us sift through applications received for a dealership in Kochi. He selected two and pointed out that one was already representing one of the other car manufacturers. So we eliminated that application and sent a telegram to the other applicant, Popular Automobiles, asking its representative to come and meet us. On the appointed day, a dhoti-clad person came to the Maruti office. He was one of the managers of Popular Automobiles and had come to check if the telegram was genuine. He said the company had applied in all sincerity, but since the proprietor did not know anyone in Delhi whom he could ask to follow up, the company was not sure anything would come of it. When the telegram reached, they wanted to check if it was a hoax! People refused to believe we could act objectively. But we did. One application from Chennai was from a relative of mine. I rejected it precisely for that reason. We selected another company, ABT, much to its surprise, as its proprietors knew that the other applicant was related to me.

Since a customer's first contact with Maruti was going to be with the dealer, I felt that a dealer should know something about the product he intended to sell and also be able to service it efficiently if a problem arose. I realized that the real success of Maruti would depend on the kind of after-sales service it was able to provide and was clear in my mind that Maruti had to earn a reputation for high quality after-sales service from the very beginning. This was possible only if the dealers and their personnel were trained, and in this I relied heavily on SMC to introduce dealers to new workshop practices. These related to not just the latest technology—much of the equipment installed in workshops was completely new to India—but also processes, like getting mechanics to follow a certain sequence while servicing a car. Apart from a chain of dealerships, Maruti also set up authorized service centres. People manning these centres were trained by Maruti.

But getting dealers to adopt a customer-focused mindset was an uphill task, and we had to keep persevering, with regular workshops and training programmes. More importantly, I relied on my time-tested formula of constant communication, which took the form of regular dealer conferences, where the message of customer satisfaction was the running theme. I always explained to the dealers that a satisfied customer would mean more business for them, something they would not get if they cut corners or had a casual attitude. The first dealers' conference was held at Kovalam in Kerala, followed by several more, to address the problems experienced by dealers. Today, most of the practices followed by car dealers are those that Maruti had introduced.

One of the problems Maruti faced was the premium collected by allottees at the time of resale. Bhargava tried various methods—computerized delivery lists, restricting the number of bookings per person, stipulating that re-sales could be made to only blood relatives—but nothing worked. The only solution was to flood the market with cars, but that took some time. This made me weak in two respects. Firstly, it weakened my argument that tax concessions were needed to make the car affordable. Because of this, people in the government wondered if Maruti still required the concessional excise duty. They thought if the market could bear the premium, then a part of it should go to the government. Consequently, the government increased the excise duty on small cars. Secondly, it became difficult for me to compel the organization to keep a constant watch on costs in order to keep the car affordable. The urge within the organization to keep costs down got eroded eventually. I consider this inability to end the problem of black-marketing of bookings as one of the biggest failures of Maruti.

~

The auto component industry in India before the advent of Maruti was struggling due to a lack of technology, low levels of demand, inadequate infrastructural support, and poor quality of inputs. Establishing Maruti's vendor development policy was a big challenge in terms of adhering to the stringent specifications for a new breed of fuel-efficient small cars and also in meeting volumes and quality. I knew that a good vendor base would determine the success of Maruti and that the objective of getting Maruti to act as a catalyst for modernizing the automobile industry could only be achieved by an improvement in the auto component industry. The vendor policy also had to take into account the fact that Maruti had to adhere to the government's phased manufacturing programme (PMP), which covered all foreign technical collaborations and involved a gradual indigenization of the imported components. We had committed to an indigenization of 95 per cent of imported components over five years. This was going to be an extremely challenging task, given the state of the components industry at that time. Besides, indigenization was also essential in order to maintain the price of the car at an affordable level.

The rigid mindset of suppliers about introducing new technology and manufacturing processes and the lax attitude towards quality and timely supplies had to undergo a drastic change if they were to become suppliers of Maruti. Since Maruti was a government company, it was bound by rules governing the selection of vendors. Besides, a lot of auto components were reserved for manufacture by small scale industry, and if they had to be developed for Maruti, they had to be de-reserved because they involved substantial investment in infrastructure.*

It was against this backdrop that we framed the vendor policy of the company. I tackled each one of the issues in a systematic manner.

First, it was decided that components that were critical for the performance and appearance of the car would be manufactured in-house and the rest would be outsourced. This

*The policy of small scale industry (SSI) reservation meant that certain items were reserved for manufacture only by SSI units. These units could not exceed stipulated caps on investment in plant and machinery.

was the policy SMC followed, and I was convinced that this was the right thing to do. Based on this principle, it was decided to manufacture 25 per cent of the components in-house and outsource the balance 75 per cent.

The second step was to forge a new relationship between the vendors and the company—that of equal partners. In this, I drew heavily on my experience in implementing the vendor development policy in BHEL, Trichy, and from what Telco was doing. I treated them with respect and dignity and drilled into them the fact that they had an equal role to play in making Maruti a success. Maruti's success would be their success too. It is an amazing lesson in human management that when a person is given respect and treated with dignity, he will go to any lengths to satisfy you.

We devised a uniform pricing system for all components. The prices were fixed on the basis of the capital investment required, the input costs and labour costs, among other things. It was a fair and transparent policy and permitted a reasonable level of profit to the vendor. This uniform policy prevented the suppliers from being subject to the whims and fancies of the officers of the purchase department. It was also decided that the price would be reviewed every year based on increases in material and labour costs and decreases in cost of production due to process improvements, etc. The price decided was a win-win for both the vendors and Maruti.

The third decision was to have just two instead of multiple vendors for each component. I felt that the quality would suffer when one product was supplied by multiple vendors, and it would lead to the creation of a huge vendor base that would be difficult to manage. In the case of low technology items, we fixed the maximum number of vendors at three. In the case of critical components, a single supplier was permitted where economies of scale did not permit another supplier. The number of suppliers gradually increased as production increased. A second or third supplier was brought in only after the previous supplier had established himself.

On the technology front, it was decided that Maruti would assist suppliers in procuring the right technology from Japanese suppliers for a reasonable price. Maruti would not directly get involved in the process but would informally help them by pointing out the right collaborator and checking out the Japanese companies through SMC. For those who required financial assistance, it was decided to offer them loans and equity participation.

Initially, it was very difficult to get companies interested in becoming Maruti's vendors. Nobody believed that the company would last very long or that it would produce 1,00,000 cars. It took a lot of convincing on our part for people to respond favourably. Maruti did a lot of hand-holding, with its managers helping vendors find collaborators, set up their factories and get loans and sundry government clearances. Maruti also offered to take 25 per cent equity in companies of vendors. This served two purposes. One, it gave them an assurance that Maruti believed that it would reach a production level of 1,00,000 cars and that business would be stable. Two, it also allayed fears that there would be a frequent change of suppliers, as was the case with public sector undertakings in those days.

The selection process itself was a very systematic one. Persons interested in producing components were invited to visit the factory where the components had been displayed. They were then asked to submit expressions of interest. The products were divided on the basis of technology required and the year in which they were required to be indigenized. Proposals were received from existing and new vendors and were evaluated and shortlisted. In those days, public sector companies had to enter into one- or two-year contracts with their suppliers.

Tenders would be floated, and the lowest bidder would get the contract. This caused a lot of uncertainty about business, and that is one reason why component manufacturers were not willing to make large investments and were tempted to cut corners to make a quick buck. The lowest tender approach also meant that very often quality was compromised. We decided to move away from this system to long-term contracts. This not only gave an assurance to vendors but also helped us maintain specified levels of quality. Maruti vendors were vendors for life, unless they chose to exit the business or their performance was consistently below par.

Once shortlisted, the prospective vendors submitted a prototype. This was then tested by the engineering department and SMC. If it passed the test, they were classified as suppliers to Maruti, and price negotiations were held. Once the price was agreed upon, a letter of intent was issued, and the vendor had to submit a larger lot of components for further testing. Here, the components were fitted in a car, which was run on a testing track for a certain number of kilometres decided for each component. This was a unique concept in India and probably one of the reasons that helped Maruti acquire the reputation of being a stickler for quality. SMC engineers were fully involved in all these processes. We never compromised with quality. We had a rigorous procedure involving many tests for the selection of vendors. Nothing could be short-circuited. One became a Maruti vendor if one passed the tests and not by influence. Many people did try to put pressure on my managers to get supply contracts by dropping names or using political clout. None of it worked. Even after the selection, there was no let-up in ensuring that products conformed to quality standards. There was a general feeling at that time that the quality of the car would suffer every time a component was indigenized. I remember an instance when a few ministers wanted early delivery of their cars before too many parts were indigenized. This prompted me to double my efforts on the quality front, and I coined a slogan within the company to convey the message that with every step of indigenization, the quality of car only improved.

A transparent system of vendor rating was introduced. The ratings were based on timely supplies, quality, rejection levels, etc. This helped in assessing the shortcomings of the vendor and also determined the future business that can be given to him. It developed a healthy competition among vendors and benefited all in the long run.

Vendor conferences were held periodically. They helped communicate to the vendors the company's future plans, and this built a sense of confidence among them. Quality was given utmost importance at these conferences, and vendors were encouraged to talk about their quality-related problems. We never missed an opportunity to tell them that adhering to quality would actually result in reduced costs for them. Suppliers were encouraged to supply the right quantity and the right quality.

There was one practice that I replicated from Trichy—that of paying vendors in fifteen days in place of the contracted thirty days. I also put an end to vendors coming inside the Maruti office to take their payments. That reduced the scope for interactions between those clearing payments and the vendors, and for demands for speed money, which was common in many undertakings, and thus avoided the loss of officers' productive time.

The vendors were unable to keep pace with Maruti's rate of growth. Timelines were missed; quality failures still continued. It was at this time we decided to get into joint ventures with suppliers for critical components, high technology components, components where large investments were required and where economies of scale dictated a single source. This enabled us to get involved in suppliers' manufacturing process and considerably eased up Maruti operations. The equity participation by Maruti in these companies ranged between 10 per cent and 50 per cent. Though the management control remained with the vendor, Maruti's equity presence represented stability and ensured quality and timely supplies.

Eventually, all this reaped dividends, and more and more people wanted to become suppliers of Maruti. Even now, almost thirty years after I left Maruti, I am asked about how we built up such a large, loyal and reliable vendor base. The answer is simple: establish credibility, be firm and fair, and treat vendors with respect. There were several other automakers that have set up manufacturing bases in India, riding on the back of the strong vendor base developed by Maruti. But even after twenty-five to thirty years, none of them has been able to match Maruti's level of indigenous integration and technology transfer.

~

A lot of the new practices that I introduced in Maruti would perhaps have not been possible without the extensive use of information technology. I had always believed in complete transparency of functioning in any organization. I realized this would be even more necessary in Maruti, since the appointment of vendors as well as allotment of cars in a market of shortage would involve a lot of exercise of discretion by individuals. I, therefore, wanted to set up systems to keep discretion to the minimum, if not eliminate it entirely. Computerization was the only way this could be done. There was hardly an operational function that we had not computerized—from personnel management to allotment of cars—and the online computer system introduced in Maruti was certainly a first and most comprehensive for any Indian industry.

The most visible aspect of this computerization programme related to the allotment of cars. Given the huge waiting list in those days and the fact that we had taken deposits from customers, we had to ensure that the allotment process was fair and did not leave scope for queue-jumping or favouritism, something that was quite common in the case of the other car manufacturers. The in-house IT department then devised a computerized random number generating programme. There was speculation that this would be rigged, but it was soon obvious to everyone that there was no scope for this. We were very strict in maintaining the sanctity of the entire process.

There was a separate quota system on the basis of which dealers got cars for customers who had booked with them. I anticipated the possibility of deals being struck with managers. So this, too, was computerized. We found that dealers were still trying to strike deals with some managers, but we took care of that by transferring the managers to some other post. The payment system for vendors was also automated, and computerized cheques were issued at the gate as soon as consignments were unloaded so that there was no need to deal with the finance department.

~

Shortly after the first set of cars was released and systems and practices were well established, I reminded Mrs Gandhi of what she had said in our initial meeting—that I should be with Maruti for two years and then discuss my future plans. She told me to wait for some more time. A few months later, she was assassinated. Rajiv Gandhi became the Prime Minister, and given the trying times he found himself in, I could hardly tell him I wanted to leave.

It was not that I was unhappy in Maruti. The company was doing well, and most of the systems I had put in place were working well. I had a sense of fulfilment that I had achieved my tasks and wanted to spend more time with my family. I had also turned sixty in 1985, and the retirement age in those days was fifty-eight.

But before I could approach Rajiv Gandhi to talk about my continuation in Maruti, he surprised me by asking me to become chairman of SAIL. I told him it was time for me to retire and SAIL required a younger person, but he was insistent on my taking up the assignment. He had called when I was in Japan on a visit and asked me to see him on my return. When I did get around to seeing him, I told him point blank: 'If you think my job at Maruti is over, let me go home.' He said, 'Who asked you to leave Maruti? You continue as non-executive chairman there but become executive chairman of SAIL.' I pointed out that this would dilute my responsibility towards SAIL. But he dismissed these concerns. In the end, I could not refuse. He reiterated that he wanted me to oversee Maruti as well. 'There is so much to be done. At this point, I don't want anyone else to come and disturb the progress in Maruti,' he said.

The question of who would become the managing director of Maruti arose. Rajiv Gandhi wanted an air force officer to take over the executive functions from me. I told him it would not be wise to bring an outsider into the organization at that point of time. If he wanted the work I had initiated to continue, Bhargava, I insisted, should be made managing director. Fortunately, he listened to me. I remained non-executive chairman for the next five years, but I kept away from day-to-day management. I confined my role to dealing with broad policy matters, giving full support to Bhargava whenever he needed it. My main objective was to ensure that Maruti did not deviate from the principles laid down in the first five years and that it met the objectives of the government in starting this venture. This is exactly what the prime minister expected me to do. Gupta, who functioned as number two to Bhargava, updated me on a weekly basis, depending on the gravity or urgency of the situation. I also kept in close touch with Suzuki in the context of development of future models. After having successfully developed the 800, Omni and Gypsy, we were very keen to introduce a 1000cc three box car. I was very happy that this project was completed before I laid down my chairmanship and the car—Maruti 1000—launched.

I was also gratified by the fact that during my period, we had established the Maruti vehicle's acceptability in foreign markets. I was also happy that before I laid down my charge, the sales of Maruti reached 1,00,000 per year. The success of Maruti triggered the entry of a number of international brands into India. Tata Motors also reversed its old policy and decided to enter the passenger car market.

One initiative I took that is continuing to date is the Auto Expo. At a time when people thought very little of the Indian automobile industry, I got CII to organize an Auto Expo on the lines of those in Frankfurt and Tokyo. I initiated the idea in 1985 when I was president of the Society of Indian Automobile Manufacturers and, in 1986, the country's first Auto Expo was held in Delhi, inaugurated by Rajiv Gandhi. It was a huge success, and it was decided that the expo would be held regularly. It is now Asia's largest auto expo and is held every two years. An interesting sidelight to the first edition is that the surplus generated from it was used to build CII's Lodhi Estate office.

My formal association with Maruti ended in March 1990 when I ceased to be chairman. Just before the 1989 general elections, I had indicated to industry minister J. Vengal Rao that it was time to make Bhargava full-time chairman. The minister said he would speak to Rajiv Gandhi since he had wanted this arrangement. He did not revert on the matter, then everybody got busy with the elections, and I decided to take it up with Rajiv Gandhi after they were over. As it turned out, the Congress lost the elections and the National Front came to power, headed by V.P. Singh. I got a sense early on that my equation with this government would not be a comfortable one, given my perceived closeness to Rajiv Gandhi. Ajit Singh was the new industry minister, and I told him he should make Bhargava the chairman. Singh said he would let me know, giving me the impression that he did not want me to leave, though I knew better. A week later, when I went to meet him, he said I should send a formal resignation and suggest Bhargava's name as successor. I duly did that and thus ended my association with a company I set up from scratch.

~

I was, however, saddened by certain developments in Maruti after this. In 1991, I was a member in the Planning Commission when the proposal for SMC increasing its stake from the 40 per cent agreed upon initially to 50 per cent came up. Suzuki came to see me and discuss this. Though we had clashed on several occasions when I was in Maruti, we had a healthy regard for each other. I advised him against the move and pointed out that having the government as the larger partner would have its own advantages. I advised him to retain the SMC stake at 40 per cent, persuade the government to reduce its stake also to 40 per cent from the current 60 per cent, and sell the remaining 20 per cent to financial institutions, dealers, vendors, employees and the public, so that Maruti would be a board-managed company and remain an Indian brand. During my initial meetings with Mrs Gandhi, I had suggested this 40:40:20 holding pattern, so that the company would be insulated from political interference and targeting. But the industry ministry advised her against it. Since Maruti Motors had just been nationalized, they told her that questions would be raised about why it was now being de-nationalized. They suggested that it could be done a little later. But that never happened.

Suzuki left my room, and he did not seem convinced by my point of view. The then government also did not consider my proposal seriously and thought that permitting Suzuki to increase its stake would attract more Japanese investment, a presumption which they later admitted did not materialize. Hence, keeping with the then policy of disinvestment, they allowed SMC to increase its stake to 50 per cent and Maruti ceased to be a government undertaking. What upset me even more was the pricing. A Rs 100 share of a highly successful company was being sold for just Rs 269! At that point of time, a Rs 10 equity share of Hindustan Motors was selling at over Rs 70 per equity share. Moreover, when management control is transferred especially to a foreign party, a control premium is demanded. But it was not done in this case.

Senior Congress leader A.R. Antulay was chairman of the parliamentary committee on public undertakings at that time. Antulay and I wrote a joint letter to then prime minister P.V. Narasimha Rao, pointing out that this was against the spirit of what Mrs Gandhi had envisaged and that Maruti should remain an Indian company. We also objected to the low price at which it was being transferred. This infuriated Rao and also permanently spoilt relations between Suzuki and me. It also turned out to be one of the causes of my exit from the government in 1992.

I clashed with Suzuki on two other issues as well. Around the time of the controversy over the stake sale, trouble broke out between Chennai-based two-wheeler manufacturer TVS Motors and SMC, which were joint venture partners in the two-wheeler segment. Venu Srinivasan, the managing director of TVS, complained to me that Suzuki was trying to edge him out of the joint venture and had written a letter saying he was unsuitable to be managing director. I thought this was the height of impropriety and spoke to Suzuki, saying that such behaviour did not become him. I also advised Srinivasan not to bow to the demands of Suzuki and to call off the joint venture if it was not working well. Given Srinivasan's stature, he was able to stand up to Suzuki, and finally Suzuki exited the joint venture with TVS. TVS Suzuki Ltd became TVS Motors Ltd.

In the late 1990s, when Maruti and the government were battling over management control, Suzuki issued a public statement saying the government's choice of Bhargava's successor as managing director—Bhaskarudu—was not suitable. I thought it was unbecoming of a Japanese partner to comment so harshly on someone who had been the director, production, until the other day and had been nominated by the government to the managing director's post. I went public with my views. Although all this did strain my personal relationship with Suzuki, it did not in any way diminish my respect for him and SMC's contribution to the success of Maruti and the modernization of the automobile industry in India.

As I look back, there is an immense sense of satisfaction about my stint with Maruti, which set several firsts for Indian manufacturing. The main objective of Maruti being the catalyst for the modernization of the Indian automobile industry was accomplished. It demolished the theory that Indians cannot manufacture a quality product. The quality was acceptable internationally and the cars found a market in Europe within five years. More importantly, Maruti was a profitable venture from the first year, a rare achievement for Indian industry and a definite first for the public sector.

Besides, it was the first and perhaps one of the very few cases since 1980 of all three objectives of foreign direct investment being fulfilled, and within five years at that: foreign capital was brought in, technology was transferred to the Indian partner, and optimum value addition was achieved. A small car at an affordable price with the highest degree of indigenous integration was achieved. Subsequent entrants like Hyundai, Volkswagen or Honda did enjoy the fruits of the Indian market but did not fulfil their obligations towards technology transfer or value addition in India.

Actual liberalization of the economy began as early as 1982 with Maruti, when the guidelines of the government were amended to permit foreign equity participation in the automobile sector on a case-to-case basis.

The objective of every public sector undertaking is to be socially conscious and develop the region where it is located. As in the case of Trichy and Haridwar, Gurgaon was also developed into an industrial hub thanks to Maruti and soon overtook Chennai and Pune in this regard. It would be interesting to note that years later, as member, Planning Commission, and chairman of the Indo-Japan Study Committee, I identified Manesar (where the second Maruti plant is located) near Gurgaon for the development of a model industrial township.

Motoring in India changed forever with the advent of Maruti. The concept of customer satisfaction in the automobile sector was introduced by Maruti. A new breed of dealers and network of service centres were created. Customer orientation was a Maruti creation.

Even after thirty years of its inception, despite large doses of liberalization, I am happy that the practices adopted by Maruti are cited as examples by one and all. Not many organizations have been able to excel the record set by Maruti.

While I am very grateful to Mrs Gandhi and Rajiv Gandhi for having reposed faith in me and for having given me the opportunity to create Maruti and drive it to success, I am to an extent saddened today only in one respect—that by giving away majority control to SMC, we lost a good Indian brand. The company has retained Maruti in its name (Maruti Suzuki India Ltd) but the distinctive logo of the M-shaped wings has now been replaced by the 'S' of Suzuki. I feel a twinge every time I see it. I wonder if future generations of the country will ever know that this was once a very strong Indian brand.

# 6

# REFORGING SAIL

In May 1985, when I was chairman of Maruti and in Japan on a visit, my phone rang in the early hours of the morning. It was Rajiv Gandhi's secretary. He said, 'The boss wants to talk to you.' Rajiv came on the line and asked where I was. When I told him, he wanted to know when I was returning. I asked him what the matter was, and he said something that startled me—he wanted me to become chairman of SAIL.

I said, 'I don't think I am in a position to take up this assignment.' I reminded him that I was sixty and that it was time for me to retire. Just as his mother had said when I expressed my initial reluctance to take on the Maruti job, he said, 'We'll try it out for two years, and then you can do what you want to.' I told him that SAIL, with its myriad problems, required a younger man who would be around for a longer period and would have the energy to deal with them. He said he had already considered several alternatives and that I should see him on my return so he could explain what was on his mind.

When I returned, I hesitated to contact his office. He could be quite charming when he wanted, and I felt I might not be able to refuse him. A couple of days later, Arun Nehru called me and said both of us were to meet Rajiv Gandhi. He picked me up and on the way also said that Rajiv Gandhi was keen on my taking over SAIL. I repeated what I had told Rajiv Gandhi. At the meeting, Rajiv Gandhi explained why he wanted me in SAIL at any cost. 'You know my passion for managing PSUs better; I have talked to you often about this. Right now, SAIL has become a big joke even within the cabinet, and my colleagues think it is a lost cause. Over and above that, there is a general feeling that I don't believe in the public sector. But you know that I believe in it and want it to be run more efficiently.' The best method of convincing people about this, he said, was to put me in charge. 'At a time when Maruti is a success and everyone knows my confidence in you, putting you in charge of SAIL will show people I am putting my best man there. I know it is a dreadful assignment, but with some luck, you may be able to turn it around.'

There was a pause. Then Nehru spoke. 'He has made up his mind,' he said, 'you better accept it and get on with the job.' After that, there was no argument. When Mrs Gandhi had asked me to take up the Maruti assignment, she said her credibility was at stake. Now another prime minister wanted to prove his commitment to the public sector. My personal wishes obviously had to come second. I said I would try and do my best.

Rajiv Gandhi must have set the ball rolling for my appointment as SAIL chairman almost as soon as I left his office. By the time I returned home that evening, the cabinet resolution appointing me as chairman had been passed. Gopi Arora, who was additional secretary in the PMO, said that I should join as early as possible.

I asked if I could join after my return from a short holiday to the United States that I had planned. After checking with the prime minister, he said Rajiv Gandhi wanted me to first take charge at SAIL and then go on my vacation. I was going to be away for only a couple of weeks, but apparently Rajiv Gandhi did not want any vacuum in the period between the announcement of my name and my taking charge. Since this was not a planned succession, he felt a vacuum could set in.

When the prime minister asked me to take over SAIL, I was given the status of secretary to the Government of India. I was also given the option of being secretary, steel, in addition to being SAIL chairman. However, I did not exercise that option since I knew that SAIL would require my full attention and I also felt that a separate secretary in the ministry would be a better arrangement to take care of the interface with the other ministries. Besides, Rajiv Gandhi had also asked me to keep an eye on Maruti, which is why I continued there as non-executive chairman.

The announcement came as a surprise to everyone; no one had any inkling that there would be a change. I joined the very next day—15 May 1985. The previous chairman, S. Samarapungavan, had laid down charge and left the city. He did not meet me. Perhaps this was for the best. It would have been embarrassing for both of us.

Within SAIL, the reaction to my appointment was mixed. People were aware of my track record in BHEL and Maruti. Besides, I was the prime minister's choice. But that did not mean they were going to welcome me with open arms. The SAIL community was a very proud one, with people wearing their association with one or the other of the five plants like a badge of honour. It would have been difficult for the senior managers—outstanding technologists who had spent thirty or more years with the company, rising from the shop floor to the top management levels, and who knew the industry inside out—to accept the fact that a complete outsider to the steel industry was now to steer SAIL. I wonder now if Rajiv Gandhi's insistence on my taking over immediately was prompted by an apprehension that any delay could give time for resistance to build up within SAIL.

As I took stock of the situation, I began to understand why Rajiv Gandhi had referred to SAIL as a 'dreadful assignment'—something he would constantly tease me about. Against the Sixth Five-Year Plan target of capacity utilization of 84.8 per cent, the actual utilization was only 73 per cent. The technology in the five steel plants was obsolete by international standards, as a result of which the plants were operating in a highly inefficient manner. The organization was hugely overstaffed, with over 2,50,000 direct employees on its rolls. To add to this, the company was highly bureaucratic and hierarchical. Each of the five plants worked in isolation, and the chairman's office, which was supposed to play a coordinating role, did not appear to be up to the task. There was a perceptible lack of leadership. After generating profits continuously since 1978-79 (the year it became an operating company), SAIL had posted huge losses for two straight years in 1982-83 and 1983-84. The combined loss in these two years was Rs 320 crore, which drew jibes that SAIL was a company making a loss of Rs 1 crore a day.

~

I soon realized that a lot of SAIL's problems—especially the lack of leadership—stemmed from the fact that SAIL as an organization had been devalued over the years and the top management did not have the authority it should rightly have enjoyed.

SAIL had been formed in 1972 as a holding corporation to manage the five integrated steel plants—Bhilai, Bokaro, Burnpur, Durgapur and Rourkela—as well as the Alloy Steel Plant and the Salem Steel Plant. It was converted into an operating company in 1978. In what was an experiment with a new organizational structure, the government had decided that the SAIL chairman should also function as secretary in the steel ministry. The first chairman of SAIL, Wadud Khan, thus became secretary, steel, and started giving more importance to his bureaucratic assignment. As a result, the interests of SAIL became subservient to that of the steel ministry. Later, the government decided to split the two posts. In 1977, Mantosh Sondhi became secretary, steel, while P.L. Agarwal became SAIL chairman. But Sondhi was a forceful personality, and the supremacy of the government only got reinforced. I was glad I had turned down the position of secretary, steel.

I realized how much the office of the chairman had been weakened when I once received a letter from an under-secretary in the steel ministry asking for immediate comments on a routine matter. I wrote to the secretary, steel, on the back of that very letter, asking him to advise his officials to stop sending such missives, that I could not be expected to waste my time commenting on such trivial matters. In another incident, I got a call from the steel secretary's office asking for the daily production figure of one of the plants. I retorted that I would put them in touch with the director, operations.

I also realized that almost every significant decision regarding SAIL and the production of steel was being taken by different government and semi-government agencies. Thus, the National Council of Applied Economic Research (NCAER) was generally commissioned by the Planning Commission to estimate how much steel and what kind of steel products should be produced. Based on this report, the Planning Commission finalized how much steel should be produced, whether new steel plants should come up and the like. Political considerations determined the location of any new steel plant. MECON Ltd (then known as Metallurgical and Engineering Consultants India Ltd) decided what technology and equipment should be used in the plant, while the Directorate-General of Technical Development in the industry ministry decided whether the equipment should be procured domestically or imported and from which country. The Iron and Steel Controller in Kolkata decided the quantity of various products that were to be produced while the Joint Plant Committee (JPC, set up in 1964 to formulate guidelines for production, allocation, distribution and pricing of iron and steel products) or the Bureau of Industrial Costs and Prices (BICP) determined the price at which these products would be sold. The prices were usually based on a cost-plus model and had little relation to demand and supply factors in the market. The steel ministry made all senior appointments while the Bureau of Public Enterprises, under the industry ministry, decided the salary and the bonus norms. The SAIL chairman, effectively, was reduced to only taking decisions relating to the internal working of the organization. How could he, then, command authority over his employees?

Some of these agencies, like the Iron and Steel Controller, were obsolete. I constantly questioned the need for this office, which was a legacy of the Second World War period when steel was scarce and had to be rationed. But to continue that office in the 1980s, with a joint secretary in Kolkata deciding how much SAIL or Tata Steel (then known as Tata Iron and Steel Co or Tisco) should produce, defied logic. Ironically, while I, as a public sector manager, was resisting state controls, the private sector Tata Steel, which was headed by Russi Mody those days, was unhappy with me for doing so. Tata Steel had always paid scarce attention to the Iron and Steel Controller, but it provided a good cloak behind which it could hide its own problems.

In one of my early interactions with the steel ministry, I made it clear that this situation could not continue and that SAIL must have a say in all matters. After that, I just went ahead and took decisions on my own. In some cases, I had to go to the cabinet through the steel ministry to get approvals. There was resentment at my exercising my authority as SAIL chairman, ignoring previous practices, but no one put up any visible opposition.

~

The external factors affecting SAIL were relatively easy to handle compared to the internal problems, which were formidable and complex. SAIL was a highly hierarchical organization. I found that the senior managers were very insular in their thinking and were not very knowledgeable about global trends in steel plant technology. I could not blame them as most of them had remained in the same place, doing the same job for decades. A person who had joined the organization at one steel plant stayed there till he retired. After his initial training in the Soviet Union (which was the collaborator for the steel plants), he may not even have gone to another SAIL plant, let alone seen the Tata Steel plant (SAIL's only significant competitor at that time). There were regular meetings for which senior managers would travel to other plants, but these would invariably be held in offices. They would not even visit the actual shop floor to see things for themselves. But they had done their job honestly and felt that the public perception of SAIL being a lost cause was unfair. They believed that they had done their best and nobody else could have done a better job.

It was obvious that their mindset and mine were quite different, and I knew it would be quite a struggle to get us on the same page. I had to proceed cautiously.

First, I had to get them to acknowledge that SAIL's problems were internal and that the solutions lay in changing their style of functioning. If SAIL was seen as a lost cause, there must have been something wrong. I had to get this message across without hurting the pride of the senior managers. It would have been easy for me to issue diktats to do things differently. But that had never been my style, as I always tried to take people along. Besides, that would only have had all of them range against me, and it would have been difficult for me to lift their morale. In my interactions with senior managers, I used to tell them, 'You have done your best, but perhaps for reasons beyond your control it has not produced the desired results. Let us now try doing things differently. If it succeeds, the credit is yours; if it does not I will take the rap.'

I realized I could not identify and understand the problems that brought SAIL to this pass by sitting in the head office and relying on second hand reports. So for the first five months, I visited each of the plants, regularly meeting managers, union representatives and workers. Earlier, when the chairman visited the plants, only the senior-most managers would be invited for meetings. I insisted that the junior and middle-level executives also be called, and I would encourage them to speak. I would organize a drinks-and-dinner evening and people—especially the younger lot—would open up more during this time.

Once, in Durgapur, after the senior executives indulged in their usual blame game, one young manager spoke up. 'You can see the symptoms,' he said. 'We are not trying to improve internally. There are issues of leadership and competency.' There was an uncomfortable silence in the room after his outburst. Later at dinner I sought out the young man, put my arm around his shoulder and chatted with him for a while. It was a deliberate gesture. I did not want him to be victimized for having criticized his seniors.

The prime minister and the steel minister, Vasant Sathe, had expected me to bring along some of my trusted people from other organizations where I had worked earlier. I did not. There is a tendency among CEOs to do that, but I strongly believe a good CEO is someone who works with new people and wins them over rather than merely relying on a trusted band of loyalists. I assured the top management that nobody would be shifted and that each person would continue to do his job. The only people I brought along with me were four young executive assistants in their mid-twenties—Alka Mishra, Vijayalakshmi Rao, Mahesh Babu and I. Raghunath. They were young managers, with one or two years of experience, who had joined Maruti as management trainees and had worked with me there as special assistants. In SAIL, I gave each of them a particular area to focus on. This was done because in SAIL I found a strong tendency among executives to tell their bosses only what they wanted to hear, and I realized that often I did not get the right picture.

I started sending two of the executive assistants, along with one person from the human resource or operations division, a couple of days before my visit to a plant. They would meet key people in the plant, including union leaders, and prepare a brief for me. Initially, they were viewed with suspicion and seen as my spies. But gradually, people realized that I was only trying to understand their problems better and began to open up to them. They started seeing them as mediums to get messages across to me.

As I started to get feedback, I thought of documenting what was ailing SAIL and what needed to be done to get it back on its feet, somewhat on the lines of the *Outline of a Corporate Plan* drawn up when I was in BHEL. But while the *Corporate Plan* had a slightly top-down approach, since it set out a vision for a relatively new organization's future, I decided that a more participatory approach was required in SAIL. I had to build morale and wanted people to feel they were part of the evolution of change. I decided to merely ask questions and let the answers come from within the organization. I sensed that there was enough talent within SAIL to give me those answers. I was not wrong.

I put my executive assistants to work on the document and they fanned out across the organization, talking to people, getting to understand the problems and seeking solutions. Some of the younger employees in SAIL were also roped in for the exercise. Senior managers wondered what four wet-behind-the-ears managers were going to achieve and saw this as the beginning of an attempt to impose my views on the organization. However, several junior managers realized that we could not afford to run an organization that was losing Rs 1 crore a day. They wanted a change and were willing to help in any way they could. Soon there was a groundswell of support.

The document went through several drafts, because I wanted to avoid overtly critical references to the previous management or prevailing practices. SAIL was such a multi-faceted organization that bringing all the issues and solutions within the scope of a single document was a huge challenge. The thirteen-page *Priorities for Action*, unveiled in January 1986, ably navigated the middle ground that I wanted it to take—steering the company along a new path without discrediting everything that had been done earlier. After highlighting SAIL's contribution to the building of 'a strong and self-reliant India', it flagged the issue of poor public perception of the organization and then posed the all-important question:

> ... Could we have done better? More so because of the general public opinion that we haven't done our best. Undoubtedly, we could have served our customers better; what then must we do to change this image and aim higher in the future?

The document set an ambitious target for SAIL—production and sale of 10 million tonnes of saleable steel by 1989 and then expansion at the rate of 1 million tonnes every year from a stagnant position then prevailing. It also set out the five priorities for action necessary to prepare SAIL for this challenging task.

The interactions across the organization while preparing the document had thrown up a plethora of suggestions. A mere listing of such a huge laundry list would not only be too daunting but could also diffuse focus. The document finally grouped the suggestions under five heads involving every section of the organization: improving work culture; making optimum use of installed facilities; increasing productivity; generating profits through control of costs; and providing better customer service. If addressed, these five priorities would solve nearly 80 per cent of the problems ailing SAIL.

I had the document translated into different languages and distributed to all the employees—from the lowliest worker to the senior-most manager. Doing this was important. As the preamble of *Priorities for Action* said, 'Each and every employee of SAIL should know about the mission of the organization, its objectives and future plans so as to feel a sense of pride and identification.'

The next step was to rope in the 685 corporate managers—executives of the level of chief superintendent and above—to take the document forward. I decided to discuss the *Priorities for Action* threadbare with them and get them to air their views frankly on the document as well as the issues facing the company.

In order to facilitate a closer interaction with each of them, I had them divided into batches of around eighty people each, cutting across levels and plants, and organized intensive four-day workshops spread over two months on *Priorities for Action*. The workshops were held at SAIL's corporate research and development centre at Ranchi, where SAIL's Management Development Institute was also located. This centre at Ranchi functioned as a training centre and had an auditorium as well as a forty-room hostel facility.

How hierarchical and status-conscious SAIL was became evident in the process of organizing these workshops. We had to put two persons to a room since the hostel had only forty rooms. One day, Mahesh Babu, one of the executive assistants, came to me and asked me to share a room at the hostel with one of my directors. I agreed but was puzzled by the request. Apparently, the general managers had raised a hue and cry about being asked to share rooms. Once I agreed to share a room, they could not refuse.

Each workshop involved four days of intense discussions on each of the topics in the document. Apart from the four executive assistants, some other young people who were part of the chairman's office, were roped in and trained to anchor each session. I would listen to the deliberations and then summarize the points that had been thrown up at the end of the day. We made sure each manager participated in the discussions in some form. They knew someone was keeping track of who was interacting and who was not. The evening sessions, over dinner, were even more fruitful. The participants were in a relaxed, informal mood and even more frank than they were in the formal sessions. By the end of the third day, everybody was a changed person, charged with enthusiasm about working for a revitalized organization which was going to achieve new heights. I was told that this was the first large-scale engagement by any chairman with all levels of executives.

In the next step, each of these managers became a messenger to take the message forward to the units and the supervisory cadres. SAIL took the help of two management gurus—Mrityunjaya Athreya and B.L. Maheshwari—for this communication exercise. I spent considerable time with them and planned out a strategy for communication down the organization. While Maheshwari took care of the senior management, Athreya dealt with supervisory and junior level cadres. Managers possessing communication skills were chosen to communicate and interact with the workers at each plant. At the risk of sounding vain, this was probably one of the largest communication exercises that any corporate organization had undertaken, surpassing even what I had done with the *Corporate Plan* in BHEL. But the result of this and the bottom-up approach to its drafting was that *Priorities for Action* got ownership across the organization.

It was now time to start acting on the document.

~

There were two overarching themes running through the various steps that were taken to ensure that *Priorities for Action* did not remain just a document. One of these was modernization of the mind and the other was a focus on costs and revenue enhancement.

Modernization of the mind before modernization of machines became my mantra while managing SAIL, even though each of its plants was practically on its last legs in terms of technology. Unless one and all opened their minds, they would not be receptive to the many new ideas that needed to be implemented to revive SAIL. As *Priorities for Action* put it, any amount of money spent on modernization will not yield results without an improvement in the work culture. This is what I concentrated on for the first two years. This covered a range of issues that ran through the entire organization—from bringing about organizational coherence to changing the way employees saw themselves in relation to the organization and to their attitudes to work. Looking back, I found that practically all the solutions to SAIL's problems lay in breaking mental barriers.

I had found senior management often blaming external pressures, which were quite common in most public sector undertakings, for poor performance or lack of it. I knew that these complaints had some basis. But I realized that the managers were often using this as an excuse for not doing their job.

It was quite common earlier for managing directors of plants to go to the ministry directly. Often they were summoned to do favours, like showing good quality steel as bad quality and selling it at a lower price to someone the ministry favoured. I put a stop to such direct contact and said that the chairman would be the point of interface between the ministry and the organization.

Fortunately, because of my personal reputation, I did not have to face the kind of pressures that other public sector chief executives had to. In the rare instances I did, I stood my ground though I did try and avoid an open confrontation. A few months after I took over, K.C. Pant became the steel minister. We had both broadly agreed that the managing director of the Bhilai Steel Plant was not pulling his weight and needed to be shifted. Soon after this discussion, Pant visited the plant along with a joint secretary, Tirlochan Singh, who let out the fact that the managing director was going to be shifted. I asked Pant about this, and he said he had told the joint secretary about the decision. He then wanted to know when I was shifting the managing director. I told him that if the joint secretary had not spoken about it, the transfer would have looked like a routine administrative decision. But now it would look as if I was acting on the ministry's orders and that all transfer-related issues would be taken up with the ministry. Therefore, I would not act immediately. I transferred the managing director in my own time.

Another incident related to the transfer of the general manager, personnel, out of the Bokaro Steel Plant. The general manager was on good terms with the then Bihar chief minister, Bindeshwari Dubey, and I had come to know that he had approached him to stall his transfer by speaking to Pant. I quickly got the managing director of Bokaro Steel Plant to relieve the transferred official of his charge. When Pant spoke to me regarding the transfer, I told him nothing could be done as the official had been relieved and his successor had taken charge and that we would try and accommodate him at some other time. When people within SAIL came to know about such incidents, they realized that I was serious about insulating them from external pressures. I told the senior management that I would handle all external issues and that, as long as they did their job honestly, I would insulate them from pressures and even protect them from any kind of harassment.

Having given this assurance to the employees, I set about trying to bring one-ness in the organization.

SAIL was a huge organization, with six plants and multifarious departments. It was also full of silos, with each plant or department acting in isolation and concentrating on doing its own job well, with little reference to how this would further the organization's interests as a whole. This affected the company's ability to leverage its size to reach its full potential. Breaking these silos was an important aspect of the modernization of the mind that I wanted because this affected the way employees thought about themselves as part of the organization. I wanted them to see themselves as part of a team, something that was missing in SAIL at that point of time. The attempt to knit SAIL into one coherent whole involved changing attitudes as well as some organizational restructuring and the setting up of new divisions. I am not among those who believe that an organization's structure is cast in stone. Every organization must review its structure periodically with reference to availability of manpower and resources and new challenges, and make necessary modifications. SAIL needed such restructuring at that point of time.

I realized that the Bokaro and Bhilai plants needed new leadership. S.R. Ramakrishnan and E.R.C. Shekar, two outstanding general managers, had earlier left SAIL and joined the private sector. I reached out to them and got them back as managing directors of Bokaro and Bhilai respectively, thereby strengthening the operating team. The fact that I brought two outstanding senior executives had a very salutary effect on the organization.

Surprisingly, a large organization like SAIL did not have a corporate planning department, a mistake I immediately rectified. The corporate planning division was set up in July 1986, and I got Arvind Pande, a bright IAS officer who had just finished his stint in the PMO and was looking for some exciting opportunities, as its first head. SAIL now had a department in Delhi looking at the organization holistically and exploring symmetries within it, though its main responsibility was to plan for the future. The division's first task was to prepare a fifteen-year strategic plan for SAIL, with the objective of the company becoming the second or the third largest steel producer in the world. This was also one way of showing that SAIL was going to set its goals itself, instead of relying on outside agencies. The strategic plan was meant as much for SAIL's employees as for the outside world. I wanted the employees to believe in their organization and to understand that their growth was linked intrinsically to the organization's growth and success.

When I came in, there was no collective thinking or coordinated policy making in SAIL. That was one reason I set up the corporate planning division, apart from wanting to reclaim SAIL's autonomy. I also wanted the division to relieve the heads of plants from work not related to the running of the factories. SAIL did not just produce steel, it was a mini-government by itself. The total estate under its control was bigger than that of the old princely states. It had a school system catering to 70,000 students and which employed 7,000 teachers. It also had five large hospitals. The chief executives of the plants would often get bogged down administering all this and tackling welfare measures instead of concentrating on the core responsibility of looking after the steel plants and planning for the future. The corporate planning division was also supposed to handle this and liaison with the state governments. But during my time, I could not accomplish some of these objectives.

~

'Improving work culture' was the first of the five priorities for action, and there was a reason for it.

Discipline was a major issue that needed to be addressed and, within this, it was the practice of overtime that proved the biggest challenge. A practice had developed of a few workers forming a group and taking leave in turns, with someone or the other working overtime in the absent person's place. As a result, the overtime bill accounted for close to 10 per cent of the wage bill. People were also working overtime in an unplanned manner, without the senior executives knowing about it. For me, this was managerial indiscipline and was absolutely unacceptable. In one of the rare instances of issuing a diktat, I gave a handwritten note to my secretary, saying that henceforth there would be no budget provisions for overtime, and told him to give the note to the personnel and finance directors.

Everyone was aghast. The managing directors of the plants and other senior managers said it would not be possible to run the company without paying overtime. Even the directors on the board were not with me on this. People said that the Damodar river* would be in flames because of this action. But I refused to budge. I told them that since I had decided to stop overtime, it was now up to them to find a way to implement this.

---

*The Damodar river valley area is home to three of SAIL's plants—Bokaro, Durgapur and Burnpur.

But I also made an attempt to communicate the rationale for this move. I convened a meeting at the Ashok Hotel in Delhi to which I invited the managing directors of all the plants, all the directors, leaders of all the apex trade unions as well as SAIL's own trade union leaders. After listening to everyone's objections, I took the mike. I pointed out that overtime was a disease that was eating into the innards of SAIL; that it was not meant to help the workers but cover up the inefficiencies of the managers who had become complacent because of the flexibility available to them to allow overtime. I pointed out that if a manager planned his work or staffing requirements properly, there would be no need for overtime.

I gave several examples to buttress my point. One was about a pump operator, who has a very critical role to play in a steel mill, being absent for three days without the manager even knowing that he was absent and for what reason because somebody else was standing in for him on overtime. I also pointed out that certain workers were paid overtime by managers because they ran personal errands for them. And then I delivered the clincher. I pointed out that only 12 per cent of the workforce benefited from overtime and that less than half of these were from critical areas in steel making; the majority were from service areas. I questioned whether the 12 per cent who got overtime were genuinely deserving candidates or favourites of managers. I concluded by saying that it was not my intention to stop payments to workers; that I would use the money saved on overtime to give more bonuses, provide better facilities for workers and step up spending on welfare measures. My slogan was, 'Everyone will be paid for the work done and not for the time spent'. This was to impress upon them that I had no qualms about giving them more welfare measures but that I would not pay them for their inefficiency in not doing the job within the allotted time. It was difficult for either the union leaders or the managers to counter these well-researched arguments.

But resistance did not disappear overnight. I wanted to start the experiment in the Durgapur Steel Plant. However, this was a strong hub of CITU, the trade union arm of the Communist Party of India (Marxist), which was ruling in West Bengal, and managing director Debu Mukherjee was not very confident of being able to implement the experiment. N.C. Naik, the managing director of the smaller Alloy Steel Plant (also in Durgapur), took up the challenge. The unions did stir up unrest and this went on for some time. When Naik had come to Delhi for a meeting, we discussed this. I then told him to visit the Paharganj market in Delhi before leaving for Durgapur and buy the strongest locks available. If and when things went out of hand, he should merely lock the factory premises, go home and take some rest. A clear message went out and the strike petered out. When the experiment was introduced in the other plants across SAIL, the opposition against it was muted and manageable.

Later, the unions backed me on this measure. It was the managers who were unhappy because it took away a tool to grant favours and made them work in a more disciplined manner. I could not stop overtime entirely, but it was used more rationally and this resulted in a huge drop in the overtime bill. From Rs 40 crore in 1985-86, it fell to Rs 2.4 crore in 1986-87.

When I went to Durgapur for the first time after my move on overtime, I saw a huge crowd at the station. I was sure the workers had come to demonstrate against me. But when I stepped out of the train, instead of seeing black flags, I was inundated with garlands, and all the top union leaders like Anand Gopal Mukherjee and Dilip Majumdar had come to receive me. They wanted to congratulate me on the various measures I was taking to improve the image of the company and to stop bad practices. This only confirmed my belief that the most unpopular of measures could gain acceptance if the rationale behind it is communicated properly.

With the most controversial decision having been accepted, it was easier to tackle other issues like high levels of absenteeism, much of which was unauthorized and, therefore, not planned for. Absenteeism in the Alloy Steel Plant and Durgapur Steel Plant in 1985 was found to be 38 per cent a day, of which 16 per cent was without permission. That meant around 3,000 people were absent without information. Taking a leaf out of Maruti's book, *Priorities for Action* set a target of bringing down absenteeism to 5 per cent. With the toughness on overtime still fresh in everyone's mind, we could manage to take tough measures to enforce this without causing any major ripples. Once again, I explained that I had no objection to people taking leave. After all, I could not complain about SAIL being overstaffed and then deny people leave. But nobody could be allowed to remain away from office without prior permission beyond a certain period.

I also saw no reason why people should not be deployed across departments on a needs basis. Earlier, if there was a shortage of staff in, say, the blast furnace, no one from the steel making unit would be deployed there even if they were sitting idle. I put a stop to this and said redeployment should be done as a matter of course. In doing so, I demonstrated that the lack of overtime would not affect operations—one of the arguments that managers generally fielded to let the practice continue.

It also came to my notice that we were losing between 5 and 10 per cent of production and energy cost when shifts changed. I, therefore, tried to implement the concept of overlapping shifts that was in place in Maruti, where people reported fifteen minutes before a shift change so that there was no break in work when they took over their assigned tasks.

I introduced certain other practices that had been initiated in Maruti, one of which was to have uniform working hours for workers and managerial staff. The former worked forty-eight hours a week and the latter thirty-six hours. I ensured everybody clocked in forty-eight hours. I was not very successful in doing this in the corporate office in Delhi. Employees pointed out that this could work at the plants where employees lived on the campus or close to it. It would not be practical in Delhi where people had to commute long distances and depend on unreliable public transport. I had to concede this logic but made sure that people started work earlier than they used to so that there was someone present in the office if managers from the plants wanted to get in touch with the headquarters.

The problem of unplanned absenteeism and excessive overtime payments was not confined to the plants but was also rampant in the country-wide marketing set-up, especially the stockyards. It would take between six and eight hours (and sometimes several days) from the time officers would settle sale details with customers to the time instructions were given to the delivery point to allow the customer to lift his supplies. There was an excessive dependence on messengers to move papers to the cashier to collect payments and then to the officer making delivery orders and then finally to the delivery point. The working time in non-plant areas was only six-and-a-half hours, and the inefficient manner of working meant the work never got completed, resulting in overtime.

To set this right, the marketing department undertook a pilot project in a few branches in the south-central zone. In consultation with the unions, we initiated an eight-hour shift and also gave some motivational incentives like subsidized lunch and more frequent interactions between the families of executives and non-executives. This was achieved without any fuss. In the next step, we dismantled all the cubicles in these branches and started an open office regime to speed up work. The success of the pilot project ensured that this system was then extended to the entire marketing set-up across the country. This increased overall efficiency led to faster deliveries and higher quantities of steel being handled at delivery points.

Another difficult exercise we had to undertake was trimming SAIL's bloated workforce, at the level of both workers and executives. There was a pressing need for this. The output per employee was much lower than international norms. Besides, given the technological changes in the steel industry, there was also an age and skills skew in the company.

A voluntary retirement scheme (VRS) was one way of bringing down employee numbers and was introduced in 1987. We designed a good package that protected the current salary, retirement as well as medical benefits of employees opting for VRS. We went about the whole exercise very carefully, training close to 1,000 internal resource persons to spread the message within the organization, explaining the need for VRS and how it would benefit employees and the organization. There were pockets of resistance, but the internal resource persons managed to overcome these. Around 10,000 employees opted for the golden handshake.

The bulk of the trimming was, however, done by not filling vacancies caused by natural attrition. Instead, we retrained and redeployed existing staff whenever a vacancy arose. By 1989, the number of employees had come down substantially for a much larger portfolio of products, and it was a signal that the organization would not be allowed to sink under its own weight.

I could not have achieved all that I did without getting the trade unions on board. Like all public sector undertakings, SAIL was highly unionized and labour militancy was the order of the day. Just before I took over, the Durgapur Steel Plant had gone through a protracted strike. The Bokaro Steel Plant had ninety-nine unions. Even the smallest incident would result in work being stopped and protracted negotiations taking place on the shop floor. All the major trade unions had a presence in SAIL. Each had its own constituency which it zealously safeguarded. Their national leaders took active interest in the company. These included Gopeshwar and Anand Gopal Mukherjee of INTUC, M.K. Pandhe, Dilip Majumdar and Mrinal Banerjee of CITU, Gaya Singh of AITUC and Raju Samanthrai of HMS .

I was very frank with them about the situation the company was in and told them that if this continued, the company would have to close down and their support base would be unemployed. I pointed out that I was not asking workers to go beyond the call of duty but only to do their duty sincerely, and that my actions did not target workers but managerial inefficiencies. I told them I was there for just two years (since that was my original agreement with Rajiv Gandhi) and asked them to bear with me for that much time, as all my actions would ultimately benefit the workers. I said that I understood the compulsions of elected trade union leaders to be populist and not openly support tough measures. 'Let me do whatever is required as a manager,' I said. 'Hold demonstrations if you must but do not block what I am doing and give sane advice to your members in private.' It was a great experiment for me to interact with such reputed leaders. Whatever their earlier stands regarding many issues confronting SAIL may have been, they were extremely considerate and supportive of my efforts to discipline the organization and improve its profitability and image. All of them cooperated because they were aware of my track record in my previous assignments and also because they were convinced that all my actions would only benefit SAIL in the long run. It is to their credit that throughout my period, there was no major industrial relation problem in SAIL. As a result, one significant outcome of the wage negotiations in 1989 was a commitment from the workers and the unions to improve productivity and quality and support positive changes in the work culture.

There was one slogan I would repeat to all employees and others who did not want the status quo to be disturbed: 'It is better to go through the discomfort of a planned change than the pain of a forced change'.

~

The executive cadres of SAIL also had their own set of issues. Morale here was extremely low and, unlike in BHEL, where the average age when I became chairman was around thirty-five years, it was around fifty years in SAIL. The retirement age in those days was fifty-eight, so motivating them to give their best even for whatever time they remained in the organization was a huge challenge. I had to kindle their pride and get them to respond to the measures taken to improve operations. They had an active association, which I met periodically and maintained good communication with. Eventually, they started to respond positively to my initiatives.

I found that some departments, though very crucial to the organization, had traditionally been ignored and that people who worked in them felt very demoralized. I set about addressing this and gave them a chance to perform. One of these was the mining department in each plant. The chairman would not visit the mines, and the mining department was seen as a punishment posting, no doubt because it meant working in remote areas in inhospitable conditions. I pointed out that a steel plant's success depended on how the raw material supplies were managed and that, therefore, mining was a very crucial activity. We started posting good managers to the mines, improved the living and working conditions in and around the mines, and gradually raised the profile of the department.

Finance was another department that was relegated to the background, and there were occasions when it was not part of discussions on matters that had large financial implications. I set about changing that, ensuring that the head of finance was present at most meetings and even involving some of the younger executives. Many of them were bright youngsters and the fact that the chairman was listening to them raised their morale immensely.

The third neglected department that got a lot of importance was the personnel department. I could not have raised the morale of others in the organization if the morale of the personnel department was low. There was a need to make them feel that they had a crucial role to play in keeping the organization ready to meet the challenges facing it and in taking it to a higher level. I ensured that the managing directors of the plants had regular meetings with them and also organized workshops for them.

I realized that there was a need to give the younger executives more opportunities, as they were the ones on whom the future of the organization rested. The VRS was one way of doing this. But it could also create insecurity and affect morale unless it was accompanied by steps to reward good performers. Unfortunately, the performance appraisal system, like that in all public sector undertakings, only put people into two slots—suitable for promotion or not suitable for promotion. There was no scientific methodology behind this and only some serious misdemeanour like corruption or indiscipline saw people being denied promotions. Promotions were automatic and given on the basis of seniority. This had disheartened a lot of the younger executives. I told the personnel department to work out a more credible way of assessing performance, which could be a tool for differentiating talent and identifying potential senior managers. I left it to them to work out the details.

As I was also chairman of IIM Ahmedabad at that time, a professor from the institute was roped in as a consultant. After six months, a new performance appraisal system kicked in. There were a lot of firsts in this system, especially for the public sector. Managers would set targets for individuals, and there would be a mid-year review before the final appraisal. It was a very advanced system for its time. SAIL was the first public sector organization to introduce self-appraisal. After the self-appraisal came an appraisal by the immediate superior. A weighted system was designed, with each level of appraisal being assigned a weight—the appraisal did not depend on the immediate superior alone. A senior group would look at all the appraisals and decide what in personnel parlance was known as the Bell distribution. The brilliant performers and the non-performers were identified and the former fast-tracked. Similar to what I had done in BHEL—identifying high-fliers and nurturing them—we rotated the brilliant performers in SAIL through different plants and functions to prepare them for senior managerial posts. Some of them were even brought to the corporate office in Delhi. Earlier, any posting to the corporate office required the intervention of the minister. I put a stop to that. Promotions were now linked to performance, something senior managers resisted, arguing that this would lead to people being superseded. They even tried to block some out-of-turn promotions but in vain.

Training was another area that got close attention. The training was completely outdated, and there had been no review in light of the needs of new technology and modern management practices. The people who needed training were not necessarily the ones who were sent for training. I remember what one young personnel executive so eloquently told me while making a presentation on training strategy in 1986: 'We are designing the wrong programmes and training the wrong kind of people.'

The performance appraisals came in handy here, with the organization now being better able to identify those who needed training. The appraisals also helped us design training programmes which were more suitable for SAIL. A training advisory board at the corporate level and unit-level committees were formed to monitor the training needs and design programmes.

In all this, we made full use of the Management Training Institute, the Ranchi-based in-house training institute of SAIL. It was a very small operation earlier, and its programmes were restricted to the lower categories of executives. I expanded its scope and got it to draw up a training calendar. MTI got a new building, better facilities and a hostel. Every executive had to undergo training once in every three years. In addition, they had to go through post-promotion training as well, without which they would not be confirmed in their promoted positions.

In addition to the workshops on *Priorities for Action*, we also organized technology workshops for engineers. These reviewed how SAIL could increase its productivity through existing technology. I found that people would often say something or the other could not be done and realized it was because they were not aware of the latest technological developments. Engineers who had not seen any steel plant other than the ones they were posted in were sent to British Steel, Japan's NKK Steel and Australia's Broken Hill Proprietary* to understand what modern steel plants were all about. Managers were also sent to steel companies in these countries in batches to get a sense of what the management of a modern steel plant required.

Soon the new human resource management practices in SAIL began to be talked about. When CII set up a national committee for human resources, it enlisted the cooperation of

*It merged with Billiton in 2001 to form BHP-Billiton.

SAIL's personnel department to upgrade the human resources side of select private sector organizations. SAIL's personnel executives gave presentations on its human resource interventions to CII and private companies like Godrej Industries and TVS Motors. The private sector was taking lessons from a public sector company on human resource policies! What better testimony could there have been to the success of our initiatives?

~

SAIL once had the reputation of having the world's lowest cost of production. By the time I joined, its cost of production was the highest. Price revisions were often delayed, sometimes by two years, and there was little SAIL could do about this. With revenues not matching expenses, it was little wonder that SAIL was in the red. As a result, we could not turn to the government for budgetary support and had to generate internal resources to fund various expansion and modernization plans.

I told the employees that since we had no control over price revision—and I had also committed to customers that SAIL would not seek price increases for three years—we had to focus on curbing our costs. That invariably evoked the rejoinder that this would result in compromising with quality. My early interactions with employees and the drafting of *Priorities for Action* revealed a lot of inefficiencies in the system. The organization was neither making optimum use of installed facilities nor doing anything to increase the productivity of men and materials, nor paying attention to waste. I pointed out that if these issues were addressed, it would cost SAIL less to produce one tonne of good quality steel than it would to produce the same quantity of bad quality steel.

The systemic inefficiencies started from the stage of sourcing raw materials. Each plant had its own iron ore and coal mines, and when supplies from these fell short, raw material was bought from outside. This was not an efficient or economical way of procurement, especially since when all of SAIL's mines were combined, the company had one of the largest mining operations in the world. Given that raw material accounted for 30-40 per cent of total cost, this kind of isolated functioning had to change. *Priorities for Action* flagged the need to encourage inter-plant transfers of raw materials and reduce dependence on outside sources.

In 1989, we set up a directorate for raw materials in Kolkata under the charge of an executive director, reporting directly to the board. The directorate had to look into the requirement of raw material of the different plants, provide the expertise and arrange for mining iron ore and coal in the most economical manner, and procure the balance requirement from other sources at the most economical price and supply it to the various plants. The mining department was made a part of this directorate, and we borrowed the services of G.S. Garcha, a very senior mining engineer from Coal India, to improve mining operations. There was some resentment that mines were being taken away from the control of the managing directors of the steel plants, but people gradually realized that this was not the intention and that the directorate was more a coordinating agency to ensure that none of the plants suffered due to the lack of either quantity or quality of raw material. As a result of this pooling of resources, to this day, SAIL gets raw material at the lowest possible price. Simultaneously, the profile of the mining department was gradually raised, yielding better results.

The largest single head of cost in steel making is energy, which accounts for 33 per cent of the total cost. In a well-managed modern steel plant, the energy input is mostly only coal and the recycled gases that are generated when coal is converted into coke. The use of purchased electricity is comparatively less. In SAIL, however, not only were the steel plants using coal as much as other comparable plants but they were also using large amounts of grid power. Moreover, the coal used for conversion into coke—known as the coke rate—was double that of most modern steel plants. I kept emphasizing the need to bring this down. I noticed that the purchase of grid power was also the result of captive sources of power not being used efficiently. Each steel plant had its own power plant, and because of the isolated nature of their functioning, one plant would have surplus power while another faced a shortage and bought power from the grid. I brought in Ranjit Chakravarthy, an executive director from BHEL, to develop a central control room that would coordinate the electricity generation and distribution by SAIL's captive power plants. SAIL also commissioned captive power plants at Rourkela and Durgapur to reduce dependence on external power. Since then, SAIL has never had a problem with power supply. An energy conservation programme launched in 1987 saw energy consumption fall 4.5 per cent over the previous year.

One of the major problems affecting SAIL when I took over was that of projects not being completed in time. While the steel plants themselves had come up in three years in the sixties, the small addition of a blast furnace or setting up a new cold rolling mill took seven or eight years. Not only did this push up costs but the technology being used also became outdated by the time the projects were completed. This only reinforced the image of SAIL being a highly inefficient organization. S.R. Jain, whom I had taken from the Bhilai Steel Plant to head HEC when I was heavy industries secretary, had completed his term with that organization and was looking for an interesting assignment. I brought him back into SAIL as vice-chairman to head a central project directorate, which was tasked with bringing about closer interaction between projects and operations. He was also made responsible for the execution of all projects under the modernization programme. Later, he succeeded me as chairman.

Simultaneously, I started laying emphasis on the optimum use of facilities and reducing waste. Capacity utilization in SAIL was low, and often this was because of low technology and poor maintenance of facilities and equipment. I first put a stop to any further capital investment and worked on upgrading and better utilization of the existing facilities. Each plant had engineering shops that would provide spares for the equipment being used. In spite of this, we found that some plants were procuring spares from outside sources. We now paid attention to making full use of these captive workshops, setting up a growth division in Kolkata headed by an executive director to ensure that these in-house facilities were better utilized.

Better discipline was enforced on the shop floor and close monitoring of production was done. There was a tendency in SAIL for production in the first quarter to be slow; the pace would pick up gradually and the bulk of production would happen in March. As a result, facilities were underutilized for most of the year. This was also one of the reasons for practices like overtime, since the pressure increased at the end of the year. I decided that this bunching of production would have to be broken. One of the workshops on *Priorities for Action* was held in the last week of March. The managing directors of the plants said they would not be able to stay away from their plants as production would suffer. I refused to accept that excuse and made their attendance compulsory. The only concession I allowed them was talking to the senior management in their plants every morning. Far from suffering, production that year touched record levels! All the incremental production recorded during my tenure was achieved by utilizing the available capacity optimally. All this did have an effect—in 1986-87, capacity utilization touched 93 per cent.

The focus on the big ticket items of expenditure did not mean that we ignored the items of minor expenditure. During my visits to plants, I found a lot of spillage of lubricant oil and use of waste cloth. I got my executive assistants to work out how much the company would lose in a year if one worker wasted 10 millilitres of oil and was extravagant in the use of waste cloth. Once again, the cost came to a few crores. We then explained to the workers that such wastage would only prevent the company from giving them more in cash and kind, since it would eat into the company's profits.

Explaining such issues to workers in a very simplified manner helped us get support on streamlining operations and making them more efficient. Boards were put up on shop floors explaining how an increase of one gcal of energy would increase the cost of steel being produced by a certain amount. I found that SAIL was incurring huge costs on demurrage and wharfage—the charges it had to pay the railways and the ports if SAIL did not unload material from railway wagons or ships within a stipulated time. This happened because there was a norm that only a certain number of wagons would be unloaded in a shift. A practice that had started during a period of low production continued without revision even when production levels increased. When workers were told what this cost the company and how it would affect them, they rearranged the work and outgo on these charges came down drastically.

What struck me was the complete lack of awareness within the organization on these matters. At one meeting, I asked senior managers of plants what they were doing to control costs. Most of them said they had asked people to travel less, travel by second class instead of first class and stay in cheaper hotels. I then asked each one of them the coke rates of their plants. I made them realize that they were using coke well above the norm, and this excess, when added up, came to a few hundred crores. I pointed out that this enormous wastage should bother them more than travel and other minor costs. I stressed that it was the big items of expenditure that I wanted to control. We then got the plants to compete with one another on all major operational parameters—using the achievements of one plant on, say, reduction in coke rate to goad others into doing better and also benchmarking each plant against its performance the previous year. Units were asked to incorporate profit improvement plans in their annual budgets and given challenging targets to meet. Each plant set up a multi-functional group under the head of operations to focus on cost control and streamline the budgetary control systems.

I laid a lot of emphasis on getting departments to understand that they were not isolated units, but that in a large, intermingled operation like that of SAIL, each should see the other as a customer and keep this internal customer satisfied. Thus, for the mines, the steel plant was the internal customer and it would have to ensure that it was procuring good quality iron ore and coal for it; within the plant, the various stages of production would treat the next stage as a customer whose requirements must be met satisfactorily. This internal customer satisfaction, I emphasized repeatedly, was an essential precursor to satisfying the external customer. A lot of my effort was spent on getting departments to talk to each other on various platforms, something that was just not happening.

Another thing that struck me when I joined was that hardly anyone talked about the financial aspect of operations. The finance department was viewed as doing little more than an accounting exercise. The performance of the company was judged only on the basis of production of saleable steel. There was no serious attempt to look at labour productivity, energy consumption and productivity of particular units. It took a lot of effort on my part to bring about an awareness of all these issues within the organization. In the course of the workshops on the *Priorities for Action*, I emphasized the fact that it was important for the public sector to make profits and that we could not keep going to the government with a begging bowl every time we needed money.

I also noticed a complete lack of attention to revenue maximization. This came out starkly in the case of the marketing of by-products. A large number of by-products result in the course of steel manufacture—waste gases from the coal burning process from which chemical products could be extracted, coal tar, benzol, ammonium sulphate and calcium ammonium nitrate apart from steel scrap. These were sold to some other industries (cement companies, for example, bought ammonium sulphate). However, this was not on the radar of the top management. There was no focus on the pricing of these by-products and how they could be used to generate additional revenue. Different plants would sell their by-products at different prices, as a result of which some were getting good prices while the others were not. Some plants had long-term agreements for the sale of these by-products that had been in force for many years, as a result of which they were getting very low prices for them. I started looking closely at this head and ensured that there was some coherent company-wide strategy in the pricing and marketing of these by-products. Even if it did not bring in huge revenues, at least I got people thinking about the cost and revenue potential of each activity.

The annual budget making exercise also underwent a makeover. Earlier, it was just the work of the finance department, which would often take the previous year's figures and increase it by a certain percentage. Now, budget making became an elaborate exercise, in which I would hold budget finalization meetings with unit heads in either Ranchi or Delhi. We would discuss every head—energy, production, costs—unit-wise, and all unit heads had to be involved.

~

When I joined SAIL, I was struck by the complete absence of a customer culture in the organization. Customers were unhappy as the quality of steel was poor, deliveries unpredictable and the costs of inefficiency were passed on to them in the form of higher prices. If any customer dared complain about either quality or delivery time, supplies would be stopped or delayed. This was not surprising. SAIL functioned in a highly protected market. There were only two significant domestic players, and there were curbs on steel imports. Demand was far higher than supply. As a result, SAIL was little more than a distribution agency for steel. There was a Central Marketing Organization (CMO) in Kolkata, headed by the commercial director, which would interact with each plant directly. Though a marketing set-up did exist within the organization, there was no service mindset.

There was also a complete disconnect between the marketing and production departments. Among the first things I had asked S.K. Ahluwalia, the director, commercial, and the head, CMO, to do was to collate information from the market to see what products customers wanted. The study showed a mismatch between the customers' requirements and SAIL's production. The iron and steel controller was, admittedly, partly responsible for this since it dictated what steel plants should produce and when. The steel plants were judged on the basis of the total volume of steel they produced. Therefore, there was a tendency to roll out certain large volume products, even if they were not in line with what the market wanted. In addition, some of these products were turned out once a year, regardless of when customers wanted it. This meant that a customer who wanted a particular product would have to wait till SAIL produced it. This attitude was probably influenced by the Soviet mindset. Some years into my tenure when I mentioned during the course of a lecture in the Soviet Union that SAIL had a 2,000-strong marketing team, it caused quite a stir. People there asked me why a state-owned entity needed a marketing arm at all.

We could have continued with the old mindset, but as in BHEL, I did not believe that being in a near-monopoly market gave any company the right to treat customers shoddily. My attempt to make SAIL a customer-oriented organization had two strands. The first was fighting the control regime represented by the JPC and the iron and steel controller. In fact, it was when addressing the marketing challenges that I had my biggest battles with them. The second was to get the entire organization to see the customer as central to its focus and to strive to meet his every need.

Once, when a representative of Japan's Nippon Steel was visiting, I asked him in the presence of senior managers what the minimum quantity was that it would supply to a customer. I asked this for a reason. SAIL would supply only a minimum quantity of 10 or 20 tonnes of steel, whereas small entrepreneurs required only two or less tonnes a month. So they were forced to buy these large quantities and run up huge inventory bills. The Nippon Steel executive was a little surprised at my question and said that even if a customer wanted one plate, the company supplied that. This was my way of educating SAIL executives that the success of any business depended on how efficiently it can give the consumer what he wants. I also showed that SAIL was not afraid of competition by arguing for reducing the customs duty on steel so that customers had a bigger choice of suppliers. This, needless to say, did not endear me to other steel manufacturers.

Just as I had met everyone across the length and breadth of SAIL to understand the organization's problems, I decided to interact directly with the customer as well to understand what they expected of SAIL. Regional customer meetings were organized in Chennai, Mumbai and Kolkata. In addition, I also visited warehouses and branch offices, where I met with branch sales officials. Based on the feedback received, I went about attempting to change the distribution mindset to a marketing mindset.

I set out three principles of marketing for SAIL. One, SAIL would absorb all costs that were within its control. Two, it would commit and maintain delivery schedules or pay a penalty. Three, SAIL should replace any supply if there were any complaints about quality. The steel sector was far from being deregulated at that time and we could have continued with the old mindset, but I was preparing the organization for life after decontrol.

Some of these measures required closer and constant interaction between the marketing and production departments. To this end, some managers in all regional centres were put in charge of market intelligence services. Their job was to understand the market and predict future trends by collating information on the products the market wanted, the grades of the products, the competitors in these products and the price. This was sent to the headquarters where the information was compiled and sent to the plants every month so that they could plan production on that basis and be more in tune with the market. We also started holding marketing meetings at plants so that the production department, the marketing department and the customers could understand each other's problems better.

Though the price of steel was controlled (only 30 per cent of products were out of this regime) and the government delayed price increases in the name of helping user industries, customers believed that steel manufacturers were passing on the cost of their inefficiencies to them. This was not an entirely wrong perception. So, even as the steel ministry was lobbying for a price increase on the grounds that SAIL needed that to survive, I made a public commitment that we would not raise prices for three years unless the cost of rail freight, coal and power, excise duties and development funds (none of which were in the company's control) were increased. Even then, the price increase would be only to the extent that the prices of these heads of expenditure increased. SAIL, I said, would absorb all operational costs that were within its control—raw materials, wages and other overheads. Having made this commitment, I did not have to keep running to the JPC or BICP for price hikes. SAIL stuck to this promise. Profits in 1986-87 dropped in spite of many improvements because we did not revise prices for two years in a row despite increases in the prices of coal, power, transportation, cess and levies since the previous price revision in 1985. When wages were revised in 1989, the costs were not passed on to the customer but were absorbed by SAIL through higher productivity.

I remember addressing a CII meeting on steel and telling all the assembled persons—representatives from the user industries—about the customer-friendly steps SAIL had taken, including capping prices for three years. There was all round appreciation by the captains of the user industries, and they publicly accepted that these steps were the best that could have been taken at that time. At the end of my presentation, I pointed out that 40 per cent of SAIL's inputs—castings, forgings, spare parts and the like—came from them. Could SAIL, I asked them, expect a reciprocal gesture—that they would not increase their prices except under similar circumstances? They were silent and could not give such an assurance. I realized I had scored a point over them, and thereafter they stopped complaining about SAIL passing on its inefficiencies to them. Once more, the public sector was one up on the private sector.

The control regime prevented SAIL from getting into long-term agreements with customers. As a result, buying steel became very much like buying vegetables for daily use—customers had to take whatever was available with little assurance of when the products they wanted would be available. So a bicycle manufacturer, for example, could not be assured that it would get enough supplies of steel to produce a certain quantity of cycles a month. Long-term contracts between vendors and the consuming industry was a very basic business practice, and so, ignoring the JPC and the Iron and Steel Controller, I told the CMO to go ahead and enter into long-term contracts with customers. There were protests from the iron and steel controller's office, but I ignored them.

Delayed delivery was another problem that customers were worked up about. I was very shocked to learn that the work order issued by Tata Steel had a line: 'Time is not the essence of the contract'. SAIL may not have said so explicitly, but there were huge delays in deliveries of supplies. A time-bound supply scheme was started in 1985, under which SAIL would commit to supply a certain percentage of the requirement within a certain time schedule. In case of any delay, it would pay a penalty of 3.5 per cent to 4 per cent of the value of the undelivered portion. Tata Steel was again very upset with me and Mody thought I was doing things that would kill the steel industry. But so appreciative were the customers of this gesture that in one case, a Chennai-based customer producing large machinery, KCP, returned the cheque bearing the penalty payment, saying this gesture was good enough and that he did not want the money.

The customer also needed to get a good quality product, conforming to the specifications mentioned in the purchase order. But this often did not happen. I made it clear that if a customer had any complaint about the quality of a product, it should either be replaced or the cost refunded. Once there was a complaint about the quality of a rake of cold-rolled coils sent to Godrej Boyce from the Bokaro Steel Plant. I ordered the entire rake to be brought back. A complaint register used to be maintained earlier, but we found it was full of unresolved complaints. I now insisted that all products returned because of complaints of quality be shipped back to the plants they came from and the managing directors asked to explain why they were manufactured and supplied in the first place.

In 1986, we started the demand registration system wherein whenever a customer raised a demand for a particular product, it would be registered and a time frame for supply indicated. After that, the onus was on the marketing and production departments to ensure that the customer got what he wanted in time, and not on the customer to keep checking whether the product was available. The order had to be built into the monthly production plan of the plant that was to supply that item. This marketing MIS (management information system) was something I insisted on. It had to be sent to the plants on a regular basis to ensure coordinated working between the marketing and production departments. I believed that the problem of timely delivery was not that of the marketing department alone. Once a commitment had been made, the entire organization had to work backwards to ensure that the requirement was built into the monthly production plan of the plant that was to supply that item.

One method of efficiently serving the small entrepreneurs, to whom SAIL could not supply in the smaller quantities they needed, was to start Steel Service Centres. These centres would buy steel in bulk from SAIL and then supply in smaller quantities or in different shapes to customers for a fee, depending on demand. This satisfied the needs of both SAIL and the customers who did not mind paying a small fee as long as they were assured of the type and quantity of product they needed. I believed that it was best to leave the service centres to be run by the private sector. Mahindra Ugine, a division of Mahindra & Mahindra, was the first company to set up a Steel Service Centre. There was a huge hue and cry over this and SAIL was accused of violating the steel control order, which stated that

SAIL could supply only to the end customer and not to any intermediary. People warned that Mahindra Ugine would hoard the steel and then sell it at a much higher price. It was another matter that unofficial intermediaries did exist, doing precisely what we were warned Mahindra Ugine would do. They would buy steel at the controlled price, pretending to be the end customer and then hoard it to sell later at a premium. Much of the opposition to the Steel Service Centres came from these sub-brokers, as they were called. Nevertheless, I felt that this was the best way of serving the small entrepreneur. However, this concept was not enthusiastically pursued by my successors.

The steel market in India faced a very paradoxical situation. While on the one hand there was a demand-supply gap, India also had the lowest per capita steel consumption in the world. What was completely missing from the entire marketing effort of the steel industry was promoting the use of steel or doing any extension activity to popularize its use. Apart from catering to the needs of small and niche customers, the Steel Service Centres were also meant to act as extension centres to show the different ways in which steel could be used. Within the CMO, I set up a technical services group which would advise customers on the use of steel and also issues related to quality. I also got the customers and the manufacturing group to interact more closely and even started plant visits by customers to help the production side understand customer needs better.

But how would it be possible to popularize the use of steel if the commodity itself was hard to get? We could supply only in bulk and not small quantities and only to the end customer and only at certain times. On top of all the restrictions on how much steel we could sell and when, there was the problem of inadequate stockyards. There were just fifty throughout the country. Dealing with these extremely ill-equipped stockyards was a trial by itself for customers. Customers would send trucks to pick up their orders but find that supplies had not reached and would get no assurance on when to come next since there was a woeful lack of communication between the production centres and the stockyards. Because of the lack of cranes and other facilities, loading of supplies would take inordinately long and trucks would line up outside the stockyards. Supplies would be released only between 10 a.m. and 2 p.m., so trucks that did not get their supplies would have to wait till the next day.

We then worked out a stockyard modernization programme. One component related to putting up better handling facilities so that the turnaround time of trucks that came to take deliveries was reduced and there was no congestion outside stockyards. Another important investment was in computerization and a wireless communication network linking all the plants and stockyards with each other so that the movement of wagons bearing supplies could be tracked. The computerization helped every branch manager know what product was available in which warehouse and in what quantity. After that, it was all about training people in a different customer-oriented mindset. Earlier, if a customer went to a stockyard in, say, Ahmedabad and his order had not been delivered, the person in charge of that stockyard thought his job ended with giving the customer this piece of information. Now the manager was obliged to check with other stockyards if the product was available with them and then give the customer the flexibility of either picking it up from the other stockyard or getting it for him from there. Stockyards were also told to service customers till 5 p.m. instead of just 2 p.m. as was the case earlier.

For the marketing department my initiatives were welcome (though there was a lot of scepticism about whether they would succeed), but the production department wondered about my strong emphasis on company discipline when we were operating in a seller's market. To all of them, my answer was that soon the political economy in India would change, bringing severe competition both from domestic and foreign manufacturers, and if this discipline was not introduced now, SAIL would fold up. It required a lot of explaining and reasoning to bring about a change in mindset. But nobody derailed any of my initiatives because of my conviction that these were the right things to do.

~

Even as I was dealing with issues relating to modernization of the mind, I started to plan for SAIL's technological modernization. The plants were obsolete by global standards and we needed to address this urgently. Modernization of the plants was vital if SAIL was to achieve the production of 15 million tonnes of saleable steel that we had envisaged. Accordingly, a Technology Plan was drawn up and a Technology Committee set up to oversee the modernization programme, which covered revamping old equipment, upgrading technology and reducing energy consumption, and the introduction of new processes. It was proposed to take up the modernization of the Durgapur, Rourkela and Burnpur steel plants in the first phase and the Bhilai and Bokaro plants in the second phase as their performance was comparatively better. The modernization of the Durgapur and Rourkela plants as well as some other smaller projects was estimated to cost Rs 10,000 crore.

But the modernization plan ran into a wall of opposition from the Planning Commission and the Public Investment Board. The internal rate of return (IRR) of the Durgapur modernization project was estimated at 8.10 per cent, which was far less than the 12 per cent which was expected by the government. But I argued that this was only a financial IRR and got an economic IRR worked out. It showed that the benefits to the economy in the form of lower foreign exchange outgo on imports and higher job generation would be much more.

After finalizing the details of each modernization programme, I focussed my attention on the mode of implementation. I insisted that these projects should be done on a turnkey basis—the agency implementing it would have to take the responsibility of all parts of the modernization work as well as the final test performance. This was how the steel plants were initially constructed and perhaps that is why they got completed within three years. Since then, not a single modernization or expansion programme had been completed on time. This had happened because the work was parcelled out between different agencies—mainly the public sector MECON and the private sector M.N. Dastur and Co—leaving SAIL to put it all together. As a result, companies that supplied close to 70 per cent of the equipment got away without any overall responsibility, either for timely completion of the project or for the final results.

The turnkey modernization that I envisaged made one agency responsible for the entire programme—from sourcing equipment to installing it and then establishing the performance before handing it over to SAIL. This did involve a slightly higher cost, but I believed it was worth paying 10 per cent extra if this could cut out delays and provide an assurance of proper performance. Durgapur (which was the first plant to be taken up) was the first to adopt this turnkey method, followed by Rourkela. This, however, angered those who had benefited from the earlier arrangement, and they got back at me later when the government changed.

I also had to deal with a campaign that all equipment required for the modernization project should be sourced from industry in and around Durgapur. This campaign had been instigated by the director of the public sector Central Mechanical Engineering Research Institute (CMERI), A. Gopalakrishnan, though he was not connected with SAIL or the modernization project in any way. This demand was impractical and would have imperilled the entire modernization project, but the fact that the director of a public sector company was raising this demand gave it more credibility than it should have got. Soon, it became a highly emotive issue, and some junior ministers in the Left Front government in West Bengal lent their voices to it.

I was apprehensive that this issue would snowball into a major controversy and so I sought an appointment with then chief minister Jyoti Basu. He called the junior ministers and the local leaders to the meeting, to which I took Debu Mukherjee along. We explained the various steps we had taken to modernize the plant and how the demands being raised had the potential to derail the project. I also used an emotional pitch, highlighting the larger benefits of the modernization programme and how it would resurrect Durgapur's reputation as a reasonable place for industrialization. Basu heard us out and then addressed the detractors: 'Here is a man who is not from the state and is trying to improve the image of Durgapur. If you can't help him, at least don't hinder what he is doing.' After that, there were no objections.

The modernization programme, however, almost got derailed for another reason. The Durgapur plant had been built through collaboration with a British consortium. SAIL did not have any construction drawings or technical or technological information available. So the natural choice was to go back to the British industry for assistance. MECON had already prepared the specifications and the essential items of the modernization programme. I was not very satisfied with this, but there was no time to waste. I put it down in a written note that the modernization plan that I was executing was not complete and that a lot more investment and downstream activities were required but that I am proceeding with the project that had already been conceived by MECON.

Steel secretary R.P. Khosla and I approached the British government and, through it, met the British steel industry. After around six months of discussions, we were close to finalizing a package that would allow the British consortium to once again collaborate on the plant. The British government was also prepared to give whatever financial assistance was required. All these negotiations were happening at the level of officials.

Around this time, Rajiv Gandhi was in Durgapur on a political visit and wanted to stay in the SAIL guest house. I was asked to be there as well. After the political event, he asked me to see him in his room in the evening, and we spent three hours discussing a range of topics. I then invited him to see the plant the next morning and said I wanted to discuss some matters with him along with the managing director of the plant.

Next morning, I discussed the plant modernization plan with him and asked if he was okay with us collaborating with the British on this. Since the project involved some government-to-government transactions, I wanted to be sure that it would get political backing. He heard me patiently and then asked, 'How soon do you want a reply?' I said as soon as possible since I did not want the momentum of the programme to be affected. He said he would let me know in Delhi. He then planted a sapling and left.

Exactly a week later, he sent for me and Pant. He said the answer to my question was both 'yes' and 'no'. 'Yes' to the modernization plan but 'no' to collaborating with the British. 'Think of an alternative,' he said. He said that the logic behind asking the British industry to help was sound but that the Indian and British governments had strong political differences over the issue of curbing the Khalistani movement in Britain. 'If at this point news comes out that a large industrial project has been given to the British government on a negotiated basis, it would send out a wrong message.' I kept silent for a moment, wondering how I was going to get out of this mess. But all I said was, 'Leave it to me.'

Fortunately, while negotiating with the British, we at SAIL had simultaneously been in touch with the Soviet Union and the German industry for the Rourkela modernization programme. I immediately picked up the threads with them for Durgapur as well. But neither had the capability of taking up the entire modernization of the Durgapur plant. The Soviets were good up to the iron-making stage, while the Germans were suitable for the steel making stage. So we divided the Durgapur package into two and within the next two months finalized a programme with a consortium of German and Soviet firms. It was all done so quickly that even within the organization people were gasping for breath. We wriggled out of the British collaboration by citing some technical excuses. To date, only Pant and I know the real reason why SAIL did not go with the British for the Durgapur modernization.

While I managed to get all the clearances for the Durgapur and Rourkela modernization plans and get the work started, it is my lasting regret that I could take the modernization of the Indian Iron and Steel Co (IISCO) plant at Burnpur only up to the penultimate stage.

IISCO is one of the two plants of the pre-independence era and was nationalized in 1972 during Mrs Gandhi's time. The purpose of nationalization was to modernize and develop the plant by infusing it with government funds. However, successive governments could not accomplish this task, and at the time I took over the chairmanship of SAIL, the plant was in an extremely bad shape, producing less than half a million tonnes of steel annually. In his initial interactions with me on SAIL, Rajiv Gandhi had even suggested that I close down the plant. After two visits, I thought it would not be in the national interest to close the plant, since it had enormous locational advantages on account of being in the vicinity of coal and iron mines and close to the industrial belt of Kolkata/Howrah. Besides, it had a highly trained and experienced workforce of 30,000 working in a most difficult environment.

We had to find a suitable collaborator for the modernization. While reading up on the plant, I learnt that the Japanese used to have a 30 per cent stake in IISCO just before the Second World War. In fact, the Japanese learnt steel making in Burnpur. During the War, the Japanese shareholding was declared as 'enemy property' and later Sir Biren Mukherjee, the industrialist who had a significant share in the company, gradually increased his stake in the company till the Japanese stake came down to 7 per cent. The Japanese finally encashed their share and left.

Armed with this information, I decided to approach the Japanese to collaborate on the project. The Japanese steel industry was one of the lowest cost steel producers in the world at that time. I told the Japanese steel makers that they had learnt the art of steel making here and that it was time for them to pay back. The Japanese agreed but said they would not be able to provide any funds or credit. On the other hand, the Indian government also said it could not provide money for this.

I was caught in a bind. Then I came to know that the Japanese had refused concessional credit because steel was not considered an infrastructure industry in their country. I went to Japan along with steel ministry officials and met practically everyone who mattered in the Japanese government, arguing that steel was an infrastructure industry in India. Finally, they agreed to give funds in the form of export credit.

The Japanese International Cooperation Agency (JICA) submitted a feasibility report, on the basis of which the government gave in-principle clearance for the modernization programme and sanctioned Rs 30 crore for the preparation of the detailed project report, which suggested that it would be best to almost completely scrap and rebuild the plant.

We now had to find the right collaborators. I found that different Japanese steel companies were good in different bits of technology and that it was beyond any one of them to undertake the entire modernization programme. So I asked five Japanese companies—Nippon Steel, NKK Steel, Kobe Steel, Sumitomo and Mitsubishi—to form a consortium and told them that whatever they spent on the modernization would be returned to them in the form of 25 per cent of the steel produced. Thus, we would have paid for all their goods and services through partial export of steel produced in IISCO within a period of ten years. There could not have been a better arrangement, and the Japanese companies agreed to form a consortium. It would have been the second landmark Indo-Japanese collaboration project in the public sector after Maruti.

An agreement was signed with the consortium in November 1988 for engineering services for modernization. The consortium worked out a basic engineering report on the basis of which SAIL submitted a modernization plan with an estimated cost of Rs 6,030 crore in September 1989. Unfortunately, just as we were moving into the final negotiations, the Congress lost the 1989 elections, and Rajiv Gandhi ceased to be prime minister. That changed everything.

The new government, headed by V.P. Singh, began looking into all decisions taken when Rajiv Gandhi was in power. The National Front government had been elected on an anti-corruption plank following the Bofors and HDW submarine scandals, and it was sure that there were more skeletons to be unearthed. My closeness to Rajiv Gandhi only strengthened their suspicions that SAIL had been used to make money for the Congress or Rajiv Gandhi himself. These suspicions were, no doubt, fuelled by those whom I had cut out of the modernization programme by opting for turnkey implementation. Perhaps the sudden cancellation of the plan for British collaboration for the Durgapur modernization added to this, since the real reason was not known to anyone. The government looked into every paper related to the modernization programme and raised a host of objections, including the decision to opt for turnkey implementation. They tried hard to find some evidence to implicate me in wrongdoing but could not.

The new steel minister, Dinesh Goswami, said he would not allow the Burnpur modernization project to go through because it was negotiated by me during Rajiv Gandhi's time. I told him point blank that if he felt that this was an underhand deal, he could negotiate the deal himself as there was still time, but he should let the project go through. But he refused to listen. There were some people at that time who were feeding him ideas that there were alternative methods of rebuilding the IISCO plant. In January 1990, the government commissioned M.N. Dastur to carry out a cost reduction study. The study suggested an alternative method of rebuilding the IISCO plant. Had any of the new alternatives suggested to the minister materialized later, I would have been happy. Unfortunately, the IISCO plant continued to languish with old technology for the next fifteen years and more.

The only lasting regret I have about my stint in SAIL is that I was unable to push the Burnpur modernization programme and close it while Rajiv Gandhi was in power. A project that would have put SAIL on a different growth path and galvanized the Indian steel industry was stalled for petty political reasons. It was the country which lost.

~

A little over two years after *Priorities for Action* was drawn up, I got another document prepared, one that would take stock of how much we had achieved and what more needed to be done. While *Priorities for Action* had refrained from adopting a critical tone, the twenty-page *The Unfinished Agenda* issued in September 1988 did not pull any punches. While it did pat the organization on the substantial progress it had made on several fronts—better capacity utilization, reduction in energy costs, improved customer service, to name a few—it was, at the same time, very blunt on the continuing problems in four broad areas—organizational culture, production and productivity, marketing and customer service, and finance and budgetary control.

It pointed out that absenteeism had not come down to desired levels (and that it was high among senior staff and executives), overtime work continued (though at very reduced levels), that the cutting down of reporting levels to reduce red tape had remained only on paper. Other problem areas were highlighted—production continuing to be low in the first quarter, schedules for capital repairs not being maintained, and poor management of working capital, among other things. It then sounded a warning about ignoring the imperatives that were set out:

> 'One thing is clear. We cannot afford to go back. Nor can we stay where we are. SAIL has to move forward—and that too quickly. All round, competition is increasing. New and small units are coming up with the latest in technologies and higher standards of quality and productivity. Internally, we must gear up to meet this challenge. Complacency will only mean that we will be left out of the race.'

By this time I was into my fourth year in SAIL—well beyond the two years Rajiv Gandhi had initially said I would be there (although in every discussion he would talk to me as if it was a lifetime assignment). When I was about to complete two years, I had thought I would be relieved of this assignment. However, the government had no such intention. At the instance of the prime minister, the cabinet secretary suggested I should continue for another three years. The task before me was incomplete and challenging at the same time. I myself did not want to leave SAIL at this stage. Hence I agreed to continue.

But by 1989, I was preparing to end my stint. I had the satisfaction of knowing that SAIL had turned around. It had been making profits steadily since 1985, clocking profits of Rs 302 crore in 1988-89. But I knew a lot more still remained to be done. The organization needed a smooth succession, and I wanted to hand over charge to someone who would have the confidence of the majority of the employees, as I had done in the case of BHEL and Maruti. So I commissioned an internal survey, covering 25,000 employees, comprising half of the senior to middle level executives, a random sample of the rest and key stakeholders like the trade unions. Called *Agenda for Tomorrow*, the survey posed three questions: what they believe should be SAIL's agenda for the next five years (1990-95); who, if any, in their opinion is best equipped to lead them; what they value most in the current top management; and what they wanted the management to do in the future.

The survey received 20,000 responses and, to my embarrassment, the majority of the responses endorsed all that I had done, suggested that the same path should be followed and doubted whether anyone in the organization could carry the legacy forward. It did not come out with any new ideas that could be followed up. To date I have not talked about this survey, let alone publicize it. It could have been seen as a self-promotion exercise to further consolidate my hold on SAIL.

In any case, a few months after the survey, my stint at SAIL came to an abrupt end. Relations between me and the V.P. Singh government became worse by the day and finally, in March 1990, I resigned. My term was to end on 15 May 1990, and I said I wanted to go to the United States on a private visit and would like to hand over charge on my return. But Goswami said there was little sense in this and that I should be relieved before I proceeded to the United States. So by the end of March, I handed over charge and left. I was sad at the way it ended, but I also had enormous satisfaction that I had fulfilled the responsibilities I was given. More than that, I carried the good wishes of over 2,00,000 employees. Even now, twenty years after leaving SAIL, many of my experiments are considered unique and have not been surpassed. The period 1985-90 is still considered the golden era in SAIL's history.

One of the criticisms levelled against me was that my ambitious Rs 15,000 crore modernization programme would burden SAIL financially. But if modernization had not been conceived at that time and work had not started, the organization would not have been able to survive. There was no financial burden on SAIL as the investment was economically very sound and made the plants more competitive. What was seen as a lost cause in 1985 had become a model institution by 1989. When steel was finally decontrolled in 1992, SAIL was better prepared for competition than Tata Steel as a result of this modernization of mind and machine.

A committee to select the 'Steel Man of the Year' in 1989 chose me and SAIL, much to my embarrassment, as it found that SAIL's performance under my leadership was much better on all parameters than that of Tata Steel led by Mody at that time. However, at my insistence, the jury headed by R.P. Khosla modified this decision and gave the award jointly to Mody and me. I did this because Tata Steel and Mody had done equally well and deserved the recognition. I greatly cherish this award as well as the Tata Gold Medal for service to the metallurgical industry, awarded by the Institute of Metals, and the Sir Jahangir Gandhi Medal for Industrial Peace.

Above all, for my work in the public sector, the President of India conferred the Padma Bhushan on me in 1986. I was awarded the 'Businessman of the Year' in 1987 by *Business India* magazine for my work in SAIL. In recognition of my services to the metallurgical industry, The Benaras Hindu University conferred on me 'The Doctor of Sciences'.

# 7

# A LIFE WELL SPENT

I left SAIL with mixed feelings—satisfaction and sadness. Satisfaction that I had put an ailing organization well on the road to good health. Sadness that the new government did not seem to believe in the need to continue with the policies and programmes I had initiated. So vitiated was the atmosphere that the government was determined to undo all that had been done during Rajiv Gandhi's time. SAIL became the hapless victim of the belief that anything that was done during my stint was meant to benefit Rajiv Gandhi personally. As a result, there was no attempt to even try and understand the larger philosophy behind my policies and actions, let alone these being followed up.

After leaving SAIL, I concentrated on mentoring my two sons, Chandra and Jayakar, who had by then established their own businesses. I also continued my association with Rajiv Gandhi, which deepened as time passed. When I was in Maruti and he was just an MP, I used to meet him regularly to brief him on developments relating to the car project. Once he became prime minister, these meetings became fewer, although he kept me informed about all important matters relating to both Maruti and SAIL, and I always knew that he was just a phone call away if I needed any help. He used to have informal meetings—sometimes over breakfast, sometimes at his office—with economists, scientists and other technocrats, and I was invited to practically all of them. Occasionally, he would use me as a sounding board for ideas that occurred to him. His confidence level in me was so high that when he took a decision to set up the Technology Information Forecasting and Assessment Council (TIFAC), he insisted on making me the chairman, with Sam Pitroda, Vasanth Gowarikar, A.P.J. Abdul Kalam, V.S. Arunachalam, M.M. Sharma and Y.S. Rajan, among others, as members. It was set up as a prestigious council to take stock of the status of the technology prevalent in Indian industry, forecast the technological needs of the country and to suggest ways and means of achieving those targets. I headed this council for three years until Kalam took over in 1992.

I always remember Rajiv Gandhi as someone with an enquiring mind, bubbling with ideas and always open to different perspectives. Both of us thoroughly enjoyed the long discussions we used to have. When he was prime minister, I had, from time to time, expressed my frustration over delayed decisions on several matters like public sector reforms and liberalization of the economy. He said he was eager to get this going but convincing his senior colleagues was taking time. Then the general elections of 1989 were announced, and he wanted to wait until he got re-elected to get the reforms going.

A few weeks after the 1989 elections, which the Congress lost, I met Rajiv Gandhi at a dinner at the Japanese ambassador's residence. In the course of our conversation, I told him that his entry into politics and his becoming prime minister were the results of accidents—one that took his brother's life and another that took his mother's. The first three years of his tenure as prime minister were filled with euphoria; the next two were spent in fire-fighting as a series of corruption allegations were levelled against his government and him personally. There was hardly any time for him to think about and form his vision of India and articulate it as an overarching philosophy of governance. I pointed out that he would become prime minister again in either five months (since the National Front government was a shaky coalition) or five years, and this was the time for him to formulate his vision and set it out, just like his grandfather and mother had.

He seemed to have taken my advice seriously because, after this conversation, he took to visiting me often at my residence on Pandara Road and discussing a range of topics with me. On his suggestion, I gathered groups of business leaders and opinion setters to meet and discuss issues quietly at my residence. I could see that he was serious about getting acquainted with the issues facing the nation. Following objections from his security personnel, these interactions later moved to his residence at 10 Janpath. Initially, only Sam Pitroda and I were present at these meetings. Gradually, we drew in experts from other fields—A.N. Khusro on agriculture, General K.V. Krishna Rao on security and M.K. Rasgotra on foreign policy and foreign economic relations. The discussions revolved around accelerating economic growth through liberalization, increasing employment opportunities, improving internal security, raising the technological status of the Indian industry and the means to integrate the Indian economy with the world economy. As a set of professionals, our emphasis was on moving government policies in the direction of what was good for the nation's development rather than being unduly mindful of vote bank politics. Rajiv Gandhi publicly called this group his 'think tank', and I acted as its convenor. We would meet regularly and would have brainstorming sessions with him as well. These sessions would usually start at 10 p.m., after he had finished all his other work so that he could give us his undivided attention, and would go on till the early hours of morning.

Fortunately for us, he reacted very positively to most of our suggestions and brief reports on different subjects given to him. Moreover, he was not satisfied with educating himself but also wanted us to sensitize the Congress to the new ideas we put forth. Accordingly, we would meet groups of Congress MPs on the lawns of the late Madhav Rao Scindia's Safdarjung Road residence and explain to them the rationale behind our new ideas and try to inculcate new ways of thinking.

When the 1991 elections were announced, Rajiv Gandhi wanted us to be involved in the drafting of the Congress manifesto. There were two ways of doing this. One was to get the party leaders to draft a document which we would modify. But that would have created resentment and so he asked Pitroda and me to set out an outline of the ideas we had discussed, approved it and then passed it on to the party. P.V. Narasimha Rao, who was involved in drafting the manifesto, did not like some of these reformist ideas. He thought they were too drastic and would result in the Congress losing its traditional support base to other socialist and leftist parties. He also did not like a bunch of non-politician professionals being involved in the party's policy formulation. But Rajiv Gandhi overruled him and retained most of our suggestions as part of the party manifesto for the elections. Later, after Rajiv Gandhi's assassination, when Manmohan Singh became the finance minister in the Congress government formed after the 1991 elections, he publicly acknowledged that he would not have been able to open up the economy if Rajiv Gandhi had not incorporated the think tank's suggestions in the party manifesto.

Rajiv Gandhi's assassination was a blow to me personally. We had shared a very good rapport and held each other in great regard. For the nation, too, it was a great loss. He was serious about rectifying whatever weaknesses he earlier had and had worked hard during the brief time he was out of power. I had no doubt that he would have made an outstanding prime minister the second time round. But that was not to be.

The 'think tank' got disbanded following Rajiv Gandhi's death. When Narasimha Rao became prime minster, I knew I would have little to do in Delhi. I did not share a great equation with him. He thought I was overrated and believed that accepting my suggestions or those of the 'think tank' would reduce the accountability of the elected ministers to parliament. I, too, did not hold him in high regard as a leader. In addition, I unwittingly gave cause for him to actively dislike me.

Shortly after Rajiv Gandhi's death, to ensure that his ideas were carried forward, on our own initiative, Pitroda and I wrote a note for discussion on what should be the attributes of the next prime minister from the Congress if it returned to power in the 1991 elections. We circulated it among a select few who were close to Rajiv Gandhi. The note discussed a number of people who were prominent leaders of the party. It clearly zeroed in on Scindia, since it spoke about the need for someone who was young, did not come with an ideological baggage and had a mystique about him (which Scindia did, given his royal background). We had meetings with Scindia regarding this, but he said he would enter the fray only if Sonia Gandhi proposed his name. We, however, had no intention of disturbing her in her time of grief and we had no means of knowing her mind. That note stressed the need for a young prime minister who could, among other things, actively engage with the international community. The stress on a young prime minister did not go down well with many of the senior and older Congress leaders who were aspiring to be prime minister. Narasimha Rao, who was a frontrunner for the post, was also not in the best of health and was, therefore, very wary of me and Pitroda after we circulated this note. Eventually, he was nominated as the leader of the party.

Given this background, I was planning to return to Chennai. When I left SAIL in 1990, I had intended to set up my own business. I had picked up stakes in a few small enterprises which were on the verge of closure, with the intention of trying to revive them. My sons and I had also set up an organization called Bharat Technologies, with the objective of nurturing and propagating a lot of technologies developed indigenously in the pursuit of self-sufficiency. I had observed the fact that we had a tendency to create assets but did not know how to manage them and get value out of them. Through Bharat Technologies, I wanted to show how this could be done. But with Rajiv Gandhi pulling me into the think tank, there had been little time to do it. I now decided to focus on this. But fate had something else in store for me.

Narasimha Rao appointed Pranab Mukherjee as deputy chairman of the Planning Commission. Before Rajiv Gandhi's assassination, Mukherjee used to be the interface between us in the think tank and the party and guided me on the political implications of the reform ideas of the think tank. He asked me to become a member in the Planning Commission. I was reluctant, given the equation between Narasimha Rao and me. So I suggested two other names instead—M. Narasimham, former governor of the Reserve Bank of India and former finance secretary, and Verghese Kurien, the father of India's milk revolution. Both, however, declined to accept. Mukherjee once again asked me to join. He said he needed a professional like me to support him in the Planning Commission. This might have been influenced by the fact that Rajiv Gandhi had made it known to a select few that, when the Congress returned to power, I would be designated as the person in charge of re-orienting the industrial policy and integrating the Indian economy with the world economy. Despite my doubts as to whether I would be a success in the new government, I agreed to Mukherjee's request. I was appointed member for industry and energy in the Planning Commission.

I could sense the discomfiture of the prime minister and his advisors—notably P.C. Alexander, who was advising him on an informal basis, and A.N. Varma, who was principal secretary to the prime minister. Neither of them liked me.

When Narasimham was appointed to head a committee on banking reforms and he wanted me as a member, the request was turned down. When Manmohan Singh wanted me to head the newly set up Foreign Investment Promotion Board (FIPB), the file remained with the PMO for some weeks and then Varma was made the head. Though I was handling the industry and energy portfolios in the Planning Commission, I was not fully taken into confidence on these matters. Whenever I made suggestions, they were well received by Manmohan Singh in the finance ministry but got stalled in the PMO. I, too, perhaps fuelled the uneasiness in the PMO. At one meeting in the Planning Commission, I was openly critical of the fact that Narasimha Rao did not appoint an industry minister and kept the portfolio with himself. I pointed out that given the lack of time, the PMO became the de facto industry ministry and that this was not the way to handle such an important portfolio at that critical juncture when major changes were effected in the policy framework.

I also favoured a more cautious approach to the privatization of power generation. Instead of signing a large number of MoUs, which was what the government was doing, I suggested taking up five experimental projects in selected locations, debugging any problems that might arise during their implementation and making them a success, instead of merely approving projects on paper. I also wanted BHEL and NTPC to be involved in the privatization programme, taking 40 per cent equity in the new ventures. These views were not given adequate consideration.

Pranab Mukherjee asked me to prepare a plan for restructuring the Planning Commission, which had over the years become unwieldy and somewhat dysfunctional. Many important subjects were dealt with by a multiplicity of members and the views expressed were fragmented. This affected sectors like education, industry, agriculture, etc. Long-term planning at the national level demanded a more integrated picture. Keeping this in view, I had suggested the division of the commission's work among five members, ensuring that one member dealt with all issues relating to a single subject. For example, a single member dealt with agriculture and rural development, another with education including science and technology and training, etc. Unfortunately, the report did not come up for any serious discussion or implementation. I hope this gets done some day.

Another important policy decision taken by me was to meter the power supplied to agriculture pump sets and enforce a minimum tariff of 50 paise per unit. At that time, there was no method of knowing how much energy was used for agricultural purposes and how much was lost on account of theft. The procedure suggested by me, with the support of then finance minister Manmohan Singh, would have given an accurate picture of the pattern and the quantum of power used for agriculture. Although this policy statement was issued during my term, state governments subsequently discontinued the practice for political considerations. Even now, I believe that if this had been diligently implemented, the finances of state electricity boards would have been far better today.

In all my suggestions, I was only being my outspoken self and had no ulterior motive. But this was not understood by those who resented me. Perhaps the last straw for Narasimha Rao and his aides was my criticism of the manner in which the shares of public sector undertakings were bundled and disinvested and Maruti transferred to SMC in a non-transparent manner. I questioned the procedure of disinvestment which resulted in the shares of some of the good companies being sold off without considering their real worth. A Rs 10 share of BHEL, for example, was sold for Rs 27, at a time when the share of BHEL's competitor Larsen & Toubro was selling at over Rs 100. Similarly, a Rs 10 share of SAIL was sold at Rs 11 per share which, I felt, did not represent the real strength of SAIL. Still worse, a Rs 100 share of Maruti was sold for Rs 269 when even the shares of Hindustan Motors were selling several times higher. The public never got to know the per share value assigned to each public sector company since the shares were sold in bundled lots and only the overall realization figure revealed.

After the first tranche of shares of several public sector undertakings were sold in this manner, I cautioned the finance minister, Manmohan Singh, and pointed out that there should be more transparency in the whole process so that the per share price of each company could be calculated on the basis of their real worth and not on the basis of their balance sheets. I feared that the decision on PSU disinvestment was taken by people who did not have full knowledge of the real worth of these enterprises. I also wrote to the prime minister, along with A.R. Antulay, who was then chairman of the Committee on Public Undertakings. We raised the matter about the share price and also questioned the wisdom of transferring the shares of Maruti to SMC when it already held 40 per cent equity, and losing control over the most successful public sector undertaking in India at that time. Manmohan Singh was quick to react and set up a committee headed by me, with K.P. Geethakrishnan, finance secretary, and Montek Singh Ahluwalia, economic affairs secretary, as members to look into the procedures for disinvestment and suggest alternative routes.

I was arguing with the government on an intellectual plane,

but some people in the PMO took it personally and, sensing danger, the dirty tricks wing got into action. That was the time the securities scam, of which stockbroker Harshad Mehta was the alleged kingpin, broke. It so happened that Mehta had met me a couple of times to talk about foreign institutional investment (FII) inflows and financial engineering of the stock market, which was a very simplistic way of addressing the foreign exchange problem. He had come to see me in the Planning Commission, and I suggested that he meet C. Rangarajan, who was also a member and looking after these matters. Rangarajan was tied up that day and Mehta wanted to speak to someone in the government before his scheduled return to Mumbai the same day. I, therefore, introduced Mehta to Geethakrishnan on the phone and suggested he meet Mehta and listen to his ideas.

Quite separately and before all this, Mehta had some business dealings with my sons Chandra and Jayakar. The Central Bank of India held some shares of one of their companies and they wanted to buy them back. Mehta had given one of their companies a loan of Rs 32.74 lakh. It was a normal business transaction—but sufficient ammunition for people out to get me. That I had known and met Mehta was enough to put out reports in the press that I had encouraged him directly or indirectly.

The Opposition was raising a hue and cry over the securities scam largely to prove that the liberalization of the Indian economy was responsible for it. I responded publicly in the press that such incidents were unavoidable in a market-oriented and fast-growing economy and that, instead of breast beating, we should get on with the job by plugging loopholes. Infuriated by the words 'breast beating', George Fernandes wrote to the prime minister complaining about my alleged involvement in the scam and suggested that I and my dealings with Mehta be investigated. Using this letter as an opportunity, the government suggested that I leave the Planning Commission. So in August 1992, I left the government. In the course of investigating Mehta, the CBI 'stumbled upon' the loan he had given to my sons' company. My meeting with Mehta was linked to the loan and quid pro quo was alleged—that I had used my official position to get loans for my sons' company. The Central Bureau of Investigation (CBI) was asked to investigate my role, and I was taken into CBI custody in August 1992.

I was kept in solitary confinement in a two-bedroom apartment for three weeks. No interrogation took place for that entire period. I was not allowed to meet my family. It was a difficult time for us, especially when Chandra was also arrested. Jayakar would have also been arrested but for the fact that he was in the United States at that time. Both Chandra and I had to surrender our passports. So Chandra, who had his professional base in the US, could not travel abroad. And Jayakar, who had his business interests in India, could not return, fearing arrest. As a result, all my sons' business ventures suffered for no fault of theirs. On the one hand, I was confident that I had done nothing wrong and that they would not find anything against me. But that added to my humiliation. A person who has done wrong will not feel humiliated at being jailed. Only an innocent person will. There is an Arab proverb: 'If you want to hurt a person the most, take him to court for a crime he did not commit.' That happened with me and my sons. The harassment continued in the form of raids on all companies owned by my family members.

An immediate fallout of the investigation and arrest was that the report on disinvestment by the committee set up by Manmohan Singh could not be completed, and my strong views against the procedure adopted for share pricing in the disinvestment policy went unrecorded. I am certain that the investigation against me was engineered either to serve as a red herring to the security scam or to scuttle the report due to a fear that my views would have been an indictment of the procedures adopted during disinvestment.

Throughout my career, I had held several responsible positions. For twenty years, I had been the chairman of a public sector undertaking or a secretary to the government. Very often, I had to bend or break rules in order to make BHEL, Maruti or SAIL success stories or to support deserving causes. But at no point of time in my long career had I ever been accused of using my official position for personal advantage nor did I have any 'audit para' on my actions. I could not reconcile myself to the fact that a normal commercial loan transaction between my sons' company and Mehta should be cited as a reason for my indictment by the CBI in court. Having been accused of a corrupt practice, I tried my best to clear my name quickly.

A joint parliamentary committee (JPC) was formed to look into the securities scam. Although Fernandes and the media had made so much noise about my involvement in the scam, the JPC did not summon me. I appeared before it on my own initiative and presented my case. The JPC did not find any of my actions objectionable. My name did not even appear in its final report.

Nevertheless, the CBI took its own time and pursued the case. It took the CBI over seven years to present evidence backing its allegations before the CBI special court. It could not find anything. On 31 July 2000, a little over eight years from the day I was arrested, the judge discharged me, pointing out that there was no case made out against me. The case did not even go into trial, so baseless were the allegations.

Even as this was going on, another case was filed against me to further harass me, this time along with Bhargava. Both of us were charged with abuse of position in getting Maruti to award a contract to supply shock absorbers to Hydraulics Ltd, a Chennai-based company. It was implied that a favour was done to this company as my second son, Jayakar, was married into the family of the promoters. The fact was that Hydraulics was supplying such parts to all other Indian automobile manufacturers and that was the only firm certified by SMC as an acceptable supplier. This case, too, dragged on for seven years, and once again the special court discharged me and Bhargava.

The person who was greatly affected by the CBI harassment was my wife, who sacrificed all her comforts throughout my career to enable me to concentrate only on my job. It was during this difficult time that my wife and I returned to my roots—to Karuveli. I concentrated on fighting to clear my name, on running my own businesses, and on doing service in my village. Throughout this period, I also continued my engagement with Rajiv Gandhi's ideas through the Rajiv Gandhi Foundation and the Rajiv Gandhi Institute of Contemporary Studies led by Sonia Gandhi.

Unfortunately, shortly after these frivolous cases against me and my sons were dismissed and, just as I was looking forward to a peaceful retired life, my wife died.

~

When Rajiv Gandhi was alive, P. Chidambaram, Sam Pitroda and I had discussed with him the idea of setting up an institute in the name of Nehru to undertake studies on contemporary subjects. It was meant to pursue many of the ideas dear to Rajiv Gandhi and also to undertake studies in contemporary issues as well as eventually equip future political leaders. After his assassination, Chidambaram, Pitroda and I floated the idea of setting up a foundation in his name on the lines of what he had discussed with us.

The Rajiv Gandhi Foundation (RGF) was set up in June

1991. The initial trustees, apart from Sonia Gandhi, were Shankar Dayal Sharma, who was the vice-president, Narasimha Rao, Suman Dubey, Amitabh Bachchan, Mani Shankar Aiyar, Pitroda, P. Chidambaram, Montek Singh Ahluwalia, R.P. Goenka and I. Wajahat Habibullah was made the secretary. The Rajiv Gandhi Institute of Contemporary Studies (RGCIS) was set up in 1992 as an adjunct to the foundation. Apart from me, Dubey, Abid Hussain, Abdul Kalam, Y.K. Alagh, Ahluwalia, Chidambaram and some others were appointed to the governing body of RGCIS. While changes were made to the composition of the trustees of RGF over the last twenty years, to the governing board of RGICS and to the executive committee, Chidambaram, Dubey and I continue to be in these two organizations, working with Sonia Gandhi, Rahul Gandhi and Priyanka Gandhi. It was while I was helping frame the management and administrative system of the foundation and institute that my troubles with the government started. Many believed that this was shadow boxing and that I was being warned to stay away from the Gandhi family. When the government announced a Rs 100 crore grant for the RGF, I advised Sonia Gandhi against accepting it, pointing out that it would then become a government foundation. The proposal also attracted trenchant criticism from other political parties. Sonia Gandhi politely declined the grant. I was given hints that the government did not like my advice to her. After my arrest, Sonia Gandhi came under tremendous pressure to drop me from the RGF. She, however, did not and continued to consult me on matters relating to it.

After Habibullah left, Pulok Chatterjee came as secretary of the RGF. Between us, we put the entire budgeting exercise and working style of the organization on a proper footing. Sonia Gandhi later formed an executive committee for the day-to-day functioning of the RGF, of which I was made a member along with Dubey and Chidambaram, and we continue to remain in those roles. Being the only organization with which Sonia Gandhi was connected, it came under close scrutiny to see if there were any irregular or underhand activities. But the affairs of the RGF and RGCIS have been conducted in such a professional manner that there was not a single point on which she could be faulted.

The social programmes initiated by the RGF had far-reaching impact on addressing the problems of the weaker sections of society, including women, children and differently abled people. The research studies initiated by RGICS helped economists, social activists and political leaders get together to discuss subjects of national importance. I was impressed by the objectivity with which decisions were taken by Sonia Gandhi and was happy that I could pursue the ideals of Rajiv Gandhi for the benefit of society.

When Sonia Gandhi became Congress president in 1998 and leader of the Opposition in 1999, she continued to take an active interest in both the RGF and RGICS, and I continued along with her. I would often tell her that while, as Congress president, she could oppose the government's policies and programmes, as leader of the Opposition, she should not merely raise objections but should also articulate her position on issues. Manmohan Singh, Chatterjee—who was officer on special duty to the leader of the Opposition—and I would identify and get experts to brief her on various topics in day-long briefing sessions. The issues ranged from the economy to education, rural development, irrigation and the social sector.

The Congress-led UPA won the general elections in May 2004 under the leadership of Sonia Gandhi. Her transformation into a leader of international stature over the years that I worked with her was indeed remarkable. She got busy with the formation of the government, and I was not sure in what way I could be of continued assistance to her. The executive side was headed by

Manmohan Singh, who had been chosen by her as the prime minister. My association with him was also very close, and I had great respect for him.

It was at this juncture that Chatterjee told me about the setting up of a twelve-member National Advisory Council (NAC) with Sonia Gandhi as chairperson, and that she wanted me to be one of the members. I agreed, and the NAC was formed on 4 June 2004. Within the council, which was mainly focused on social sector issues, I largely confined myself to economic issues, pointing out that economic development and growth were equally important. I argued constantly that wealth creation was as important as subsidies and doles and that there was a need to make people self-reliant by developing their skills. I also helped develop the mechanism of interaction between the NAC and the ministries so as to ensure that the council's recommendations did not remain on paper. It was through this mechanism that we managed to get the Right to Information Act and the National Rural Employment Guarantee Act through the government system.

Two years later, Sonia Gandhi had to resign following the controversy over her holding an office of profit (MPs are not supposed to hold an office of profit). For some time, until the NAC was disbanded, I presided over meetings and also followed up with the government on the status of recommendations that had already been sent. During my period in the NAC, I was able to highlight the need to create more employment, the need to develop skills for the same, and to closely integrate the development activities of the government with this object.

Soon after I became a member of the NAC, Prime Minister Manmohan Singh would often talk about how I could play a more active role in assisting the government. I was clear that I only wanted an advisory role, given my age. He left it to T.K.A. Nair, advisor to the prime minister, and Chatterjee, who was now in the PMO, to discuss the kind of assignment that would interest me. We discussed various options, including heading the Bureau for Restructuring Public Sector Enterprises (BRPSE). Everyone thought I was best suited for it and I also knew what was to be done. But having worked with the public sector all my life, I was not greatly enthused by the idea. The last option was a body to suggest ways to improve the competitiveness of Indian manufacturing. This was one of the important agendas in the Common Minimum Programme adopted by the newly formed government. It interested me, as the concept was new to India and it was an overarching assignment. The government wanted me to head this as well as the BRPSE, but that would have been too much of a burden on me.

Therefore, in September 2004, I took over as chairman of the newly formed National Manufacturing Competitiveness Council (NMCC). I decided I would not confine myself to manufacturing alone but also look into the competitiveness of the economy as a whole. I had a lot of ideas and believed that with Singh as prime minister, I would be able to put these into action. As a matter of principle, I decided to take on this assignment without receiving any remuneration and many of the perquisites while I was given the rank of a cabinet minister. For me, this was an opportunity to give back to the country the benefits of my experience.

The NMCC was a well-formed council and was modelled after a similar body that functioned in the United Kingdom. While the competitiveness council formed in the United States comprised mainly the private sector, the British one was a partnership of the public and private sectors. Hence, the NMCC comprised twelve senior business leaders, six senior secretaries to the government, two eminent economists, two academicians, and the serving presidents of the three apex chambers of commerce. It got off to a good start, and the prime minister agreed to oversee its function even though, for administrative reasons, the council was placed under the ministry of commerce and industry.

~

The economic reforms initiated in 1991 did a lot of good, but the expected results for the manufacturing sector did not materialize. The liberalization process was based on the assumption that the main problem of Indian entrepreneurship was the myriad shackles tying it down and that the sector would soar once it was free of controls. However, this did not happen. As a result, the share of the manufacturing sector in GDP has stagnated at 17 per cent since the 1990s, when it should have been closer to 35 per cent. This is not a good sign, since this sector has huge spinoffs for other sectors, especially the services sector. Poverty is a pressing problem in India, but this cannot be alleviated with subsidies and freebies. These are temporary palliatives. A permanent solution involves generating meaningful employment for the 10 million youth coming into the employment market every year. That is possible only by giving a fillip to manufacturing activities, enabling people to move from agriculture and related activities progressively to small, medium and then large industries.

A weak manufacturing sector will make it difficult for India to become a strong nation. This weakness manifests itself in many forms. In the information technology and telecommunications industries—currently the sunshine sectors of the economy—our demonstrable strengths lie on the software side. The manufacture of supporting hardware is non-existent. In the power sector, over 50 per cent of our equipment needs are now imported. Most of our defence hardware is imported, and the domestic manufacturing support to defence is less than what it was in the seventies. Only 20-30 per cent of machine tools needed by our domestic industry are produced in India whereas more than 80 per cent of our needs were met from indigenous sources two decades ago, and practically all our textile manufacturing equipment is imported.

This is a sorry situation for a country that aspires to be a global economic power. It is an indication that the incentive to manufacture in India is inadequate. That is because imports have become easier and import duties have been lowered to the 0-5 per cent range in a large number of industries. Besides, the spate of free trade agreements entered into with several countries made it difficult for domestic industries to compete, and the internal reforms in the areas that push up costs for domestic manufacturers were neglected.

Indian manufacturing faces many handicaps. These include, among other things, a double whammy of an inverted duty structure coupled with high domestic indirect taxes, labour laws and regulations that entail multiple inspections of factories, high interest rates and abysmal infrastructure.

In addition, there is a huge problem on the skills front, with most of those graduating from various engineering and technical institutes not being employable. There is also a woeful lack of facilities. In 2005, there were facilities for training 7,00,000 engineering graduates, while those for training diploma holders were only 2,70,000 when they should have been several times that number. The number of industrial training institutes was only one-fourth of what is required. Soon after I started my work in 2005 at NMCC, I came to the conclusion that this kind of situation cannot help achieve a manufacturing sector growth of 14-15 per cent a year, double that of the current 7 per cent. Due to NMCC's efforts in the past few years, this situation has been remedied to an extent and efforts are still on.

The liberalized Indian political economy freely allowed foreign firms that wanted to invest in India and tap its huge market. Three benefits should normally flow from foreign direct investment—additional capital, modern technology and domestic value addition. In a majority of cases of foreign direct investment that came in after 1991, these objectives have not been fulfilled. When majority holding was allowed to foreign participants, there was very little incentive on their part to associate themselves with an Indian partner or transfer technology to India. While capital has certainly come, neither has technology been shared nor has there been much value addition within the country. The majority of multinational companies are merely assembling their products with imported inputs and components and exploiting the large Indian market. These issues got further compounded by inadequate attention paid by the Indian organizations towards domestic R&D. Thus no Indian brands emerged.

Often in our deliberations a question arose: whether my emphasis on increased domestic value addition would mean reduced emphasis on foreign direct investment. I was able to convince everyone that the NMCC was concerned with increasing value addition in India, whether it came through public, private or foreign companies. Our emphasis was on increased manufacturing activity in India and consequential increased employment from whichever source it came from. I was equally concerned about increasing the scale of activities in India in every sector to reach an optimum level which alone could ensure competitiveness. Given the economic conditions in India at that time, my emphasis was on increasing employment. A question was raised about whether this would diminish the possibilities of Indian industry becoming more competitive. I felt both were not mutually exclusive, and the intention was to increase employment by increasing the scale of operations from the present levels.

I believe there is a need to periodically review whether the benefits that we anticipated in 1991 are being fully realized. Any argument against lower import duties or restrictions on foreign direct investment may be misconstrued as an argument in favour of protectionism. That is not my case at all. There is a very delicate balance to be struck between exposing an organization or industry to competition (which is good and which is what I did in the three companies I headed) and giving the right amount of protection to ensure that it competes without one hand tied behind its back. Lowering of import duties should be preceded by internal reforms or else it will kill the industry. Similarly, foreign direct investment may be a good instrument for accelerated growth, but there should be a mandatory stipulation regarding transfer of technology to India and local manufacture.

These are some of the issues with which I am engaging in the NMCC with varying degrees of success. Its brief is to identify sectors where India can be globally competitive, work out sector-specific strategies to increase competitiveness, suggest measures to improve the physical and social infrastructure. It has been doing significant work. In 2006, it unveiled a 'National Strategy for Manufacturing ', which highlighted some of the ideas outlined above. This document was prepared after extensive consultations with industry and other stakeholders. It highlighted the need for a sustained level of growth of 14 per cent in the manufacturing sector for fifteen years, which would take the share of manufacturing in GDP to 25 per cent. It suggested urgent and specialized attention to four of the more important sectors which had high growth and employment potential—textiles, leather, food processing and the electronic industry. Various suggestions for the development of these sectors were reviewed by the high level committee on manufacturing presided over by the prime minister.

In order to consider the recommendations of the NMCC and

to place them on fast track, the prime minister constituted a high level committee on manufacturing presided over by him, with the finance minister, the industry minister and I, in my capacity as NMCC chairman, as members. The minister concerned with the subject was also an invitee to these meetings.

I have been arguing that domestic value addition should be the government's primary concern. There should be a judicious balance between protecting domestic industries, getting appreciation for opening up our markets and lowering import duties. I found that the Indian manufacturing industry faced unfair competition through goods coming into India, with little or no restriction through bilateral trade agreements entered into without deep examination. On the NMCC's advice, the prime minister stopped the commerce and foreign ministries from taking any unilateral decisions and ensured that all proposals for free trade agreements were cleared by a committee called The Trade and Economic Relations Committee under his chairmanship. Thereafter, the NMCC, as a member of the committee, was consulted on such matters.

A National Manufacturing Competitiveness Programme to support small and medium enterprises was also formulated by the NMCC and implemented by the ministry concerned. Personally, I believed that the small and medium enterprises required lot of attention and support from the government, as they formed the backbone of the manufacturing sector. I had a fear that most of the small and medium entrepreneurs were not able to be in business due to inadequate institutional support and the onslaught of cheap Chinese goods. The NMCC also passionately argued that unless certain curbs were introduced on the import of low cost Chinese goods, the future of the medium and small industries in India would be bleak. I even cautioned the government that soon small entrepreneurs would become traders of cheap Chinese goods. Already, the Chinese currency was deliberately kept undervalued and the Chinese industry had access to unlimited finance at as low as 3 to 4 per cent interest. Moreover, there was no check on the quality of Chinese goods entering India. All these resulted in heavy import of manufactured goods, 80 per cent of which were imports from China into India in 2010. In contrast, more than 80 per cent of India's exports to China consisted of raw materials. I also found that until the time the NMCC raised this subject, large quantities of imported power equipment came with manuals in the Mandarin language, giving me the impression that we just bought the goods because of their price, without fully examining their quality or suitability to Indian conditions. The manufacturing industry created in India for power equipment was damaged to a great extent because of these imports from China. While most of the departments appreciated the NMCC's concern, the situation unfortunately has not fully been remedied.

Since independence, considerable efforts have been made by various national research laboratories to develop products and solutions that could help the Indian economy. But little effort has gone into translating their experiments into projects and assisting in the manufacture of those products in India. The NMCC, serving as a catalyst, tried to identify critical areas where such a collaboration would be beneficial. The NMCC helped in developing a scheme for the production of potash from seawater. This process was developed by one of the laboratories of the Council of Scientific and Industrial Research, but further work in proving the process was lacking, although 100 per cent of the potash required for fertilizer production was being imported year after year. Under the NMCC, we have launched a pilot project funded by the Department of Science and Technology, roping in Tata Chemicals for proving this process and for the production of the much-needed potash indigenously. If this experiment succeeds, it will completely defeat the international cartel which has so far been dictating the availability and the price of potash in India.

Based on our study, a National Skill Development Corporation was formed to assist in speeding up the process of skill development. A high level council, of which I am a member, was also notified under the prime minister to promote skill development across the country.

The efforts taken by the NMCC resulted in sensitizing all wings of the government and the public about the need for a renewed emphasis on manufacturing activity. People became conscious of the fact that increasing the tempo of domestic manufacture is the only solution to providing meaningful job opportunities to the estimated 10 million boys and girls coming every year into the employment market. Unfortunately, the tempo of increased manufacturing activity seen between 2005 and 2007 slowed down in 2008 because of certain measures taken by the Reserve Bank of India (RBI) to curtail money circulation in order to check inflation. The higher interest rates, decrease in investment in new projects and reduced flow of foreign direct investment resulted in the slowdown. Fearing a setback to the economy, the prime minister appointed a group with me as well as the secretaries of the departments of finance, revenue, commerce, industry and textiles to suggest ways and means to accelerate industrial growth. We made a detailed study and gave a number of suggestions in September 2008. Implementation of some of the suggestions is in progress.

Because of the concern repeatedly expressed by the NMCC over the delay in implementing major public sector projects costing over Rs 1,000 crore, the PMO nominated member secretary, NMCC, Ajay Shankar to resolve inter-ministerial tangles and speed up the projects so that economic activity could go on at a reasonable pace and also to help the public sector remove hurdles placed by environmental and other regulations. This monitoring by the NMCC has helped these projects to be expedited.

The NMCC studies revealed that the lower rates of growth in manufacturing in India is hurting the strategic sectors which have a direct bearing on the security of the country. At the instance of the prime minister, I was asked to head a committee to study the feasibility of associating with the Indian private sector in building submarines. The committee included secretary, defence production, scientific advisor to the defence ministry, and the deputy chief of naval staff. As chairman of the committee, I was strongly of the view that some of the companies in the private sector had the potential to build submarines, and the hesitation of the department of defence production to associate with the private sector was ill founded. The committee has made its recommendation to allow the private sector to build submarines. Unfortunately in this case, as it happens in many others, the ministry of defence has not been able to find a satisfactory method to associate with the private sector by meeting its vital demand for sophisticated equipments.

The NMCC considered indigenizing ship building and manufacture of equipment for aerospace as they are vital for national security. Practically all ocean-going ships and equipment required for aerospace are imported. The NMCC has brought this anomaly to the notice of the government and is engaged with all stakeholders in crafting a set of feasible measures to achieve a breakthrough.

At present, India completely depends on the import of civilian aircraft. The NMCC has stressed on the need for both the public and private sectors to manufacture Indian-designed civilian aircraft in a time-bound manner by using the available Indian expertise in different organizations. The prime minister has constituted a committee with me as chairman for the implementation of this project.

Thanks to the ministry of telecommunication and information technology, the NMCC's views that at least 30 per cent of the requirement of the telecom industry should be procured from domestic manufacturers was accepted, and suitable policy guidelines were issued. Several foreign organizations directly and through diplomatic channels tried to resist this development, but the government of India stood firm. We were clear that without this support from the government, there would be no beginning of the manufacture of telecom equipment and associated electronic components in India. To carry this programme forward, Pitroda and I recommended the setting up of two fab facilities which would be fundamental to the growth of the electronics industry. An empowered committee was set up with Pitroda and me to identify foreign and Indian collaborators for the fab facility. Our recommendation has been forwarded to the government, and hopefully this will place manufacturing in the electronics sector on a firm footing.

Stretching beyond its terms of reference, the NMCC also helped in the formulation of the programme for the development of solar energy and the setting up of a National Solar Mission. It got off to a good start, but the objectives which the NMCC had in mind while suggesting the setting up of the solar mission were not fully realized. The NMCC's idea was to parallelly develop the domestic manufacture of the equipment that goes into the system. This did not take place, and much of the equipment is being imported.

While everyone in India recognized that more than 40 per cent of food, fruits and vegetables perished between the farm and the table, the efforts on food processing were minimal. The NMCC helped the ministry of food processing in evolving a national plan for industrial parks dedicated to food processing and got it approved by the high level committee on manufacturing.

The NMCC helped in setting standards for ensuring quality

of operations, wherever these did not exist. There is a compulsion to have national standards in critical areas, particularly where there are multiple implementing agencies. One such area is the Metro. With the success of the Delhi Metro, many other cities started setting up their Metro rail projects. Each ordered equipment according to their own specifications, largely dictated by their chosen suppliers of equipments. I thought this was hardly the way in which such an important development addressing public transport should be handled. Soon, hundreds of cities will have their Metros, and unless there are specified standards, domestic efforts in manufacturing will suffer. The NMCC initiated a series of discussions with the ministries of urban development, railways and industry to set up a mechanism wherein, with the assistance of the Delhi Metro and the ministry of railways, national standards were established for all future installations.

Most of these ideas of the NMCC have found a place in the National Manufacturing Policy which aims to create 100 million jobs by 2020. The manufacturing industry, when it grows large, would require a large number of leaders. Anticipating this, the NMCC, in association with JICA, IIT Kanpur, IIM Kolkata, IIT Madras and the CII, developed the Visionary Leaders for Manufacturing Programme, which envisages the annual nurturing of 300 executives, CEOs and entrepreneurs capable of breakthrough thinking with the help of Professor Shoji Shiba, a very eminent management consultant from Japan. I had secured the support of the Japanese government for this programme, which later culminated in an agreement between the two countries for technical assistance to this programme.

Over time, the NMCC came to be respected as a very useful instrument by the government in resolving inter-departmental conflicts and in sensitizing the need for faster economic growth.

I have been NMCC chairman for over nine years now.

During this period, I was able to institute a series of studies/reports/suggestions for various sectors hitherto not attempted. The importance of the manufacturing sector, particularly for India, was continuously emphasized. The members of the council, most of them senior business leaders, found their work in the NMCC interesting and were able to contribute greatly to identifying problems and suggesting solutions. Soon the entire industry started looking up to the NMCC to solve their specific problems. The government, the prime minster and various ministries acknowledged the overarching role played by the NMCC and the objectivity of its recommendations.

Unfortunately, on account of the global economic meltdown combined with the policies adopted by the RBI in restricting the availability of funds and raising of interest rates, the Indian manufacturing industry, both large and small, suffered. On my part, I impressed upon the RBI that growth is more important and that any attempt by it to curb inflation should be done in such a manner that it does not affect the flow of capital to the manufacturing industry. Towards this end, I also made several recommendations to the government, suggesting a slew of major projects like building a million houses per year for the lower sections of society, a Delhi-Kolkata freight corridor, inter-city high-speed trains, development of airports, and speeding up the execution of power projects and highways. I suggested that these recommendations should be taken up by them to stimulate the growth either in the public sector or by the PPP mode on an annuity basis.

When I took over chairmanship of the NMCC, I thought its life would be of two or three years, as was the case with similar councils formed by the government. I did not bargain for a longer period. But as the NMCC got established and became an essential link between the government and industry and an overarching organization, it came to be regarded as a permanent establishment of the government. The government did not countenance any change in the leadership or the composition of the council.

I could have retired in 2009 when the second UPA government was formed, but the prime minister wanted me to continue. By that time, there was a general acknowledgement of the effective role played by the NMCC in advising the different departments of the government, on the one hand, and in serving as an effective link between the government and industry, on the other. In retrospect, I could have organized the NMCC in a slightly different manner had I known that it would remain a permanent establishment or the type of gaps it had to fill within the government. Constituted in the present manner, I had to be content with playing an advisory role, leaving it to the executive to implement the ideas.

I am happy that I have helped the government in finding ways of achieving a higher rate of economic growth, identifying policy gaps and pointing out that a market-oriented economy was not the panacea for all ills and that the state still has a role to play and that the stage has not come to open up the economy to external forces without internal liberalization and that the emphasis should be on generating gainful employment for the new entrants into the job market. Since implementation has always been my strength, when some of the suggestions I have made are not put into practice at the speed of my thoughts, there is just a slight sense of disappointment.

During this period, the president conferred the Padma Vibhushan on me and the Emperor of Japan conferred on me that nation's highest civilian honour, The Grand Cordon of the Order of the Rising Sun. Eleven national associations honoured me with life-time achievement awards.

The last nine years, thus, have more than made up for the eight years I spent in fighting to uphold my reputation. As I look back on my life and career, I cannot help but feel that it has been a life well spent.

# CONCLUSION

Management of a business enterprise in India is a lot more difficult than in other countries. There are far more uncertainties that an Indian manager has to encounter while performing his tasks. Besides, the managers in the public sector have to face far more severe constraints than their counterparts in the private sector. My personal experience has shown that there is no general prescription for all situations. For example, the type of problems that I had faced, the circumstances under which they had to be tackled, and the instruments of change that I used were different in each of the three public sector companies that I helmed. There are, however, a few factors which are universally applicable.

Any company, whether in the public sector or private sector, cannot prosper if it does not engage in marketing and in keeping the customer at the centre of all its decisions. Despite being in the public sector, my emphasis in all my assignments was on marketing and customer orientation both at the national and international levels. I was constantly striving for new markets, new business and new methods of customer satisfaction. In each of my assignments, I could have continued with the business-as-usual approach. BHEL was operating as a monopoly. Maruti had some competition from Hindustan Motors and Premier Automobiles, but since we were operating in a sellers' market, I need not have invested the time and effort in a customer culture that I did. SAIL, too, was in a sellers' market, and its only competitor was Tata Steel. But it was the focus on marketing and customer satisfaction that put all three companies on a sound footing.

Every company, whether in the private or public sector, must ensure that it is technologically strong and sound and, over time, self reliant. I was very keen to ensure that the companies I headed were all up-to-date with the latest technological trends in their respective industries. I made a conscious effort to get BHEL to move away from outdated Soviet bloc technology to more modern Western technology in the seventies, even before the collaboration agreements with the Soviet Union and Czechoslovakia ended. It was this that stood BHEL in good stead. Upgrading of technology did not mean securing more modern designs for the products manufactured. It was equally important to ensure that the organization had the correct policies, standards, systems and procedures to help optimize its functioning. Hence, to achieve these, efforts were made to get an inside view of the organizational structure, systems and procedures of the collaborators. In case of the omnibus agreement with Siemens, an effort was made to secure access to their in-house management training facilities. Most CEOs pay considerable attention to plant and machinery and people, but the organizational software is hardly seen as an important element for the successful running of an enterprise. It is my experience that a technology-based enterprise in India needs to adopt American enterprise practices for marketing, innovation and organization design; German enterprise practices for systems, procedures and organizational discipline; and Japanese company practices for shop floor, cost and quality culture. The collaborations with Combustion Engineering and GE, Siemens Group and SMC will endorse this. Transplanting any of these practices without adapting them to our needs will not yield results. Many make this mistake. We have to carefully blend them with our ethos and develop our own 'culture'.

Upgrading technology does not mean only joint ventures and collaborations. There is no substitute for in-house efforts on research and development. I laid special emphasis on R&D in all my organizations. Some of the other public sector engineering companies like HEC, Mining and Allied Machinery Corporation, Hindustan Machine Tools and Indian Telephone Industries could not grow beyond a point and evolve as organizations only because they did not pay enough attention to in-house R&D and engineering to upgrade their technology.

Every company, whether in the public or private sector, must be quality conscious. A strong focus on quality has been a running theme of my work. I laid emphasis on quality even when I was general manager at Trichy at a time when no one in the public sector was even talking about it. In each of my subsequent assignments, I scaled up the quality consciousness in the organizations I headed. When CII became active, I advised it to move away from the general tendency of industry associations to lobby for concessions and to focus instead on areas that would help its members become better managed institutions. CII then looked at issues that would make companies competitive, and one of these was quality. It approached me to head the initiative on quality, and I agreed. I formed a group within CII, comprising around fifty top executives of industry, and called this the National Committee on Quality. I insisted that the meetings of this committee should be attended only by CEOs; they could not depute anyone else as people are wont to do. I believed that unless the CEO himself is committed to this task, the culture in the organization will not change. This group, headed by me, made quality consciousness central to the functioning of companies and emphasized that there could be no short-circuiting of the process. Since then, the quality movement has caught on in the country, and I look back with a sense of satisfaction about having pioneered it. I continue to be involved in the quality movement in the country and am currently the president of The Indian Society for Quality. In recognition of my work in the area of quality, I was conferred with the Nakajima Award for quality by the Japanese authorities.

People often ask me how I, with absolutely no knowledge of automobiles or steel, made a success of Maruti and SAIL. For me, it was not important to know how cars or steel were made; my main task was to identify people who knew the work, wherever they were, and get them on board and also to create an environment where they could perform unhindered in a professional atmosphere. This is what I did in the three organizations that I helmed.

No company, whether in the public sector or private sector, can achieve success if it ignores the people that make the organization. An organization can pour money into acquiring the most sophisticated technology and hiring expensive consultants to advise it on business strategy, but all that will come to nought if the employees of an organization are not driven by a sense of purpose. During my days in BHEL, there was no money for state-of-the-art technology or even to subscribe to foreign journals on management. If we could still make it one of the best performing public sector companies, it was only by investing money, time and energy in people.

There are many ways a chief executive can motivate people. For me, motivating people was a question of convincing them about their ability to do something constructive. I reposed great confidence in my managers and never interfered but also never distanced myself and was always available. The most important element in motivating people is to be accessible and also to listen. This not only gives the employees a sense of confidence that they can discuss their ideas freely but it also gives the CEO first-hand knowledge of the state of the organization instead of relying on what other managers relay to him. The best solutions, I have found, come from open discussions where everyone has a say. I believe that everybody has a story to tell in an organization, even the lowest person in the hierarchy. But there is a tendency to listen only to those who are more qualified or in higher positions, even though what people working on the shop floor or in the field have to say can also be of immense value. The middle level managers, of course, resent this and will try to block access, but it is up to the CEO to check such attempts.

It is also important to treat people with dignity. This is not always about giving more money or perquisites, but can take different forms. It can be something as simple as knowing people's names or noticing some problem they are facing and addressing it proactively. In all the three companies I headed, I made it a point to interact with all levels of employees, especially the workers, asking after their personal welfare and their families. Many wondered why I frequently visited the shop floor. For me, it was part of a relationship-building effort with the workers. It was also the only way I could identify myself with the larger body of employees and also observe for myself the working conditions and find out in reality if there was any method by which I could make their job easier and help them be more effective. It is an almost euphoric feeling for a person at the bottom of an organization's hierarchy to know that the head is not treating him as an anonymous cog in the wheel but actually recognizes him and is interested in what he says. It creates a bond that is stronger than what motivational lectures can create. At SAIL, when I came to know about the kind of pathetic travel allowance employees got, because of which they could not afford to eat at the hotels they stayed in, I got the allowance increased. When I asked senior managers of plants at SAIL for suggestions to cut costs and they started talking about travelling second class and staying in less expensive hotels, I made it very clear to them that this was not what I was seeking. I told them that I wanted people to travel in comfort and with dignity.

Dignity can also be about the nature of the work people are doing. At Maruti, one of the reasons I pressed for—and got—certain automated processes from the Japanese was that I did not believe people should be relegated to boring, repetitive jobs that did nothing to enhance their skills or develop their minds.

The morale of employees will be low if they feel that they are being treated unfairly or that one section is more privileged than another. This is particularly true of the workers and the supervisory staff. It does not take much to ensure that both workers and executives have, broadly, the same set of rules governing them, or even that the workers are given preference in some matters, like payment of bonus or wage revision. It is important for employees to know that there is no privileged or underprivileged class.

At the same time, it is important to ensure that qualified and unqualified persons as well as bright performers and laggards are not treated on a par. One major handicap any public sector manager faces in motivating employees is the belief that promotions or salary hikes will come automatically and are not based on performance. In each of the companies I headed, I ensured that salary increases or promotions were merit-based. I did it using whatever elbow room hide-bound public sector rules allowed me. It makes a huge difference to the way people approach their jobs, once they know that their performance is going to be rewarded.

The most important quality I looked for in a person was merit. The other factors to which I gave equal importance in judging people was their knowledge of the job, their ability to carry people along with them, their willingness to learn and change, and their levels of integrity. For me, the age of the individual did not matter. If I felt that a young executive had reached a position where he could do challenging jobs as well as other senior persons, I gave a chance to that young executive. Some senior people were uncomfortable with me and felt that I did not respect seniority, but that was not the case—I was only encouraging people who deserved it.

The job of a chief executive who takes charge of an ailing organization is particularly difficult. Resistance and resentment are inevitable, especially if he is an outsider to the company or the sector. How is one to deal with this? Many CEOs begin by purging the existing top management and bringing their own people in. I completely avoided this route. At BHEL, two people were removed when the government appointed me as chairman, but I never got rid of anyone reporting to the chairman. Later, I got some people from outside the company, but this was more to address a lack of talent in certain areas than any attempt to pack the organization with my own people. The hallmark of a successful manager is to convert people to his point of view instead of merely ensuring that he is surrounded by like-minded people.

The other mistake people commit is to disparage everything that has been done earlier and issue diktats about new ways of functioning. This will only put people's backs up and make the task of turning around the organization even more difficult. I never claimed I knew everything, especially at SAIL where I had no knowledge about steel making or the industry. I would constantly say that the employees had done their best, but since it had not yielded results for whatever reasons, it might be good to try and do things differently and see whether that works. More importantly, I eschewed a top-down approach and invited suggestions from within the organization and took employees on board. That gives employees a sense of ownership in all that is being done to revive an organization. Without this ownership and involvement, I could not have turned SAIL around.

In order to get this involvement, it is necessary for a good manager to constantly communicate. Communicating your ideas once may not be sufficient. I believe that you have to communicate at least five to six times over and again in different ways to get a point across. Communication is the only way to overcome resistance to a new style of working. Explaining why something needs to be done, I found, is half the job done. I rarely got anyone on board through an executive fiat. People will follow orders to avoid the charge of insubordination. But if they are not convinced about the rationale of that directive, they will follow it in a half-hearted manner, and that is of little use. Every employee needs to be convinced about and committed to whatever he is doing. It was this desire to take employees along that made me circulate the *Outline of a Corporate Plan* at BHEL and *Priorities for Action* at SAIL among all the employees. At Maruti, too, I was constantly communicating with employees by way of circulars and letters and also verbally. My communication was not limited to employees alone but also extended to trade unions, customers, suppliers and other stakeholders of the companies I headed. The success of a company depends on all of them being on the same page. Another attribute which helped me a lot was active listening. Listening precedes good communication. The best solutions I have found have been drawn from intense discussions and active listening.

Every company should have a vision about what it stands for. It is the business of the chief executives to articulate a vision for the company and then work out a strategy to meet that vision. The vision must be extensively shared with the people, and in fact it must evolve from the people. The articulation of a vision kindles hope and pride and inspires the employees to perform better.

Change in an organization is inevitable. Every time a change is made in the larger interest of the organization, it will create discomfort in a few. This must be addressed. Unless it is recognized and addressed effectively, the benefits of the change will be slow. The employees have to be first prepared mentally to accept the change, after which the changes should be introduced across the organization in a phased manner and then, finally, the pace of change should be increased.

A successful CEO also needs to foster team spirit within the organization so that individuals do not function in isolation but see themselves as part of a group and each group recognizes that it is part of a larger whole. Often, managers fail to realize the importance of this. I have learnt that a few simple ideas diligently implemented can deliver far better results than numerous complex ideas indifferently pursued. Individually, we may achieve a great deal, but, as a team, we can achieve results seemingly impossible. The first step towards building a team is to make its objectives independent but at the same time ensure that it is in congruence with the larger goal of the organization. The next step is to get everybody on board by reconciling their differences and then encourage them to think of various other alternatives before taking any decisions. The most essential requirement for team building is to ensure that everyone is open to learning and changing themselves.

It is unfortunate that team work is not practised even in management schools, as I observed during my stints as chairman of IIM Ahmedabad and Bangalore. While at BHEL, I had once given a consultancy assignment to IIM Ahmedabad. I expected the entire knowledge of the faculty would be available to us. To my extreme disappointment, the professor to whom the consultancy was given worked alone and did not consult anyone else. It was obvious that the management schools themselves needed lessons in managing themselves.

Every organization has problems, and every CEO will face hurdles in resolving them. The trick to being a good CEO is to anticipate these problems and hurdles and plan for tackling them when they do surface. I have always believed in parallel processing and not sequential processing. When I take an action, I think of the consequences that could follow and plan for them simultaneously, instead of waiting for them to manifest themselves.

~

Strategic thinking and long-term planning are crucial for every organization. I strongly believe that long-term goals should not be forgotten. For the sake of short-term benefits, there should not be a compromise on long-term goals—something most CEOs with short tenures are prone to do. I generally planned things for fifteen years, which were subdivided into five-year and annual plans. I also tried to inculcate an entrepreneurial spirit and strategic thinking in senior and middle management levels through the corporate planning process. BHEL, Maruti and SAIL are still reaping the benefits of the long-term planning and the guidelines I developed during my tenure.

One major handicap that public sector managers face is external interference—from some ministers, bureaucrats and politicians—the result of the distortions that crept into the management of state-owned enterprises after Nehru's time. It is, no doubt, a serious problem and has been one of the reasons for the poor performance of the public sector. However, it is possible to insulate the organization from such interference to a significant extent. It requires courage of conviction and the ability to explain the rationale of one's actions. In managing the external environment, I followed certain principles. I never complained about someone to any higher authority and took responsibility for all decisions in my organization. Whenever I approached any ministry for help, I would always explain the benefit that the help would yield to the nation, organization and individuals. I religiously stuck to the commitments which I made publicly, and at no point of time did I fail in my promises. More importantly, I always maintained a certain degree of humility.

When I became chairman of BHEL in 1972, public sector bashing was very common, and any negative newspaper report would spark off a few parliament questions. In the garb of seeking answers to these questions, day-to-day decisions were being questioned. Whenever a member of parliament wrote a letter, the industry minister, T.A. Pai, would forward it to me. I collected three or four of them and went to him and said: 'I don't know if you want to do the chairman's job, but I don't want to do my general manager's job.' I told him that BHEL is run according to a set of policies. He was welcome to change them, and I would abide by them. But there are many areas in which decisions are taken by units and not by me. I said, 'If you ask me questions like these and I ask the general manager of the Haridwar or Bhopal plant about them, he will stop taking decisions and start leaving them to me. I want the decentralized set-up to continue.' Pai understood the point I was making, and the ministry refrained from meddling in the working of BHEL. At SAIL, too, I quietly re-asserted the position of the chairman's office, which had got devalued over the years.

Asserting independence, however, does not mean adopting a confrontationist stance, especially with regard to politicians. A public sector manager does need to interact with the political establishment. I recognized this fact and did not shy away from it.

When I was general manager at Trichy, I met the industry minister of Tamil Nadu every alternate month and kept him informed of what the unit was doing to help the local industry, local population and the state. BHEL was a central public sector undertaking and I need not have done this, but I recognized the importance of building channels of communication with the state government. This helped me a lot in keeping local disruptive elements at bay.

For example, when the Communist Party of India (Marxist) and its trade union arm, the Centre for Indian Trade Unions, complained to the state government that they were not allowed to hold public meetings or take out processions on the BHEL campus at Trichy, the chief minister, M. Karunanidhi, asked them if these curbs were being imposed only on them. When they said no, he said they had no reason to complain since the rule applied to everyone. When I raised the issue with him of an officer of the local employment exchange taking bribes from every person he sent to BHEL and insisted that he transfer the person or else I would not take anyone sent by that employment exchange, the chief minister acted on my request.

Contrary to popular impression, I have found that politicians have regard for people who are demonstrably professional in their approach and are firm and fair in enforcing discipline.

When I was taking a hard line on labour unrest over bonus at Trichy, the local Dravida Munnetra Kazhagam (DMK) legislator sought the chief minister's intervention. Karunanidhi suggested I meet him, and I went to Chennai. At the meeting on Marina Beach, where the chief minister used to hold court regularly after 9 p.m., the local legislator briefed him once again about the issue. I then explained to Karunanidhi the current rules about bonus and what I was trying to do to give workers better benefits. I pointed out that what I was doing was in the long-term interest of the employees and that I would have no solution but to impose a lockout if indiscipline continued. After some more discussion, Karunanidhi silenced his party men, pointing out that they did not know how to put across the workers' point of view. 'I find the general manager is in a better position to take care of the workers than all of you. Go back and listen to what he says. He is doing a good job; don't disturb him.'

Engaging with the political establishment, however, does not mean ingratiating oneself or giving in to requests that are clearly unwarranted. I used to tell my ministers, 'I am flexible but not that flexible, and that I will give advice that is good for the organization, the government and them personally.' If they still wanted me to pursue a course of action I had advised against, I would do so but not without having my say.

Like all public sector CEOs, I, too, was constantly being approached to do favours for someone or the other. In Maruti, first there was pressure to collaborate with Renault for the manufacture of a small car and then to bend rules to give dealerships and supply contracts to particular persons. In SAIL, the pressure related to giving local contracts and to transfers. Those who came with such requests would often drop names. A favourite line would be, 'I am coming straight from breakfast with the Prime Minister.' I would listen to them but not oblige them if it involved bending rules and compromising with quality in any way.

During my Maruti stint, when people approached N.D. Tiwari, who was the industry minister, for recommendations for dealerships or supply contracts, he would say, 'If you want me to recommend, I will do so. But knowing Krishnamurthy, if it is above board, he will do it. If it is not, he will not do it. And the next day, Mrs Gandhi will come to know about it.' Invariably, the person concerned would withdraw his request.

But that did not mean I was absolutely rigid. I knew the pressures ministers faced and would not refuse to do petty things which would not harm the organization or dent my reputation. I told Dinesh Goswami, who was steel minister in the V.P. Singh government, not to send me all the requests for favours that he got because they would just get filed. If there were one or two he was particular about, I suggested, he should give them to me directly or through his private secretary. One day, when I had gone to see him, his secretary gave me the resume of a girl with an engineering degree in electronics from Assam, the minister's home state. I was ready to give her a job in SAIL. But then Goswami told me she was his daughter. I then told him I would not employ her in SAIL because people would say that this was the first thing he did as minister. Goswami was not very happy about this. But when I got back to my office, I rang up P.P. Gupta, who was the managing director of the public sector computer maintenance firm, CMC, and asked him to give her a job, which he did.

But earlier in BHEL, when Mrs Gandhi had wanted one of our general managers to be appointed as director, I had my reservations. I knew he was an unsuitable person and that the only reason she was asking was that his wife was known to her and the person was publicly flaunting this link. There was tremendous pressure on me to oblige her. I had to politely tell my minister to find another chairman to do this and that I did not want to lose my credibility. This was during the Emergency, and I could have paid the price for this non-cooperation. Mrs Gandhi did not pursue the matter and got him appointed as chairman of the Central Electricity Authority. When she became prime minister for the second time, he joined the BHEL board. But by then, I was not part of the organization.

I also stood up to Mrs Gandhi on the appointment of the director of IIM Bangalore when I was chairman of the board in 1983. N.S. Ramaswamy had been the director since 1973 when the institute was set up. I had identified Praxy Fernandes for the post, but Mrs Gandhi rejected his name because he had given evidence against her before the Shah Commission, which was looking into alleged atrocities during the Emergency. I then resigned as chairman of the board, since my recommendation was not accepted.

It is often said that my ability to stand up to pressures and the free hand that I got in all my assignments had to do with the fact that I was the blue-eyed boy of, first, Mrs Indira Gandhi and then Rajiv Gandhi. But this is not true. When I stood up to Karunanidhi in Trichy, I had no political backing. Mrs Gandhi did not personally handpick me to head BHEL; she had heard of my work at Trichy and my name had been suggested to her. She was openly sceptical of any Indian manager's ability to turn BHEL around. I had to wrestle with governmental and political interference. Nobody insulated me from all that. It was only after I had made a success of BHEL—and probably because of it—that I had an easier time at Maruti and SAIL and got some of that much-touted insulation from interference. But the so-called 'patronage' that I am supposed to have enjoyed was predicated on my delivering results. I was under no illusion that I could continue in the posts I held even if I failed to discharge my responsibilities. When I was heading BHEL, some other public sector chief executives complained to the finance secretary that the ministry agreed to every demand that I made. The finance secretary responded, saying, 'Yes, that is because he is the only one who keeps his side of the bargain; others don't.'

Every time I felt I had achieved something, the euphoria would evaporate soon. A divine discontent would then take over and generate the agenda for further action. This continuous play of the sense of achievement followed by the eternal divine discontent has been the engine that has propelled me on. I believe that it is only those at the helm, who have this divine discontent propelling them on, who will become transformational leaders and leave a lasting impact.

These are the few tenets by which I conducted my long

career in the public sector. What Dr Kalam said about the work I had done in BHEL being talked about thirty years later no longer surprises me. Even in 2014, in many discussions, there is talk about replicating the BHEL, Maruti and SAIL experiments that I undertook.

Each experiment was a unique experience. I did not even realize that I was passing through such diverse experiences or that I was transforming these organizations. So when people started asking me about my style of management, I could not give a cogent answer. But on the suggestion of no less a person than Dr Kalam, I captured the essence of my work in this book so that others could also share the richness of my experience. And in doing so, I understood myself and my style of management better.

# INDEX

# ACKNOWLEDGEMENTS

I had made several attempts to write a memoir over a long time but could not make much headway for some reason or the other. A few others tried on their own, with inputs from me, but their work remained incomplete. I had almost given up when I met Seetha Parthasarathy, a senior journalist, who had come to interview me for an assignment. Sometime later, I happened to read her work. Impressed by it, I sought her help in writing this memoir.

Over a period of two years, she had numerous sessions with me, analysed my earlier speeches and writings, interviewed many of my former colleagues, visited the archives of different organizations and the Planning Commission, and thus helped me frame and write this book. Her penchant for detail and the thoroughness with which she approached the project helped me jog my memory, explain my actions and articulate my philosophies better. But for her help, I daresay this memoir would never have been written. My sincere thanks and heartfelt appreciation to her.

A number of my former colleagues—juniors and seniors who had worked with me at BHEL, Maruti, SAIL, the ministry of Industry, the Planning Commission and the NMCC—spent a lot of time with Seetha Parthasarathy and me, supplementing the effort. My thanks to each and every one of them for having evinced interest and spared their valuable time. A special word of thanks to K.R. Paramesvar, Krishna Shankar, Naresh Chandra, D.S. Gupta, Mahesh Babu and Ajay Shanker for their contributions.

K. Raghunathan and Rekha Raghunathan gave me great support in this project. They worked with me and Seetha Parthasarathy at all stages—right from conceptualization to publication. Their inputs added to the quality of the project and I thank them.

My wife would have been the happiest to see my life's work laid out in a book. She had been my greatest support and strength throughout my career, especially in my difficult years when I had to fight the government on its unfair accusations. The biggest regret of my life is that she did not live long enough to see me 'At The Helm' once again. My sons Chandra and Jayakar have always stood by me, and I appreciate their moral and physical support in bringing out this memoir.

This book could not have been completed but for the blessings of Lord Venkateswara of Tirupati and Lord Sarguneswar and Goddess Sarvangasundari of Karuveli. To them I am eternally grateful for all that I have experienced and could achieve in life.

# ABOUT THE AUTHOR

V. Krishnamurthy is the doyen of Indian management, having headed the country's largest and most challenging public sector companies.

He was Chairman and CEO of Bharat Heavy Electricals Limited, Maruti Udyog Limited and Steel Authority of India Limited. He has been Chairman of IIM Bangalore and Ahmedabad; IIT Delhi; Xavier Institute of Management, Bhubaneswar; and the Centre for Organization Development, Hyderabad. He has also been Chairman of the Technology Information, Forecasting & Assessment Council. He was Member of the National Advisory Council from 2004-08. Among other positions, he has served as Member, Planning Commission, and Secretary to the Government of India in the Ministry of Industry.

Presently, he is the Chairman of the National Manufacturing Competitiveness Council, holding the rank of a Cabinet Minister. He is also a member of the Prime Minister's Council on Trade and Industry, Prime Minister's Trade & Economic Relations Committee, Prime Minister's Energy Coordination Committee, Prime Minister's High Level Committee on Manufacturing and a High Level Advisory Group on Climate Change. He is the Chairman of the group set up by the prime minister for design and manufacture of civilian aircraft in India and the Co-Chairman of the empowered committee for setting up facilities to manufacture chips for the electronics sector in India.

He is Chancellor of the Central University of Tamil Nadu and the Indian Maritime University. He is Member, Board of Governors, Administrative Staff College of India, Hyderabad, and President, Academy of Higher Education (National College), Tiruchirapalli.

He is Member of the Board of Trustees and Executive Committee of the Rajiv Gandhi Foundation and Member of the Governing Council of the Rajiv Gandhi Institute of Contemporary Studies, based in New Delhi.

He studied to be a Chartered Engineer and holds a Doctorate in Economics from the Soviet Academy of Sciences, a Doctorate in Sciences from the Banaras Hindu University and a Doctorate in Letters from Pondicherry University.

He has been Member of the Energy Advisory Committee, the Public Enterprises Selection Board and the Telecom Restructuring Committee. He has chaired various committees including the National Committee on Quality, a committee to prepare a comprehensive white paper on the public enterprises in India, a committee to determine the policies on disinvestment in the public sector, a group to restructure oil companies in the public sector and a committee to assess the capability and infrastructure of the private sector to build conventional submarines. He was also the co-chairman of the Indo-Japan study committee.

He was conferred the Padma Shri in 1973, the Padma Bhushan in 1986, the Padma Vibhushan in 2007, the Grand Cordon of the Order of the Rising Sun by the Government of Japan in 2009, the Business Leadership Award by the Madras Management Association in 1975, the 'Businessman of the Year' title by *Business India* magazine in 1987, the Sir Jahangir Ghandy Medal in 1988, the 'Steelman of the Year' title by The Indian and Eastern Engineer in 1989, the Tata Gold Medal by the Indian Institute of Metals in 1989, the National HRD Award in 1989 and the Special Nakajima Award by the Japan Institute of Plant Maintenance in 2007.

As a mark of respect to his eminence as a visionary leader and an institution builder, and for his pursuit of excellence, the Centre for Organization Development, Hyderabad, honoured him by establishing the 'V. Krishnamurthy Award for Excellence' in 2000.

He lost his wife Rajam in 2001. He has two sons, Chandra and Jayakar, and lives in New Delhi and Chennai.